Shakespeare Scholars in Conversation

Shakespeare Scholars in Conversation

Interviews with 24 Leading Experts

MICHAEL P. JENSEN

Foreword by Jeffrey Kahan

McFarland & Company, Inc., Publishers
Jefferson, North Carolina

All interviews originally appeared in *The Shakespeare Newsletter.*

Library of Congress Cataloguing-in-Publication Data

Names: Jensen, Michael P., interviewer. | Kahan, Jeffrey, 1964– writer of foreword.
Title: Shakespeare scholars in conversation : interviews with 24 leading experts / Michael P. Jensen ; foreword by Jeffrey Kahan.
Description: Jefferson, North Carolina : McFarland & Company, Inc., 2019 | Includes bibliographical references, filmography, and index.
Identifiers: LCCN 2019002420 | ISBN 9781476670607 (paperback : acid free paper) ♾
Subjects: LCSH: Shakespeare, William, 1564–1616—Study and teaching—Interviews.
Classification: LCC PR2987 .J37 2019 | DDC 822.3/3—dc23
LC record available at https://lccn.loc.gov/2019002420

British Library cataloguing data are available

ISBN (print) 978-1-4766-7060-7
ISBN (ebook) 978-1-4766-3495-1

Printed in the United States of America

McFarland & Company, Inc., Publishers
Box 611, Jefferson, North Carolina 28640
www.mcfarlandpub.com

To the people who made "Talking Books" possible,
John W. Mahon and Thomas A. Pendleton.
They gave my strange column a home
in *Shakespeare Newsletter.*

Contents

Foreword by Jeffrey Kahan

How do you know if you've made it in your chosen field? For bankers and businessmen, there's that sweet corner office, stock options, a Christmas bonus rivaling the G.D.P. of a small country; for actors, there's the Emmys, Oscars, and Tonys; for musicians, there are the Grammys and various musical halls of fame. But in academia, specifically Shakespeare studies, you've made it, really made it, when Mike Jensen interviews you for his "Talking Books" column in *Shakespeare Newsletter*.

For more than 17 years Mike has ... but Mike will tell you those details himself. What he won't tell us—frankly, what I think he doesn't fully realize—is the impact that he's had on the field. When Mike began "Talking Books," Shakespeare studies was in the midst of a cultural revolution—the term is significant. No, we weren't burning books and jailing dissidents or sending older academics to work camps, but the repudiation of the past, signaled by Roland Barthes's famous essay, "The Death of the Author," the poststructuralist destruction of definitive meaning, and finally, New Historicism, which emphasized political concerns over aesthetics, left many scholars confused and frustrated. If nothing valid could be said about literature, then why bother saying anything about it? If art was just politics misspelled, then any serious student was better off as a poli-sci major. That's not to say that there weren't important, seminal works produced in the 1980s and 1990s—(a shameless plug here for my old Shakespeare prof, Ed Pechter) it's just that in the eye of the storm we didn't really have a sense of what would make it to port and what would be left adrift on the high seas of critical confusion.

Mike played a role on that voyage, I think a significant, perhaps even crucial, role. Having somehow convinced ourselves that we had entered into a brave new world wherein Shakespeare's place in academia owed more to accident than aesthetics, that authorship was at an end, that words were worthless, along came Mike, quietly but firmly reasserting Humanist values, asking difficult questions and citing historical counter examples (I'm thinking here of his *Shakespeare Newsletter* piece on Donald Foster, Gary Taylor and Brian Vickers—not in this anthology of "Talking Books" interviews but well worth seeking out). Mike refused to play our game. He wasn't alone; there were still plenty of bibliographers and legit historians, New and Old, bucking the trend by writing engaging, thoughtful and fact-filled essays and weighty tomes. What "Talking Books" did and, 17 years on, continues to do, is give the deconstructed author a *local habitation* and voice.

What probably aided Mike in his project was (and is) that he's not one of us. Mike doesn't have a Ph.D., and while he briefly taught Shakespeare at the university level, he has no formal degree in the field. That's not to say that he's untrained. At a recent Shakespeare Association of America conference, I toured the book room with Mike, who picked up some new titles. We chatted about some topic (I can't now recall which), and he confessed that he didn't know much about it; he only had (some number I can't remember—it was large) books on the subject. Just how many books does he have on what he thinks is important? Mike is an expert in Shakespeare film and stage production, radio adaptations, and, outside of Shakespeare studies proper, can legitimately call himself an expert in all things *Peanuts*—think Charlie Brown, not the groundnut (*Arachis hypogaea*). I have never visited Mike's house, but I imagine that he has ten books for every page that Stephen King has published. Do the math on that!

More than just a bibliophile, Mike has instant and near complete recall for names, dates, facts, titles, publishers. It's really remarkable and more than a bit intimidating to find out that Mike knows more about your particular field of study that you do—heck, he probably recalls more of your writing than you do! The point here is that as an outsider, Mike observes the inner workings of the Borg-Mind without being assimilated. Mike is more like the Shakespeare Association of America's resident shrink, taking notes on our ticks, slips, neuroses and night terrors, asking a few pertinent questions, but mostly just listening a lot. Sure, Mike is invested in what he does; but his investment is of a different kind than academics bedwetting over tenure or publishing contracts. Mike's independence has, paradoxically, made him indispensable to the profession.

Sure, journalists (really, if we were to give Mike a title, he'd probably be happier with that moniker than academic) have been around a good long while; some have even interviewed authors. Some were even interested in Shakespeare and interviewed scholars active in the field (William Hazlitt's *Table-Talk* comes to mind), but who has month by month, year by year, kept up with all the major trends, and interviewed all the major players in Shakespeare studies? We've been writing about Shakespeare for hundreds of years, so you would think someone would have done this before. Finally someone has. His name is Mike Jensen.

More than just a keen observer and contributor, Mike has also proven himself to be a genuinely kind soul. When, recently, I confessed that I felt that my own career had stalled, Mike quietly had a word that put me on the Board of *Shakespeare Newsletter*. What a guy!

As for other careerists out there, keep writing: Mike is probably reading your stuff. And he's always thinking about who would be the right person for the next "Talking Books" column. He might even be ringing you right now.

Jeffrey Kahan is the author of *Reforging Shakespeare, The Cult of Kean, Bettymania and the Birth of Celebrity Culture, Getting Published in the Humanities* and *Shakespiritualism: Shakespeare and the Occult, 1850–1950*. His scholarly editions include *Imitations, Parodies and Forgeries, 1710–1820* in three volumes and editions of *Pericles, Prince of Tyre* and *Coriolanus* for the New Kittredge Shakespeare. Kahan is a professor of English at University of La Verne in La Verne, California. He wrote and edited *King Lear: New Critical Essays*.

Preface

The "Talking Books" column in *Shakespeare Newsletter* has a simple concept: readers eavesdrop on many of the most prominent Shakespeare scholars of our time as we talk about the books that have influenced their work, refer to often, or think are just plain fun. The column is a Shakespeare geek's dream come true, and I should know since I am one. "Talking Books" is the most popular feature in *SNL*, as we call it. Many people have urged me to collect the columns in a book, and here it is.

Reading these interviews again and reading them together showed me two things I had not realized when conducting the interviews months and years apart. The first is that my older guests tend to mention certain older scholars and their books that my younger guests do not mention and possibly do not know. None of these older books is mentioned more often than M. C. Bradbrook's *Themes and Conventions of Elizabethan Tragedy*. Bradbrook's excellent work seems to be neglected due to its age. I hope the recommendations in this book will motivate you to seek out Bradbrook's works and those by the other older scholars we discuss. Their books are well worth reading.

The second is an insight into how the field is changing. Lukas Erne's book *Shakespeare as Literary Dramatist*, to give one example, was published after "Talking Books" began. Ann Thompson was the first to mention the book in our 2003 interview, and many of the scholars I now interview continue to praise it. I am not persuaded by Erne's premise that Shakespeare wrote multiple versions of some of his plays, one for the stage and another for publication, but my skepticism is beside the point. *Shakespeare as Literary Dramatist* has a profound impact on Shakespeare scholars and their work even now, which is the point. The impact of *Shakespeare as Literary Dramatist*, and books and authors of similar influence, is measurable in these pages. Cumulatively, these interviews give us a unique snapshot of what Shakespeare scholars think and how their thinking is changing as we go deeper into the twenty-first century.

This book presents the columns in chronological order, starting with the first, my interview with Stanley Wells in 2001, and ends with the Robert

S. Miola interview from 2009. A very few changes to some interviews were necessary due to the passage of time, and I cleared those with the guests that are still living. I otherwise treated all answers as sacred. To make this book as useful as possible, the introductions to every interview have been thoroughly updated by adding books written by my guests after our interviews, including books that are forthcoming. A bibliography of all the books mentioned has been added. There are many interviews in which guests mention an author, but not the title of the book they had in mind. I have supplied these. You are invited to treat the bibliography as a reading list of the great books in Shakespeare studies past and present, because you will not find one that is better or more comprehensive.

This is not really an academic book, but it is on an academic subject, so there is some jargon. In scholar-speak, the name of a journal followed by numbers such as "52:4," means "volume 52, number 4." I saw no advantage to typing this out each time, so I used the correct bibliographic style.

"Early modern," is the politically correct term for what we once called the Renaissance, but now without the tacit implication that this era was superior to the Medieval. It also usually substitutes for Elizabethan and Jacobean, since it covers both eras. I sometimes playfully shorten "early modern" to "early mod."

Readers should know the words *quarto* and *Folio*. A quarto is a small book from early modern times. When discussing Shakespeare, a quarto is usually one of Shakespeare's plays printed as a standalone book. Folio designates the 1623 First Folio that published thirty-six of Shakespeare's plays, eighteen for the first time. Guests follow the standard practice of designating the number when they discuss the Second, Third, or Fourth Folios and, still following the standard practice, do not always use the number when discussing the First.

Just to keep things complicated, some guests added a few publication dates to make points about dates or chronology, and so do I in some introductions. There are also a very few instances in which a book was written in one year, but was not printed until decades or centuries later. The composition dates are next to the titles of these books with the first publication dates in the bibliography. Titles otherwise appear without dates in the interviews, but you will always find publication dates in the bibliography along with publisher names, when applicable. Publisher names are not always applicable because the rise of formal publishing houses did not occur until long after some of the books we discuss were printed. There is, in addition, an appendix listing Shakespeare films mentioned in these interviews.

I want to thank Mick Hattaway, Peter Holland, and Lois Potter for supplying some page numbers for the bibliography that I was unable to find.

Introduction

To understand this book, it helps to know a little about the "Talking Books" column in *Shakespeare Newsletter* where I have interviewed many of the prominent Shakespeare scholars of our time. I did not set out to be an interviewer.

I had been publishing short pieces for almost a decade before my first interview, if it was an interview. I attended a *Hamlet* conference in Berkeley in October 1990. The actor Mel Gibson made a brief appearance to plug his 1991 *Hamlet* movie and take a few questions. I asked Mr. Gibson a couple of additional questions in the hall and wrote up his comments for the *Shakespeare on Film Newsletter*. I did not think of this report as an interview, but it was called an interview in the several books and articles that cited the piece, so I played along.

I continued to pile up publications until my first book appeared seven years later. It was written with Helen D. Davies to help newly diagnosed Alzheimer's patients cope with the next few years of their lives. We had dozens of media interviews and personal appearances to support the book, so most of my interviews up to that time were on the other side of the microphone.

I wanted a different direction for my writing career, which coalesced around my long-held interest in William Shakespeare. I liked that Shakespeare scholars are a community that speaks to one another in print. I wondered how I might become part of their conversation, especially since I lacked some obvious qualifications such as a Ph.D. and was not faculty at a college or university at that time. Perhaps an interview column on the topic of books about Shakespeare could get me in the side door, but who would want to publish it? All Shakespeare journals publish scholarly articles and reviews, but *Shakespeare Newsletter*, hereafter *SNL*, prints an unusual mix of scholarly articles, book reviews, and Shakespeare–related news. *SNL* was the only hope for this idea.

SNL had been around for fifty years at that time, and so it had longevity despite its unpromising title. The newsletter also had, and still has, by far the largest number of subscribers to any Shakespeare journal. I put a toe in by writing a couple of reviews for *SNL*, and those went well. I could work with these people, but would they want a genre of column that had not been tried before in one of the journals? Could I show the editors that the column would check all three of their boxes in a fresh way: scholars, books, and newsy seeming interviews?

I had already made the acquaintance of a number of well-known Shakespeareans, as we call ourselves, when I contacted *SNL* with my proposal. Without consulting my friends, I promised to deliver them in a series of interviews that would discuss the books that were the most useful in their work and influenced their ideas. Take a step back and you realize that these interviews are really about the careers of my interview guests and the state of modern Shakespeare studies, because the guests are the people shaping modern Shakespeare studies. Books are the way we get into that discussion.

I was crestfallen when *SNL* Editor John W. Mahon replied that he and his co-editor, the now late Thomas A. Pendleton, would try one interview to "see how it goes." I put the best face on it and proceeded, asking Stanley Wells to be my first guest.

There is no bigger star in the Shakespeare world, then or now. Stanley had privately reached out to me a few times, showing great kindness in his responses to comments I made on a Shakespeare listserv. Not long before my proposal to *SNL*, the late Shakespeare scholar Terence Hawkes made one of his frequent vitriolic public attacks, the first of several that he directed at me. Stanley wrote a very nice note. I did and do think the world of him. I was delighted that Stanley consented to be the guest in my first, and perhaps only, "column."

It was a smashing success, mostly due to Stanley Wells. He took some rather generic questions and energized them with very specific and insightful answers that often pointed the way to learning more. This approach was exactly what the column needed, which I recognized when I saw Stanley's answers. The quality of those answers assured that there would be a second column, a third, and it is still going more than 17 years later. The success that followed is very much due to Stanley Wells opening my eyes to what "Talking Books" could be, and my learning over time how to make it that.

I relied on those generic questions for the first few interviews, but noticed that the same questions sometimes received the same answers, which would be a problem if readers began to notice. The solution was to spend more time with the books written by my guests and develop extra questions specific to them.

After five interviews, I exhausted my circle of friends who had enough of a public profile to be of interest to *SNL* readers. I needed to find other scholars I did not know. Anne Barton was at the top of my list.

Barton was the great American-born Shakespearean whose career was mostly in the U.K. She was one of editors of the first edition of the *Riverside Shakespeare*, the text assigned for my undergraduate Shakespeare class. I read her fantastic introduction to *Twelfth Night* in the *Riverside* years later as I prepared to study the play. It was so remarkably good and unfailingly insightful that I made a point of seeking out the books Anne had written up to that time. These were even greater than her introduction, if only because there was more space to develop ideas and let those ideas play together. I was thrilled again when this hero of mine consented to be a guest in "Talking Books."

So it went. Peter Holland, who wrote the fascinating book *English Shakespeares: Shakespeare on the English Stage in the 1990s*, is editor of the important annual *Shakespeare Survey* and was then director of the Shakespeare Institute in Stratford-upon-Avon. I asked Peter. He said yes. Ann Thompson is one of the General Editors of the third series of Arden Shakespeare editions and co-editor of the controversial new editions, plural, of *Hamlet*. I asked Ann. She said yes. Finding new guests was easy. I simply asked the person whose work fascinated me the most at that moment. Nearly everybody said yes. The most astute amongst you have already wondered, "What about all the great scholars whose work does not fascinate you?" I have a confession to make.

I will not spend weeks, sometimes months, reading books that bore me, nor will I give myself whiplash from rolling my eyes at a hundred miles per hour by reading books with approaches that I think are wrong. As soon as I see a dust jacket or catalog copy that praises an author's psychoanalytic, feminist, cultural, or Marxist approach to Shakespeare, I move on. These and other literary approaches are sometimes grouped with French literary theory, an outgrowth of late twentieth century French philosophy, commonly just called "Theory," and note that not all the writers are French. Each of these schools of thought has a distinct approach to critiquing literature, but I discuss them together here because my purpose is to give some of the reasons they fail to address the literary matters that interest me and to question their long-term viability. It is also a matter of principle, and that needs some defending.

It is impossible to make the case here. To do it properly would take a book that I have no desire to write, so briefly and incompletely, most of these approaches are political and judgmental at their cores. People who use them are more interested in condemning the ways that Shakespeare, to use the example dear to me, has been used to consolidate the power of nations than they are in understanding what Shakespeare actually wrote. Theory even denies that Shakespeare's texts are understandable, and so settles for judging Shakespeare for not seeing the world through the eyes of modern feminists, supporting power structures based on owning property, and other perceived moral failures. My friend Samuel Crowl put it well, "It is surely one of the goals of current theory—when practiced at its most lofty level—to rival, if not supplant, the text."[1] I have sympathy with those who want to expand Core educational reading to a multicultural canon that includes literary texts that relate to non-white, non-male, and non-straight readers instead of forcing traditional and less relatable texts upon them; I have no use for the ego and judgmental politics too often taken by many approaches to literature, and that puts me out of the mainstream of current scholarship.

These scholars usually reply to criticism of their political approaches by claiming that everything is political, including their critics, as if saying that somehow makes their methods right. That claim is really just a lazy way of not grappling with the arguments against these approaches and allows the speaker to dishonestly avoid admitting defeat. It is absurd to pretend that the overt polemic of a Jonathan Dollimore is the same as the textual excavations of a theatre historian such as Alan C. Dessen, and that difference exposes the claim that everything is political to be a rationalization, a false equivalence asserted as a matter of faith, for it lacks substance. Shakespeare studies should deal with the issues raised by Shakespeare, his contemporary writers, and the theatre and book trade of his time. "Scholarship" based on the ideas of one theorist or another, one movement or another, and then applied to Shakespeare, too often results in expressing opinions dressed in fake objective language. It cedes authority to the movement.

I do not claim that all feminist, cultural, and similar scholarship is worthless. I once heard a half-brilliant lecture by a leading scholar. If I remember her argument accurately, the talk was given several years ago, she spoke of Innogen in *Cymbeline*, spelled Imogen in older editions, whose husband makes a bet with a villain that Innogen will stay true when the villain tries to seduce her. This scholar used a feminist approach to say that for all of her life, others took responsibility for Innogen's sexuality: first her father, then her husband, and now the villain who tries to make it his. It never occurs to any of these characters that Innogen's sexuality is hers to withhold or bestow. This is a brilliant insight, really. It tells us very little about Shakespeare, but it tells us quite a lot about the time the play was written and the then prevailing understanding of sexuality, and these are assumptions Shakespeare seems to share, at least in this play. *Antony and Cleopatra* is another matter.

I do not remember the speaker saying that in marrying Posthumus, Innogen took responsibility for her own sexuality, so I may have figured that out on my own. If so, I am grateful that this lecturer put me on the path to realizing this. Unfortunately, and if I still remember her remarks correctly, the speaker later claimed that Posthumus defends Britain from a Roman invasion by guarding a pass so narrow that it could be successfully secured by one man. That pass was then equated to the vagina that Posthumus also guards. This is Freudian lunacy, and does not acknowledge that by taking the wager in the first place, Posthumus did a lousy job of guarding Innogen's vagina. She had to repel that invader herself, so this is another false equivalence. At a less lofty level, the speaker got the defender of the vagina, um, pass wrong. It was Belarius and his adopted sons who repelled the invaders, three people, not Posthumus by himself, as Posthumus makes clear in 5.5.14–51.

Feminist, Marxist, psychoanalytic, cultural, French, and other critics are very, very smart people and, as in the lecture, some portion of their work can be enlightening. Marx showed that economic forces help shape our lives and society. Freud showed that the unconscious helps shape our lives and behavior. Theory shows that we always have subjective responses to the texts we read. Unfortunately, all of these are guilty of the reductionist fallacy: they reduce something complex into something simple. Our lives and society are shaped by more than economic forces, there is more to us than our subconscious mind and the drives it energizes, and we do not project everything that we read into a text.

I am confident that someday these theoretical approaches will be understood to have limited value when studying literature, and there are already signs that this is changing. My brief critique is expressed in negative terms. In our interview, Robert S. Miola gives a wonderful positive expression to the alternative work now being done in Shakespeare studies that go beyond these questionable literary approaches. That is the nature of philosophy. Each generation invalidates the assertions of the previous, with rare exceptions. It is just a matter of time.

Despite the impression I may have left above, some of the people interviewed in this book use these methods. Life is too complex to rigidly divide scholars into those who practice these critical methods and those who do not. Certain people use them some of the time, but these methods are less useful when performing other acts of scholarship, such as editing a play. I interviewed Ann Thompson, for example, who co-edited the influential feminist anthology, *Women Reading Shakespeare 1660–1900*, with Sasha Roberts. This was still early days for "Talking Books," and I would do several things differently now, one of which is include questions about feminist scholarship. What drew me to Thompson, however, was her work as an editor of texts. Sam Crowl and Tony Dawson are two favorites of mine for their books on Shakespeare performance. As you will see, both praise several theoretical approaches and even I agree that at times their work is better for what they have learned from these approaches. I once succumbed to several suggestions that I interview a scholar whose work is steeped in cultural criticism. I think the interview is mostly successful, though not entirely. I did not enjoy the experience at all, so I no longer make exceptions to the rule that at least some of a scholar's work must fascinate me before I send an invitation to be a guest in my column. If you feel that "Talking Books" and this volume are flawed because I do not emphasize theoretical approaches, please know that I believe this is a virtue. I hope my interviews show the best these approaches offer and avoid their excesses, at least most of the time. We now turn to the mechanics of "Talking Books."

Once a guest agrees to be interviewed, I spend a few weeks gathering their books and more weeks reading them. It sometimes takes months, since some guests have been quite prolific. I then write an introduction and a few dozen questions which are sent to my guests via email in a Word document. I ask guests to only answer the questions that interest them. It is OK if a comment does not really fit a question. I can change the question later. I get the interview back and, if necessary, suggest ways my guest might give more helpful answers. I usually add some follow-up questions. We pass the interview back and forth a few times until we are both happy with it. I add comments here and there in response to some answers. I realize that these comments make the interviews read as if my guest and I had an oral conversation, but my reason is to make a point, add my own endorsement to a book I admire, tell readers where to look in the bibliography to find the book when needed, or ease the transition to a new topic. This illusion of conversation makes the interviews more readable, I think, so it has that stylistic advantage. I do not do this to trick people into thinking they are reading a transcript of a conversation, though I imagine many do.

I use this method of interviewing for two reasons. The one that matters less, perhaps, is that I am lazy. I have transcribed excerpts of radio programs for articles about Shakespeare radio, and it is a lot of tedious work. It is even more work once I have a transcript. I then have to go over it carefully while listening to the recording to make sure the transcript is accurate. In both parts of the process, there is much starting, stopping, rewinding, and listening for the place I want on the tape or audio file. I just hate it. Doing that for a much longer "Talking Books" interview would be agony, and I would quit.

The more important reason, however, is the manuscript format allows my guests to make sure their answers are clear and polished, that they say what they really want to say. Few people have such polish in conversation. One invited guest only wanted to do a recorded interview. He is a great scholar and a wonderful guy, a household name to people in the Shakespeare business, so I really wanted to talk about books with him. I toyed with doing all that work to accommodate him, but I thought the quality of the interview would suffer along with my sanity, so we ended it there.

My guests seem to enjoy the process for several reasons. Most have read the column and know that previous guests came across well. An editor's job is to make writers look good, so that is what I try to do as the Contributing Editor, my title, of "Talking Books."

I think there is a certain implied flattery when I ask someone to be a guest. About half say something such as, "Wow, I love 'Talking Books' and I am flattered that you asked." They are flattered? I am flattered they didn't tell me to go fish!

It does not hurt that I always credit my guests when I receive praise for an interview, and that is not flattery. I just ask questions and, if needed, suggest ways to make the answers better. It is my guests who must rise to the occasion and be informative and fascinating. They really do deserve the praise.

Most of us write our articles and books one at a time, concentrating on the ideas at hand without always realizing that our ideas gain deeper meaning with each new publication. Several guests thanked me for making them understand that their publication history has a beginning and middle, if not yet an end. They see the arc of their work for the first time.

Though I try to be supportive of my guests, I cannot ignore it when one has written something controversial. I ask questions that I hope are so subtle that neither the guests nor readers realize I am challenging them. This allows them to present their ideas from their own perspective, even when I am skeptical of that perspective. I want to see if they can convince me, and you will see that happen in my interviews with MacDonald P. Jackson and Katherine Duncan-Jones, for example. Unfortunately, that led to one guest dropping out after our first draft interview was returned to him with my follow-up questions. He never spoke to me again, not even to say that he was no longer willing to be interviewed. A mutual friend had warned that he would behave "like a child" if challenged. I hoped my subtlety would prevent him from realizing I had doubts about certain claims he has made. I guess he saw through me. He should have played along, for my guests always have the last word and, who knows? He might have convinced me.

It is a little disappointing when books are recommended that are written by authors with whom I have strong philosophical or personal disagreements, and indeed books by my nemesis Terence Hawkes are recommended by several guests. Of course, I let those recommendations stand, and I do not at all mind being corrected by a guest if I have a fact wrong or misunderstood something. Though this goes against the current political climate in the United States, facts matter very much and I'd much rather get things right than have people think I was right.

I hope these comments give you everything you need to know about "Talking Books," and this reprint of twenty-four past columns. Put it all together, and this book is a collection of interviews with many of the greatest Shakespeare scholars of our time talking about some of the landmark books in our field. Most of these scholars are also some of the nicest people I know. I am lucky that I get to do this. I think you will enjoy eavesdropping on our conversations.

Note

1. Samuel Crowl, *Shakespeare Observed: Studies in Performance on Stage and Screen* (Ohio University Press, 1992), p. 51.

Stanley Wells

While most scholars specialize in one or two areas, Stanley Wells has excelled in many, including bibliography, textual editing and annotation, journal editing, close readings, and theatre history and criticism. He directed The University of Birmingham's Shakespeare Institute from 1988 to 1997 (where he is now Emeritus), has lectured in many different countries, is a past chairman of the International Shakespeare Association, and co-led the team that produced both editions of the sometimes controversial *Oxford Shakespeare* (1986 and 2005). Wells now operates from the Shakespeare Centre, home of the Shakespeare Birthplace Trust in Stratford-upon-Avon, of which he was Chairman from 1991–2011. He is now Honorary Emeritus Chairman of the Royal Shakespeare Theatre, of which he was Vice-Chairman at the time of our interview. It would be easy to triple this list of affiliations.

Wells's first book was not about Shakespeare, but the 1964 edition *Thomas Nashe: Selected Works*, the first volume in the Stratford-Upon-Avon Library. Shakespeare read Nashe widely and imitated some of his linguistic tricks, and while this was not known in 1964, they collaborated with others on *Henry VI, part one*. This is an excellent starter collection for Nashe readers, if you can find it.

A few of Wells's many Shakespeare books include *Re-Editing Shakespeare for the Modern Reader*. It explains editing standards for the Oxford edition. *Shakespeare: A Dramatic Life* was published in America by W. W. Norton & Company and as *Shakespeare: A Life in Drama* in the U.K. The book studies the plays, not the man. *Shakespeare in the Theatre: An Anthology of Criticism* has some of the finest theatre writing about Shakespeare ever published from c. 1700–1996. Wells edited the quarto text of *King Lear* for the Oxford Shakespeare multi-volume series, of which he is General Editor, and is co-editor with Michael Dobson and substantial contributor to the *Oxford Companion to Shakespeare*. Shortly before our discussion, he completed *For All Time: Shakespeare and His Legacy*, an amply illustrated volume that looks at the mark Shakespeare left on the world.

Some of the books Wells has published since our interview are *Looking for Sex in Shakespeare* and its unintended companion, *Shakespeare, Sex and Love*. The former looks at specific texts such as Shakespeare's sonnets and A *Midsummer Night's Dream* to understand how Shakespeare understood sexuality. The latter is a big picture study of sexuality as understood and practiced in Shakespeare's time with examples drawn from Shakespeare's contemporary writers as well as the Bard. Wells takes a direct look at those contemporaries in *Shakespeare and Co.: Christopher Marlowe, Thomas Dekker, Ben Jonson, Thomas Middleton, John Fletcher and the Other Players in His Story*. Shakespeare may be the gorilla in the literary room, but the best works by his fellow playwrights are as fine as anything Shakespeare wrote, just different. This book is an excellent introduction to these writers and their work.

Wells has never written a Shakespeare biography, but has worked the edge of that field often. *Shakespeare's Sonnets*, co-written with Paul Edmondson, is one of the better introductions to those poems and finds that at least some have autobiographical elements. The delightful *Is It True What They Say About Shakespeare?* debunks, confirms, or qualifies many of the common claims made about Shakespeare. It is a fantastic introduction to him and so is *Coffee with Shakespeare* published by Duncan Baird in 2008. This one has the conceit of

Sir Stanley Wells

and a question and answer session with Shakespeare who has come back from the dead for a cup of coffee with his interlocutor. Shakespeare supposedly answers Wells's questions, though, of course, the answers were written by Wells who draws on his knowledge of Shakespeare biography. He is honest about the gaps in our knowledge and makes clear what is known and what is speculation. This book was reprinted as *Shakespeare ... off the record* in 2011 by Watkins Publishing, one of Duncan Baird's imprints. These short books are more reliable "biographies" of Shakespeare than many of the more traditional but speculative biographies past and present. A cunning and very different approach to Shakespeare biography is *The Shakespeare Circle: An Alternate Biography*, co-edited with Paul Edmondson. This is an anthology of biographical essays about the people Shakespeare (mostly) knew. This unusual approach fills in different parts of the Bard's life that are missing with a Shakespeare-centered approach. A more direct book is *William Shakespeare: A Very Short Introduction* for the Oxford University Press series of "Very Short" introductions in 2015. It is not a formal biography, but an introduction to his life and works for those with just an hour or two to spare. A non-biographical companion piece, *Shakespeare's Tragedies: A Very Short Introduction*, followed in 2017.

Great Shakespeare Actors: Burbage to Branagh surveys the careers of some of the finest Shakespearean actors over the centuries. A kind of book seldom published anymore is the collection of previously published essays. It is a testimony to Stanley Wells's stature as a Shakespearean that Oxford University Press brought out a book of twenty-five essays culled by Paul Edmondson from Wells's long career. It is entitled *Shakespeare on Page and Stage: Selected Essays.*

Welles is one of the "go to" scholars called by the British media when Shakespeare is in the news. He received a C.B.E. in the Queen's Birthday Honors List in 2007 and was knighted in 2015. Our interview appeared in *Shakespeare Newsletter*, 51:3, #250, Fall 2001.

•••••••••••••••••••••••••••

MPJ: *Which books helped direct your career?*

Stanley Wells: After leaving University College London, where I took my first degree, I worked for several years as a schoolmaster in the country—as Shakespeare is supposed to have done (though I attach no importance to the resemblance). During that period I maintained my scholarly interests partly by reading successive issues of *Shakespeare Survey*. I had no idea at the time, of course, that for nearly twenty years, I should be its editor, but I valued it for its accessibility and informativeness, qualities that I strove to preserve during my editorship.

Which books influenced you the most?

It may seem too obvious to say so, but the book that has had the biggest influence on my life since I was a schoolboy is the collected works of Shakespeare. Or, more accurately, various editions of the separate plays and poems. When I read a play I usually do so in an annotated edition. Sometimes of course one wants to be able to read the text without interruption: "Annotation," as Dr. Johnson said, "refrigerates the mind." But I think the Introductions to the best of the multi-volume editions are often underrated as sources of both information and criticism. The editor of a play lives closely with it for a long time, has to think about it from many different points of view, and so is in an exceptional position to write illuminatingly about it. Naturally I have a predilection for the volumes of my own *Oxford Shakespeare*.

Some of the books that have influenced me most have been ones that are not directly, or primarily, concerned with Shakespeare. As an undergraduate I was passionate about John Keats's letters, partly because his prose is Shakespearean in its glancing allusiveness, its vigor, and its coherent inconsequentiality, so that as he writes we seem to enter into his very thought processes, as we do in for instance Hamlet's soliloquies. And of course Keats has fine things to say directly about Shakespeare, too. Shakespeare was his god, with whom he rightly sensed a close creative affinity. If Keats had lived he might have developed into a great dramatist.

As a young man I also enormously enjoyed reading theatre criticism, especially the collected reviews of Bernard Shaw and Max Beerbohm. They stimulated and fed my interest in the history of the theatre. And of course they are both, in their very different ways, great stylists, Beerbohm the master of urbane, deadpan irony, Shaw amazingly vigorous, bursting with intelligence and wit at every pore, often outrageous. I was reading his review of Forbes-Robertson's Hamlet again the other day, and thought really, this is one of the masterpieces of English prose.

At the same time, it has to be said that both Shaw and Beerbohm had serious limitations in their response to Shakespeare, Shaw notoriously because he was such a devotee of the social dramas of Ibsen. In fact to read, for instance, Shaw's diatribe on *Cymbeline* is enough to make one think that critical understanding of Shakespeare genuinely has advanced over the past century. Still, he's always a pleasure to read. Quality of writing is important to me. I feel that scholarship and criticism are subdivisions of literature which deserve the same kind of concern for clarity and grace of expression, for imaginative engagement and courtesy to the reader. I find this in some of the older critics, such as C. S. Lewis, F. P. Wilson, and my one-time tutor Harold Jenkins, and in some more recent ones, such as Stephen Greenblatt, Stephen Orgel, Jonathan Bate, and Terry Hawkes. At other times, as I wade through acres of impenetrable jargon, I wonder why I'm not reading Jane Austen instead.

Yes, I understand. She restoreth my soul. Are there any books that you refer to frequently?

Along the most thumbed volumes on my shelves are those of my old friend Sam Schoenbaum, especially *Shakespeare's Lives* and the *Documentary Life*. They're packed full of fascinating information, and almost Shavian in their witty intelligence. Maybe he overdoes the irony at times, but they're wonderfully readable—and, as you can tell, that matters to me.

I think it does matter, and I find your books wonderfully readable. Who isn't read any more who should be rediscovered?

I'm pleased to have been working at a time when the importance of studying Shakespeare's plays as scripts for performance has been adequately recognized. Americans have made great contributions to the history of the English stage. A pioneer was Arthur Colby Sprague, whose books have been important to me. I especially admire his *Shakespeare's Histories, Plays for the Stage*, which I think is under-rated as a work of criticism. It's too easy to pigeonhole him as a theatre historian without seeing the relevance of his work to critical thought.

I also admire the work of Charles Shattuck, and the wonderful volumes of *The London Stage* and the sixteen volume *Biographical Dictionary of Actors, 1600–1800* by Philip J. Highfall, Jr., Kalman A. Burnim, and Edward A. Langhans. As you see, I tend to value books full of facts above ones that are full of ideas.

So do I. Are there any major studies that should be replaced?

G. C. D. Odell's *Shakespeare: From Betterton to Irving*, though it's opinionated, out of date, and often critically inept, is an invaluable pair of volumes which I wouldn't be without. If I had another lifetime or two, I'd love to try to write a replacement! The other book that I should like to write if I had world enough and time would be a discursive history of Shakespeare editing. My forthcoming book includes substantial chapters on Shakespeare's life and career, but although I admire both Park Honan's and Katherine Duncan-Jones's recent full-length biographies, I have no ambition to write one myself.

Stanley, thank you for getting this column off to such a great and informative start. It has been a pleasure talking books with you.

Alan C. Dessen

Alan C. Dessen has been helping Shakespeareans understand the early modern theatre more accurately since 1971. That was the publication year of his first book, *Jonson's Moral Comedy* in which Dessen showed that Ben Jonson's comedies were influenced by the moral plays of the late sixteenth century. *Shakespeare and the Late Moral Plays* is something of a companion piece, for it reads Shakespeare in light of the moral plays of his boyhood, finding parallels in language and character. The anonymous comedy *The Trial of Treasure* presents two protagonists and their companions, which parallels with the *Henry IV* plays, for example. The Vice character is reincarnated often as characters such as Richard III and Parolles in *All's Well That Ends Well.*

Elizabethan Drama and the Viewer's Eye uses the tools of historians to identify things seen on early modern stages that we may not imagine when simply reading old texts and *Elizabethan Stage Conventions and Modern Interpreters* also illuminates early modern staging by looking at properties, movement, and teases out the meaning of the stage directions repeated across plays, among other conventions.

My four favorite Dessen books come next. *Recovering Shakespeare's Theatrical Vocabulary* builds on earlier work by determining what audiences actually saw on Shakespeare's stage, reveals how we can determine this, and what this means for modern readers. The book is a heady work of textual archaeology. *A Dictionary of Stage Directions in English Drama, 1580–1642*, written in collaboration with Leslie Thomson, explains stage directions that may seem simple but are actually complex. So, for example, the stage direction *flame* indicates "an effect linked to supernatural events, evidently produced from under the stage, through the trapdoor." This is a book to have on hand when reading early modern plays. *Shakespeare in Performance: Titus Andronicus* surveys notable productions of that underrated play through 1988. The first edition was published in 1989 by Manchester University Press, and then the book was expanded by Michael D. Friedman who added more recent productions in 2013. Dessen told me at that time that he declined to update the book because he said what he wanted to say in the first edition. Dessen's last book, *Rescripting*

Shakespeare: The Text, the Director, and Modern Productions, is on omissions, insertions, transpositions, and reconceptions made by directors to the received text in productions he saw during twenty-five years of theatergoing. This book gets into the details of changes made when Shakespeare is put on the modern stage.

Alan C. Dessen

Until 2013, readers of *Shakespeare Bulletin* enjoyed Dessen's annual review of performance choices on the stages in London and Stratford-upon-Avon, and from 1994 to 2009 he edited the "Shakespeare Performed" section of *Shakespeare Quarterly*. From 1994 to 2001, he was the Director of ACTER, the semi-annual American tour in which five English actors perform one of Shakespeare's plays.[1] His British Academy lecture, "Staging Matters: Shakespeare, the Director, and the Theatre Historian," was delivered in 2005. Alan is the Emeritus Peter G. Phialas Professor of English at the University of North Carolina, Chapel Hill. This interview appeared in *Shakespeare Newsletter*, 51:4, #251, Winter 2001–2.

••••••••••••••••••••••••••••

MPJ: *Which books helped direct your career?*

Alan C. Dessen: My undergrad background was primarily New Critical and ahistorical, so a series of books I confronted in graduate school opened up whole areas. Some of these items are now past their sell-by date, for example, Willard Farnham's *The Medieval Heritage of Elizabethan Tragedy* and M. C. Bradbrook's *Themes and Conventions of Elizabethan Tragedy*.

How are they dated? Are they still worth reading? I have all of Bradbrook, but never got around to reading her through, just for reference when I found something in an index.

Bradbrook's "themes" in figures such as Christopher Marlowe, John Webster, and Thomas Middleton, do not seem as pertinent today, but her notions about "conventions" got me started on my ongoing project, the attempt to recover the original stage conventions or theatrical vocabulary, that led to my *Elizabethan Stage Conventions and Modern Interpreters*, and shows no signs of completion. Indeed, a case could be made that, after publishing four books going back to 1977 that deal with the same set of problems, the finish line is not even in sight.

Farnham's 1936 book now seems very heavy-handed, but his chapters on *de casibus* tragedy, the moral plays, and *The Mirror for Magistrates*, originally edited by William Baldwin and George Ferrers, introduced me, and I suspect others of my generation, to important materials.

Other books still provide material or formulations that I find useful. A. P. Rossiter's 1950 *English Drama from Early Times to the Elizabethans* provides a succinct overview from a very shrewd reader. Bernard Spivack's 1958 *Shakespeare and the Allegory of Evil* is reductionist as Shakespeare criticism, but provides a detailed and engaging (if overstated) introduction to the Vice. The Marlowe chapters in David Bevington's 1962 *From "Mankind" to Marlowe* may have been superseded, but his analyses of the Elizabethan moralities and interludes "offered for acting" (e.g., structure, doubling and tripling of roles) remains basic to any understanding of the development of popular drama in this period.

Whose books influenced you the most?

The two books I encountered early, and still consider foundational, are Madeleine Doran's *Endeavors of Art* and Bernard Beckerman's *Shakespeare at the Globe 1599–1609*. Indeed, Beckerman is one of my few academic heroes. Yes, some sections of his 1962 book have been superseded, but I regularly find, after great effort teasing out a "new" insight into stage technique, that same point made in one of his paragraphs. For me, he represents that ideal combination of academic theatre historian and shrewd director that I do not find elsewhere—myself included.

Doran's book is a distillation of what she gleaned from over twenty years of reading in plays and treatises of the period. I was told that a colleague had to pry the manuscript away from her and send it to a publisher, because there were always more items to read and digest. Since I started with Jonson and the moral plays, I drew heavily on or reacted against Spivack, Bevington, and Jonas Barish's *Ben Jonson and the Language of Prose Comedy*, but over the long haul the Doran and Beckerman books have had the greatest impact on how I think about English drama of this period.

I should note that as a theatre historian I inhabit a tiny corner of the far-flung Shakespeare empire, and, moreover, my own pet questions place me on the margins of even that space since I don't "do" buildings, biographies, or theatre companies. I distinguish between "performance history" (how Shakespeare's plays have been staged since the Restoration) and "theatre history" (how they were staged in those first productions). There are a wealth of studies in the first category, but, largely owing to the limited evidence, the pickings are much smaller for the latter, hence my recent obsession, along with my colleague Leslie Thomson, over stage directions.

I do draw regularly on the excellent work of theatre historians of my generation: Andrew Gurr (e.g., *Playgoing in Shakespeare's London*, among his many books), William Ingram (*The Business of Playing: The Beginning of the Adult Professional Theater in Elizabethan London*), Roslyn Knutson (*The Repertory of Shakespeare's Company*), Scott McMillin (*The Queen's Men and Their Plays*, co-authored with Sally-Beth MacLean, and also his earlier gem, *The Elizabethan Theatre and The Book of Sir Thomas More*).

Is there anything published lately we should know about?

Some recent books have changed the map for the theatre historian. I would single out in particular Bruce R. Smith, *The Acoustic World of Early Modern England*; Robert B. Graves, *Lighting the Shakespearean Stage, 1567–1642*; and Tiffany Stern, *Rehearsal from Shakespeare to Sheridan*. Stern's conclusions (e.g., about the likely absence of group rehearsal in our sense) are controversial, but as an indefatigable researcher she has churned up new evidence in a fashion not matched by anyone else in recent years.

Since you've read every extant English play of the early modern era at least once, and many several times, I'd dying to know: what are the really wonderful, unsung, under-appreciated plays?

That's not an easy question to answer. I've not found any totally neglected masterpieces, though there are lots of plays off the beaten track that serve my purposes well, just as there are plays now "canonized" that I deem sub-par (e.g., *Roaring Girl*). I think the major plays of Christopher Marlowe, John Webster, Thomas Middleton, John Ford, Jonson, etc., deserve their press clippings. In my estimation, Jonson's *The Alchemist* is the great non–Shakespeare play of the period. I haven't read it in many, many years, but there's an outrageous anonymous play c. 1600 called *Look About You* which has more tricks and disguises per square inch than anything else I've read. I need to revisit it to see if it's as wild as I remember. When I retire from teaching and grading, I want to revisit primary sources—perhaps starting with the entire Fletcher canon.

I should note that current critical consensus gives the authorship to The Roaring Girl *to Thomas Middleton and Thomas Dekker. Readers will find the play in the bibliography under their names. Name a Shakespeare book that is just plain fun.*

Given my quirky sense of humor, I confess that my all time favorite piece of "Shakespeare criticism" is not a book or even a scholarly essay, but rather James Thurber's "The Macbeth Murder Mystery."

I'm embarrassed to reveal that I spent two years researching the writers of the Algonquin Round Table and reading their books, but somehow I never got around to "The Macbeth Murder Mystery." Alan, thank you for mentioning it and for talking books with me.

Note

1. ACTER has undergone a name and location change. The new name is AFTLS, for Actors from the London Stage, and is administered from Notre Dame.

Jill L. Levenson

Jill L. Levenson has made her mark on the way we think about *Romeo and Juliet*. I first read her book on important productions of the play in Manchester University Press's *Shakespeare in Performance* series published in 1987. There is the possibility of a revised edition. She has chapters on the play in *Shakespeare's "Romeo and Juliet": Texts, Contexts, and Interpretation*, edited by Jay L. Halio, and in two Modern Language Association books, *Teaching Shakespeare Through Performance* edited by Milla Cozart Riggio and *Approaches to Teaching Shakespeare's "Romeo and Juliet,"* edited by Maurice Hunt. She edited the Malone Society reprint of the first quarto with Barry Gaines, and the Oxford World Classics edition, which she considers her major work so far. Levenson is also the co-editor, with Jonathan Bate and Dieter Mehl, of *Shakespeare and the Twentieth Century: The Selected Proceedings of the International Shakespeare Association World Congress, Los Angeles, 1996*. Levenson contributed chapters and articles to many other books and journals on both Shakespeare and contemporary drama, Tom Stoppard in particular, and edited the international quarterly journal *Modern Drama* for more than a decade.

Since our interview, Levenson co-edited *The Shakespearean World* with Robert Ormsby. The book's thirty-six essays by fifty scholars from around the world look at Shakespeare's global impact. I contributed a chapter making the case for including audio Shakespeare when writing performance histories, surveying the history of worldwide audio Shakespeare as I go. Current projects are a book for Oxford University Press titled *Shakespeare and Modern Drama* for the Shakespeare Topics series and contributing the performance history component to the new Variorum edition of *Othello*.

Levenson is a past president of the Shakespeare Association of America and former chair of the International Shakespeare Association, serving as convener of the Eighth International Shakespeare Congress in Brisbane, Australia in 2006, and the Ninth International Shakespeare Congress in Prague, 2011. She is an honorary vice president of the International Shakespeare Association, a fellow of the Royal Society of Canada, and emeritus professor of English at

Jill L. Levenson

the University of Toronto. This interview appeared in *Shakespeare Newsletter*, 52:1, #253, Spring 2002.

....

MPJ: *Aside from yours, of course, what are the really great books on* Romeo and Juliet?

Jill L. Levenson: Besides the earlier editions by Brian Gibbons and G. Blakemore Evans, my favorite publications on *Romeo and Juliet* are essays or chapters in books: Nicholas Brooke's chapter in *Shakespeare's Early Tragedies*, M. M. Mahood's in *Shakespeare's Wordplay*, Harry Levin's "Form and Formality in *Romeo and Juliet,*" Rosalie L. Colie's chapter on "*Othello* and the Problematics of Love" in *Shakespeare's "Living Art,"* which begins with her analysis of *Romeo and Juliet.* These are seminal pieces of criticism that began to release the play from the stereotypes to which it had become attached, especially a very narrow concept of tragedy. They took a close look at the second quarto text and helped the rest of us see how dynamic it was. On the subject of genre specifically, there are two helpful short pieces more than a generation apart that draw attention to the comic component in this early tragedy: H. B. Charlton's "*Romeo and Juliet* as an Experimental Tragedy," a British Academy lecture delivered in 1939 and published in 1940;

and Susan Snyder's chapter on *Romeo and Juliet* and *Othello* in *The Comic Matrix of Shakespeare's Tragedies*. Among recent essays, I like two which have already been reprinted: Edward Snow's "Language and Sexual Difference in *Romeo and Juliet*," and E. Pearlman's "Shakespeare at Work: *Romeo and Juliet*." Both of these analyze the play's composition in revealing detail.

Which books helped direct your career?

That's an easy question: everything written by Alfred Harbage by the early 1960s. For some reason I began to read his books on the English Renaissance theatre and audience when I was an undergraduate, and I decided that I wanted to study with him. There was something about the kind of research he did and the clarity with which he wrote about it that made me want to work in the same field. By a wonderful stroke of good fortune I was accepted at Harvard and began to take courses with Professor Harbage during my first year. He became my supervisor, mentor, and professional role model.

Which books influenced you most?

To paraphrase the well-known comment, I was influenced most as an undergraduate by whatever I was reading at any given time in my English courses. Originally I intended to major in education and to teach in elementary school. But my first required half-course, an introduction to prose fiction—we read everything from American short stories to Fydor Dostoevsky's *Crime and Punishment*—began to turn my mind towards an English major; and William Faulkner's *The Sound and the Fury* clinched the decision. At that point I expected to teach high-school English, but the half-course in Shakespeare's tragedies (we used Thomas Marc Parrott's edition of twenty-three plays and the sonnets) was so exciting that I began to consider a career in university teaching in order to pursue research. I lived at home while I attended Queens College, and I remember bursting out of my room after reading each Shakespeare play to tell my long-suffering mother about the experience, usually while she was trying to prepare dinner. With *King Lear*, I was so overwhelmed that all I could convey was a plot summary. Several years later my mother and I attended a performance of *King Lear* by Daniel Seltzer at Harvard (1964), and I realized that on her first exposure to the play she understood it far better than I ever had.

That's fascinating. I'm envious that you could share something like this with her. Are there any books that you refer to frequently?

Yes, there are books I keep near my desk all the time for preparing classes, and any other work that involves close reading of texts: the microscopic two-volume *Oxford English Dictionary* with its magnifying glass;

E. A. Abbott's *Shakespearian Grammar*; several standard handbooks on rhetoric and poetics; Stephen Booth's edition of *The Sonnets*; at least six or seven Oxford World Classics editions of Shakespeare, as well as a few third series Ardens.

Are any non-lit-crit books particularly enriching in your thinking and writing about Shakespeare and early modern theatre?

Because of the Topics project on Shakespeare and modern drama, I've been reading a lot of modern Shakespeare adaptations, not only dramatic adaptations. One chapter, for example, deals with women's rewritings of Shakespeare plays, and because theatrical versions are scarce, I'm looking at these dramatic versions in light of other forms of revision, such as novels. In fact, I'm currently supervising a Shakespeare Association America seminar on adaptations of Shakespeare—of all kinds—since Stoppard's *Rosencrantz and Guildenstern Are Dead* (1966).[1] The first papers are beginning to arrive, and I'm now reading the subject of one of them, Barbara Kingsolver's *The Poisonwood Bible* (classified as an Oprah's Book Club selection!). I find all of these adaptations enriching in the classroom as well as in my own thinking and writing: observing an artist, or even a would-be artist, as s/he interprets Shakespeare usually unsettles views of Shakespeare that may have begun to calcify. Margaret Atwood's novel *Cat's Eye*, for instance, is a brilliant deconstruction of *King Lear* which makes Shakespeare's play part of an artist's vocabulary for describing the way she came of age.

What needs are there crying out for a book that perhaps you don't want to write?

Charles Shattuck's catalogue of Shakespeare promptbooks needs to be updated, with all of the shifting that's happened in collections over the four decades since it was compiled. I wish I had the time, and travel expenses, to do such a worthwhile project.

Jill, I know how busy you are, and how we had trouble scheduling this interview. Thank you so much for finding the time to talk books with me.

Note

1. This seminar took place on March 23, 2002 in Minneapolis.

Brian Vickers

In the preface to his book *Returning to Shakespeare*, Brian Vickers writes, "Shakespeare is always there, in my consciousness, as an enrichment and a challenge, partly because I find it necessary periodically to move away to other literary forms and other periods. However great the writer, or composer, to limit oneself wholly to one *oeuvre* is unhealthy, as specialism cramps and confines the imagination. How little they know of Shakespeare who only Shakespeare know!" Thus Vickers has written about Greek drama in *Towards Greek Tragedy: Drama, Myth and Society* and early modern science in *Occult and Scientific Mentalities in the Renaissance* as well as edited the comprehensive anthology *English Renaissance Literary Criticism*. These are just three of several books *not* in one of the four areas where Vickers has published most often: William Shakespeare, Francis Bacon, rhetoric, and authorship.

Editions of Bacon's works are *The History of the Reign of King Henry VII: And Selected Works* for the series Cambridge Texts in the History of Political Thought. *The Essays or Counsels Civil and Moral* was published by Oxford World's Classics in 1999 with a revised edition, now entitled *Francis Bacon*, out in 2008. These were preceded by the monograph *Francis Bacon and Renaissance Prose* in 1968. Vickers's first book, *Essential Articles for the Study of Francis Bacon*, was published the same year.

A kind of companion volume also published that year is *The Artistry of Shakespeare's Prose*, which won the Harness Shakespeare Essay competition, and this brings us to Vickers's Shakespeare publications. A short book on *Coriolanus* was expanded and included in *Returning to Shakespeare*. The controversial *Appropriating Shakespeare: Contemporary Critical Quarrels* takes a hard but very logical look at French literary theory as practiced in Shakespeare studies. The monumental six volume *Shakespeare: The Critical Heritage* presents all the significant and much of the less significant Shakespearean criticism published between 1623 and 1801. A follow-up essay, "Recreating a Tradition: Some Reminiscences on Editing *Shakespeare: The Critical Heritage*," explores some of the lessons Vickers learned about the history of Shakespeare criticism and the sources for learning it when he put together these volumes. Vickers later became the hands-on General Editor of a new series designed to continue the documentary history of Shakespeare's reception down to 1920 or 1940, depending on the play. Entitled *Shakespeare: The Critical Tradition* and published by Continuum, six volumes were produced: *King John* edited by Joseph Candido, *Richard II* by Charles R. Forker, *A Midsummer Night's Dream* by Judith M. Kennedy and Richard F. Kennedy, *Measure for Measure* by Georg L. Geckle, *Coriolanus* by David George, and *The Merchant of Venice* by William Baker and Vickers.

We did not discuss rhetoric, because at the time of our interview my knowledge was not deep enough to ask interesting questions, but Vickers publications on the subject read later are an education in themselves. *Classical Rhetoric in English Poetry* is a history of the use of rhetoric first in Greek and Latin, then in English literature through the end of the eighteenth century. *In Defense of Rhetoric* looks at the rise and fall of rhetoric over a couple of millennia, with predictions about its future. Vickers is also the editor of *Rhetoric Revalued: Papers from the International Society for the History of Rhetoric.*

Brian Vickers

Three books on authorship appeared after our interview. A look at the attributions of the lyric "Shall I die?" and the *Funerall Elegye*, entitled *"Counterfeiting" Shakespeare: Evidence, Authorship, and John Ford's Funerall Elegye* was published in 2002 and *Shakespeare, Co-Author: A Historical Study of Five Collaborative Plays* was released by Oxford University Press at the end of that year. In 2007, came *Shakespeare, "A Lover's Complaint," and John Davies of Hereford.* It attempts to prove that "A Lover's Complaint" was written by Davies, not Shakespeare. It convinced many scholars until MacDonald P. Jackson published a counter argument. See the introduction to the Jackson interview for more. Subsequently, Vickers has published many attribution articles and reviews of books on the subject of attribution including a review of Jackson's refutation in the *Times Literary Supplement* (24 April 2015). His most recent Monograph is *The*

One King Lear which attempts to show that most of the differences between the quarto and the Folio versions of that play may be explained by the quarto compositor not having enough paper for the printing. Vickers is also the General Editor of the new edition *The Collected Works of John Ford*. Volume one, co-edited with Gilles Monsarrat and R. J. C. Watt, was published by Oxford University Press in 2012. Volumes two and three, just out as I revise this in 2018, include Ford's collaborative play and the evidence for his participation in them. Two of these plays are attributed to Ford for the first time. Volumes four and five will contain the solo-authored plays. It is in preparation. Vickers has also announced a two volume *Collected Works of Thomas Kyd* forthcoming from Boydell and Brewer, and as I write this the editorial team is not quite assembled. Vickers's Kyd attributions have been controversial, so it will be interesting to see how the scholarly community will receive the edition when it is eventually published.

Vickers retired as Professor of English Literature and Director of the Centre for Renaissance Studies at ETH Zurich (the Swiss Federal Institute of Technology) after 27 years and is now Emeritus, but is spending his retirement as a Distinguished Senior Research Fellow at the School for Advanced Studies at the University of London and a Senior Research fellow at the Institute of English Studies. Current projects are his directorship of *The Oxford Francis Bacon*, with eight volumes of a projected sixteen in print, and he directs the London Forum for Authorship Studies, created in 2005. Sir Brian was knighted in 2008. This interview appeared in *Shakespeare Newsletter*, 52:2, #253, Summer 2002.

••••••••••••••••••••••••••••

MPJ: *Brian, I am under-read in Bacon. Have you any suggestions?*

Brian Vickers: I think the best place to start would be with some of Bacon's early works. For instance, there is the "device" that he wrote in about 1592 called "Of Tribute; Or, Giving That Which Is Due" (pp. 22–51 in my anthology, where I print for the first time the complete text, newly discovered by Peter Beal, which I have co-edited with Henry Woudhuysen). In this debate four speakers meet to argue their case, the first praising "the worthiest virtue" (Fortitude), the second "the worthiest affection" (Love), the third pleading for "the worthiest power" (Knowledge), the fourth celebrating "the worthiest person" (Queen Elizabeth). So often in early Bacon one feels that he is about to launch into drama. Alternatively, one could start with the first book of *The Advancement of Learning*, which is a marvelous defense of the importance of study against its detractors. The best single modern account of Bacon is by an American scholar, Perez Zagorin, called *Francis Bacon*. I don't think he's got the *Essays* right, but everything else is clearly expounded and well documented.

Since you have two books on authorship/collaboration coming out, how can someone lacking a background in these issues inform themselves about them?

Well, that's not easy, since there is no single book that can answer your question. Unfortunately, a lot of suspicion and misunderstanding exists in Shakespeare circles concerning attribution studies. Some scholars simply mistrust statistics; others don't understand them. It's entirely typical of this stand-off that the last four editions of *Titus Andronicus* all ignore the overwhelming case for George Peele as author of 1.1, 2.1, 2.2, and 4.1. I hope that *Shakespeare, Co-Author* will show people that attribution studies can be trusted.

Ah, a preview of your results. Thank you. One disadvantage of the language barrier is that English-speaking Shakespeareans usually read books by other English speaking Shakespeareans, and miss a lot of the literature in other tongues. As a multi-lingual scholar, are there any books you want to bring to wider attention?

Although outstanding works by German scholars (such as Wolfgang Clemen and Dieter Mehl) have been translated, several other excellent studies in German ought to be better-known, preferably by having English translations issued. For instance, there is the outstanding book on Shakespeare's language by Jürgen Schäfer, *Shakespeares Stil. Germanisches und romanisches Vokabular*, which combined historical and statistical approaches to the question of Shakespeare's use of Anglo-Saxon as against Latin-derived words. Many of the great German nineteenth century scholars, such as Nicholas Delius and Gregor Sarrazin, who were not lucky enough to be widely read in English translation (as were August Wilhelm von Schlegel, Georg Gottfried Gervinus, Hermann Ulrici) are always worth consulting. Also, there are still many valuable dissertations on specific aspects of Shakespeare's language, and that of his contemporaries, produced when German universities still had a strong philological tradition based on a good classical education at the Gymnasium. Alas, since the Second World War German universities seem to have lost their autonomous intellectual tradition, and younger German scholars often seem to be playing catch-up with current literary theories, mostly of a fashionable but insubstantial nature. In Shakespeare studies, as everywhere else, literary scholarship has been contaminated by so-called "political" attitudes, from which German critics have not been immune. I wish they would re-establish their own scholarly traditions.

Let's hope an English Language publisher will take an interest in the best work. Whose books helped direct your career?

Looking back, I think two books that specially influenced me placed

Shakespeare's language and style in its historical context, the humanist curriculum (that is, the *studia humanitatis*, involving rhetoric, moral philosophy, history, and poetry), were both by American scholars: T. W. Baldwin, *Shakspere's Small Latine & Lesse Greeke* (1944), and Sister Miriam Joseph, *Shakespeare's Use of the Arts of Language* (1947). These were the first two detailed historical studies of the grammar-school curriculum as Shakespeare absorbed it, and of his knowledge of the expressive devices of rhetoric. I have worked on these topics from time to time in my career, but am convinced that an enormous amount may still be learned about Shakespeare's creative forging of an individual style and his debt to these traditional disciplines.

Which books influenced you the most?

I studied at Cambridge between 1959 and 1964, and learned a great deal from the teaching of Muriel Bradbrook and Leo Salingar. Of their books, I would recommend anyone to read her *Themes and Conventions in Elizabethan Tragedy*, and his *Shakespeare and the Traditions of Comedy.* Both books put Shakespeare in the context of the dramatic traditions on which he drew and re-shaped, and both bring out all the playwrights' reliance on theatrical conventions. Here, too, I am convinced that a good deal of fruitful work can still be done. I have also learned a great deal from books on the practicalities of writing and staging Elizabethan drama by such scholars as G. E. Bentley, Andrew Gurr, and Alan C. Dessen. I remember once being stimulated by Alfred Harbage, *Shakespeare and the Rival Traditions*, although like many people I now find it too schematic in its contrast between the private and the public theatres. However, it does contain much illuminating criticism. Another scholar whom I greatly admire is G. K. Hunter, whose book *John Lyly, The Humanist as Courtier* showed an admirable grasp of the actual literary situation confronting writers trying to start a career in London, and which includes a brilliant account of what Shakespeare learned from the plot-structures of Lyly's plays. Hunter's recent volume in the *Oxford History of English Literature, English Drama 1586–1642, The Age of Shakespeare* is the distillation of a lifetime's involvement with this genre, and should be on everybody's shelf.

Do you refer to any books frequently?

I am a great admirer of properly prepared reference works. Among those I consult most frequently are W. Ebisch and L. L. Schücking, *A Shakespeare Bibliography*, with the *Supplement*; Gordon Ross Smith, *A Classified Shakespeare Bibliography 1936–1958*; John W. Velz, *Shakespeare and the Classical Tradition: A Critical Guide to Commentary, 1660–1960*—an outstanding tool: would it were updated; Bruce T. Sajdak, *Shakespeare Index: An*

Annotated Bibliography of Critical Articles on the Plays 1959–1983—a gargantuan task—would it were also updated; and the invaluable *World Shakespeare Bibliography* produced by *Shakespeare Quarterly* over the years, brought up to modern standards first by Harrison T. Meserole, ably continued by Jim Harner, and now available online.[1] I also use that magnificent work compiled by Peter Beal, *Index of English Literary Manuscripts, Vol. 1, 1450–1625*, in two parts, *Vol. II, 1625–1700*, in two parts: I gather that an updated online version is being considered. I am also looking forward to Steven May's extension of William Ringler's *Bibliography and Index of English Verse Printed 1476–1558*, which will cover the period up to 1603. Having been privileged to see draught excerpts, I can report that, among other things, it will provide for the first time an inventory of English verse forms, a little-studied but important topic.

What book needs to be written that perhaps you don't want to write?

I remember once reading a report in the *Guardian* newspaper about the international Shakespeare conference at Stratford-upon-Avon one year, where John Dover Wilson was interviewed, including his remark that "everything in Shakespeare studies is yet to be done!" I would like to draw attention to the paucity of studies on Shakespeare's language: on his grammar (although Jonathan Hope is now producing a sequel to Edwin Abbot's *Shakespearian Grammar*, which dates back to the 1880s); on his metrics (the statistical analytical studies of Philip Timberlake, Ants Oras, and Marina Tarlinskaja are all outstanding in tracing the gradual development of Shakespeare's verse style in its use of feminine endings, internal pauses, and the distribution of strong and weak stresses within the line, but there are hardly any intelligent studies of the functions of verse in relation to character and situation as they metamorphosed during Shakespeare's career).

There are, equally, no good studies of Shakespeare's use of alliteration (although with modern computer programs adequately modified to take account of similarities of pronunciation across differences in spelling this would seem to be a relatively straightforward matter). There are no detailed studies of Shakespeare's use of rhyme—even the fact that Helge Kökeritz, in his book *Shakespeare's Pronunciation*, included an inventory of all of Shakespeare's rhymes (running to over 8000) seems to be an unknown fact to many scholars today, even those working in the field. The only usable book on Shakespeare's syntax is the all-too-brief study by John Porter Houston, *Shakespearean Sentences: Study and Style in Syntax*, which has many intelligent comments on syntax in relation to speaker across the whole of Shakespeare's career. But a professional linguist today would find the methodology inadequate, although he or she would not have the interpretative skills that Houston had. This, to me, is the greatest problem, how we can educate future Shakespeareans who know his plays inside out, know the work of at least 10 other Elizabethan, Jacobean and Caroline dramatists, and have the curiosity and self-discipline to do proper interdisciplinary study in some of the many areas on which his works touch. If anyone has ideas on how to solve this problem, I would be glad to hear from them.

Maybe, if I live forever, I'll work on it. Brian, I know how hectic your schedule has been, and that we even had to delay this interview. Thanks so much for taking the time to talk books with me.

Note

1. The current editor is Laura Estill.

John W. Velz

John W. Velz is best known for his work with Shakespeare and the classics. He compiled *The Tragedy of Julius Caesar: A Bibliography to Supplement the New Variorum Edition of 1913* and wrote a chapter in *Shakespeare's Ovid: The Metamorphoses in the Plays and Poems* edited by A. B. Taylor, but his best known work is *Shakespeare and the Classical Tradition: A Critical Guide to Commentary, 1660–1960*, a bibliography that Brian Vickers recently called, "outstanding."[1] Over three decades ago, Velz was contacted by the librarian at the University of Illinois who said both of the library's copies had been stolen. "It's the best review I ever received." Everyone at the University of Illinois will be happy to learn that *Shakespeare and the Classical Tradition* is now available online.[2] A later bibliography was a collaboration with Clifford Chalmers Huffman, *Shakespeare's Roman Works: Titus Andronicus, The Rape of Lucrece, Julius Caesar, Anthony and Cleopatra, and Coriolanus.* Add twenty-five journal articles and chapters in books, and this part of the Velz bibliography is considerably longer.

With Richard Hosley and Arthur C. Kirsch, Velz edited *Studies in Shakespeare, Bibliography, and Theater*, collecting essays by James G. McManaway, and with Francis N. Teague Velz co-edited *One Touch of Shakespeare: Letters of Joseph Crosby to Joseph Parker Norris, 1875–1878*. Velz also edited *Shakespeare's English Histories: A Quest for Form and Genre* which features nine essays that look at chronicle plays from a non–Historicist perspective. He is also a medievalist who has given many papers at medieval conferences.

After three decades at the University of Texas, Austin, Velz enjoyed a busy retirement. In 2002, he participated in Audrey Stanley's *Troilus and Cressida* workshop at the Shakespeare Association of America meeting, gave a lecture in Vienna on "Shakespeare and Classical Barbarism," and prepared a number of articles on Shakespeare and Christianity. Two that were published in books are "Shakespeare and the Geneva Bible" in *Shakespeare, Marlowe, Jonson: New Directions in Biography*, Takashi Kozuko and J. R. Molryne, eds., and "The Parliament of Heaven in Two Fifteenth-Century Dramatic Accounts of the Fate of Humankind" in *New Approaches to European Theatre of the Middle Ages: An*

John W. Velz

Anthology, Barbara Gusick and Edelgard E. DuBruck, eds. John and I were already friends when I interviewed him for "Talking Books," and we remained in frequent contact until his final illness made it difficult for him to stay in touch. He died in November 2008. His last book was published in his last months. *Exit Pursued by a Bear: Encounters with Shakespeare and Shakespeareans* is a memory book in which he wrote some very nice things about me, this interview, and many other Shakespeare scholars. I became weepy when I reread the inscription to revise this introduction, "Thanks for all you have done for me!" Believe me, I received far more than I gave. This interview was originally published in *Shakespeare Newsletter*, 52:3, #254, Fall 2002.

••••••••••••••••••••••••••••

***MPJ:** Shakespeare and religion is an area that has received a lot of abuse. It is getting renewed attention in light of suggestions that the Shakespeare family had papist sympathies. Is there an indispensable book on Shakespeare and religion?*

John W. Velz: No one work is indispensable. Because many have their own agendas to plead for specially, one should read as widely and alertly as possible, watching for inconsistencies and narrowness of vision. There is a plethora of very recent material; the *Shakespeare Survey 54* is "Shakespeare and Religions," in part based on the conference on that subject in the summer of 2000. I know of another volume of collected essays on Shakespeare and the Reformation in the pre-publication stage.[3] Shakespeare moved in Huguenot circles in London and he read carefully from a Geneva Bible. Yet his family had strong Catholic leanings, and he shared those feelings. At the same time, Shakespeare was a "good Anglican" in that he kept his ears and his mind alert in Holy Trinity Church when he was a boy; he had the Elizabethan Psalter by heart and an amazing number of passages from the Bishops' Bible as well. If there is one book to start with, it might be Ernst Honigmann's *Shakespeare: The Lost Years*, which posits Shakespeare's working in two Catholic households in Lancashire. Making sense of the three religions in Shakespeare is a daunting task that no one has yet completed.

Which probably explains why there are so many assertions, but little agreement. Who are the great authors of books on Shakespeare and the classics?

I think the two scholars who get the palm are Brian Vickers and Robert Miola. There are many other good scholars in the field and some are remarkably good, but these two stand out above us all. Miola's *Shakespeare's Rome* finds a place for Virgil in Shakespeare's conception of *Romanitas.* Virgil had been largely shut out in favor of Plutarch until Miola brought him forward. Miola's books, *Shakespeare and Classical Comedy: The Influence of Plautus and Terence*, and *Shakespeare and Classical Tragedy: The Influence of Seneca*, are both more penetrating and more broadly inclusive than other books in the field. Vickers' most famous works are the books he wrote early in his career on rhetoric. But I am most taken with two later books, *Appropriating Shakespeare*, that takes on the post-modern critics of Shakespeare, and a retrospect of Vickers' best essays, *Returning to Shakespeare*, which is prefaced by an intellectual autobiography. In writing about Vickers' British Academy lecture on the *Consolatio* in Shakespeare, I used words like "close-packed," "exhaustive," and "virtually definitive." These two students of the Classical Tradition are as close to being polymaths as one gets in our profession. And neither of them forgets what it all means while leading us through the labyrinths of ancient lore.

Whose books helped direct your career?

T. W. Baldwin's two relentless, scholarly volumes on *William Shakspere's Small Latine and Lesse Greeke* to start with. Baldwin was a better Forscher than he was an interpreter of what he turned up, but his kind of digging must begin it all for everyone who is interested in Shakespeare's background in the ancient world. The second book, Virgil K. Whitaker's *Shakespeare's Use of Learning*, picks up where Baldwin leaves off, providing scholarly interpretation of what Baldwin discovered about Shakespeare's education. The book showed me how one scholar can build on another's foundation. Whitaker had a big influence on my career in another sense. In 1964 at the Marlowe/Shakespeare Festival at Rice University, Whitaker, an invited speaker, befriended a callow assistant professor and told him that no one should get a Ph.D. in Shakespeare unless s/he signed an agreement to spend the next summer working as a dogsbody in a Shakespeare festival; running lines with actors, building sets, making costumes, coaching beginning actors, etc. I took Whitaker quite literally and was taking part in campus productions before a year was out. First role: The Bear in *Winter's Tale*. From there to directing medieval plays and later Shakespeare productions, and eventually to working at two Shakespeare Festivals, in one (Odessa, Texas) as Dramaturg and Assistant Director, and in the other (Ashland, Oregon), teaching a shortcourse in the Festival repertory.

Are there any books that you refer to frequently?

Lately to my well-thumbed reprint of the *Geneva Bible* and my new *Oxford Classical Dictionary, 3e*, edited by Simon Hornblower, and Antony Spawforth. There is a small three-shelf bookcase beside my computer that is chock full of library books on various aspects of the classical tradition; I get into one or another of them daily if possible.

Are there any books that you think deserve more attention than they have received?

Irvin Leigh Matus, *Shakespeare, In Fact*. This is the best single refutation of the Oxfordian theory, but it is seldom recognized in discussions of the authorship question. The worth of this book is well spelled out in the full review in *Shakespeare Newsletter* by Thomas Pendleton some years ago.

I'm glad you plugged Mautus. What is the most important book on Shakespeare himself?

S. Schoenbaum's *William Shakespeare: A Documentary Life*. I use it constantly to look up facts or to look at documents. Schoenbaum's *Shakespeare's Lives* is wonderful also, wry about those who have written about Shakespeare's life over the centuries. At a time when everyone is writing a bio of Shakespeare, it would be salutary for us all to reread *Shakespeare's Lives*.

What kind of books do you greatly admire?

In general books that are solidly grounded but open-minded. My dissertation director, Huntington Brown, told me more than forty years ago, "Mr. Velz, scholarship that does not inform criticism is pedantry. But criticism that is not informed by scholarship is frippery. Never forget this." And I haven't.

What area is crying out for a book that perhaps you don't want to write?

At the end of the Introduction to *Shakespeare and the Classical Tradition*, I proposed that some half dozen books be written on special areas of Shakespeare's participation in the classical tradition. To date I can think of only two areas that have been fully covered. One is mythology, covered brilliantly by Jonathan Bate's *Shakespeare and Ovid*. The second is the influence of Plautus and Terence on the mature comedies, which has been partly covered by Wolfgang Riehle's *Shakespeare, Plautus, and the Humanist Tradition*, and further covered by Robert Miola's *Shakespeare and Classical Comedy*, even to the extent of including *Hamlet* and *Lear*.

The four topics not yet fully treated are the pastoral as an ongoing interest in Shakespeare, rhetoric in the mature plays, classical influence in the last plays, and Shakespeare's varied responses to Platonism. There is a lot left to do beyond these books I suggested 34 years ago. It is difficult, for instance, to conceive that it was not until 1997 that a book of new and probing essays on Shakespeare and Plutarch appeared.[4] It is just as difficult to conceive that a comparable anthology of new essays on Shakespeare and Ovid did not appear until Taylor's anthology in 2000. I am glad to hear that Routledge is continuing the collections of new essays on given works of Shakespeare that Garland made famous.

That is great news. Thanks, John, for talking about books with me.

Notes

1. See the Sir Brian Vickers interview, p. 33.
2. http://web.uvic.ca/shakespeare/Library/SCT/index.html
3. I have not been able to identify a book published within a few years of our interview that meets Dr. Velz's description. Possibly the editor was unable to find a publisher.
4. This is under the name of editor Mary Ann McGrail in the bibliography.

Anne Barton

Anne Barton did not know we had a history when I asked her to be a guest in "Talking Books." Before I had heard of Shakespeare journals and scholarship, I read Shakespeare for pleasure in the first *Riverside* edition. The introduction to *Twelfth Night* was so fascinating and helpful that I made a point to notice that it was written by Anne Barton. With due respect to the other members of the *Riverside* team, and the respect due is enormous, her introductions consistently made the biggest impression on me. I soon read more by her, beginning with her first book *Shakespeare and the Idea of the Play*, written under the name Anne Righter. It was my joy to later give a rave review to her *Essays, Mainly Shakespearean* and though I didn't review it, *Ben Jonson, dramatist* also greatly impressed for Barton's textually sensitive readings and contextual knowledge. She has been recognized by Richard Harp for redeeming the reputation of Jonson's late plays with this book. Also receiving excellent reviews is *The Names of Comedy*, in which Barton considered comedy in Shakespeare and classical authors. She edited *The Tempest* for the New Penguin Shakespeare and wrote the introduction to the New Penguin *Hamlet*. Demonstrating a later interest in Lord Byron, Barton wrote a short book on his *Don Juan* for the series Landmarks in World Literature, plus many other articles on Byron and other writers in many journals.

Shortly before our interview appeared, Barton wrote a 30,000 word general introduction to the Pléiade edition of Shakespeare's works published by Gallimard, in Paris. The first two volumes on the tragedies were published in 2002. She contributed a chapter on Shakespeare and Byron in the *Cambridge Companion to Byron*, edited by Drummond Bone, and with Eugene Giddens edited Jonson's *The Sad Shepherd* for the *Cambridge Edition of the Works of Ben Jonson*, finally published long after our interview in 2012. While updating the introductions for this book, Cambridge University Press announced the publication of a posthumous book entitled *The Shakespearean Forest* which is described at looking at the ways that forests were represented across early modern English literature. The catalog copy describes it as "exploring the forest as a source of cultural and psychological fascination, embracing and illuminating its mysteriousness." The book was prepared for publication by Hester Lees-Jeffries and includes a foreword by Adrian Poole and an afterword by Peter Holland, two of the executors of Barton's estate.

Anne Barton

Though born in New York City and partly educated at Bryn Mawr College in Pennsylvania, Barton has spent her professional life in the U.K. She was Grace II Professor of English at Cambridge University from 1984 to 2000, a Fellow of Trinity College and Honorary Fellow of New College, Oxford. She was also a Fellow of Academia Europæa and the British Academy, where she gave the annual Shakespeare lecture in 1991 entitled "Parks and Ardens," later published. Barton was on the editorial boards of *Shakespeare Quarterly* and *Studies in English Literature*, and her work regularly appeared in *The New York Review of Books*. She credits her marriage to Royal Shakespeare Company director John Barton for bringing her "closer to Shakespeare as realized in the theatre." Anne Barton and I became friends during the interview and stayed in touch for many years. She died in November 2013. This interview was first published in *Shakespeare Newsletter* 52:4, Winter 2002–3.

••••••••••••••••••••••••••••

MPJ: *You are just the second person I've interviewed to work so much with Jonson. What are the indispensable books on Jonson and his works?*

Anne Barton: Reading your draft introduction makes me realize with mild dismay that literary criticism has never had all that much of an impact on me. The texts themselves have always been the thing. My interest in Shakespeare's contemporaries—not just Jonson but others too—and in Renaissance and Restoration literature generally is just as great. The Jonson work that has most influenced me (apart from the great Herford and Simpson edition, which Ian Donaldson and others are now re-doing) included

Jonas Barish's *Ben Jonson and the Language of Prose Comedy*. It made me understand Jonson's sentence structure—both prose and verse—and how different it is from Shakespeare's. There is John Creaser's innovative edition of *Volpone*. The Introduction challenged all the old clichés about Jonson's characters as "monolithic," "caricatures," "flat" as contrasted with Shakespeare's "round" characters. He persuasively demonstrated that Jonson's people—although less clear-sighted about themselves than Shakespeare's tend to be—are psychologically complex nevertheless.

I also like Stephen Orgel's *The Jonsonian Masque*, and of course his great two volume work, with Roy Strong, *Inigo Jones: The Theatre of the Stuart Court*, and that extraordinarily perceptive article by Edward Partridge on the *Epigrammes*, called "Jonson's Epigrammes: The Named and the Nameless."

Whose books helped direct your career?

This is trickier, in a way. I suppose, Logan Pearsall Smith's *On Reading Shakespeare* (1933) which came my way (I can't think how) when I was very young, certainly long before I went to Bryn Mawr. It was the first book of literary criticism I ever read. I have not re-visited it (don't dare), but it made me venture into the complete Shakespeare (with vivid illustrations by Rockwell Kent), that some godparent or other had given me, with more enthusiasm than I might otherwise have had.

Whose books influenced you?

Both M. C. Bradbrook, my Ph.D. supervisor at Cambridge, and my mentor at Bryn Mawr, Arthur Colby Sprague (who was responsible for getting my undergraduate essay published) influenced me a lot, but less for any books they actually wrote than for themselves as people and scholars. Sprague taught me the importance of Shakespeare as performed on the stage, and Brad the importance of casting one's net as widely as possible in Renaissance literature generally.

Books that have influenced me: Frank Kermode's *The Sense of an Ending*. Kermode made me think fruitfully about the problem of "endings," above all in Shakespeare. C. L. Barber's *Shakespeare's Festive Comedy*, and Northrop Frye's brilliant article "The Argument of Comedy" and its extension in *The Anatomy of Criticism*. Frye's remains, to my mind, the most stimulating and provocative attempt to construct a theory of comedy.

Ernst Kantorowicz's *The King's Two Bodies: A Study in Medieval Political Theology* entirely changed the way I read Shakespeare's history plays. He led me to see how the "doctrine" of the king's two bodies not only operated in them, but had a logical extension Kantorowicz didn't see: the actor too (like Christ and like kings) has two bodies (his own and that of the

character he plays), and this lies behind all the theatre imagery so characteristic of these plays.

I have also been influenced, and accept, the idea of Shakespeare as reviser of his own plays, hence the essays in Gary Taylor and Michael Warren's *The Division of the Kingdoms*, and its spin-offs. It is important, I think, to say that the greatest influence on my study of Shakespeare has been the work of his contemporaries—Jonson, John Ford, Philip Massinger, Christopher Marlowe, etc., etc.

On that subject, are there any great neglected works from this era?

I suppose most keenly I'd want to put in a word for Ford, especially that great play *Perkin Warbeck*, first performed c. 1630, but also for Thomas Heywood's *The English Traveller*, for George Peele's *The Old Wives Tale*, and for John Lyly's *Gallathea*—all eminently stageable today.

Which books do you refer to frequently?

Bullough's invaluable *Narrative and Dramatic Sources of Shakespeare*, the Spevack *Concordance*, the two volumes of Sam Schoenbaum's *William Shakespeare: A Documentary Life*, and *William Shakespeare: Records and Images*, Alan Dessen and Leslie Thomson's *A Dictionary of Stage Directions in English Drama 1580–1642*, and Dessen's two books *Elizabethan Stage Conventions and Modern Interpreters* and *Recovering Shakespeare's Theatrical Vocabulary*, though I don't always agree with his conclusions, and the Wells and Taylor *Textual Companion* to the Oxford Shakespeare, though I often don't agree with it either!

What have you found particularly enriching in your thinking and writing about Shakespeare and early modern theatre?

I have gained a great deal from reading adaptations of Shakespeare—John Dryden, Thomas Shadwell, Edward Ravenscroft, etc., in the Restoration, and "sequels" such as Francis Godolphin Waldron's *The Virgin Queen* or John Fletcher's *The Woman's Prize, or the Tamer Tam'd* (c. 1611), not to mention W. H. Auden's "The Sea and the Mirror." They are often enormously illuminating of the original.

Whose books do you greatly admire?

I greatly admire John Jones's book *Shakespeare at Work* for its perception, formidable intelligence, and fineness of detail. I also like Michael Neill's *Issues of Death: Mortality and Identity in English Renaissance Tragedy*, especially for the way it combines a close investigation of Shakespearean with one of non-Shakespearean drama. Colin Burrow's new edition of all of Shakespeare's non-dramatic poems, for Oxford, is stunningly good. It is a magnificent edition, by far the best, with wonderful commentary and introductions.

It is an extraordinary edition. Name a Shakespeare book that is just plain fun.

Mary Cowden Clarke's *The Girlhood of Shakespeare's Heroines* from 1879. Not to be condescended to, either! As a series of "prequels" to Shakespeare plays, it is not only imaginative and highly entertaining—and often very candid, for its time, about sexual matters—but perceptive about the plays themselves.

Anne, I've received some great ideas from our conversation. Thanks for talking books with me.

Peter Holland

Peter Holland recently mentioned a previous guest in this column, Anne Barton, as "the person who made me into a scholar, if I am one." Let's see.

Holland is an editing phenomenon. An incomplete list of works edited before our interview include six of Shakespeare's plays for Pelican Books, *A Midsummer Night's Dream* for Oxford University Press, several Jacobean and Restoration plays, and the collection *The Plays of William Wycherley*. He is an associate general editor of the Oxford English Drama series of non–Shakespearean plays by early modern English and Restoration playwrights. This general editorship is shared with later "Talking Books" guest Martin Wiggins, so much later that Wiggins is unfortunately not included in this collection of interviews.

Holland is the General Editor of a series of volumes published by Palgrave derived from several Huntington Library conferences called "Redefining British Theatre History." These are edited by Holland with different co-editors. In addition to co-editing the series, Holland contributed the chapter "Theatre Without Drama: Reading REED" on the Records of Early English Drama database to the volume entitled *From Script to Stage in Early Modern England*. He is also General Editor of the well received Oxford Shakespeare Topics series with Stanley Wells, and has edited *Shakespeare Survey* since volume fifty-three. Prior to that, he was the *Survey*'s performance reviewer. In our interview, Holland mentions that he wrote the Shakespeare entry for Oxford University Press's *New Dictionary of National Biography*, edited by H. C. G. Matthew and Brian Harrison, forthcoming at the time of our interview. His entry was published as a separate book in 2007.

Holland is a superb performance critic, writing the delightful *English Shakespeares: Shakespeare on the English Stage in the 1990s*. One of the best pieces of Shakespeare movie criticism is "Film Editing," about Kenneth Branagh's handling of a couple of words in *Hamlet*, and how this opens some fascinating ways to think about the film. It is in the book *Shakespeare Performed: Essays in Honor of R. A. Foakes*. An early book was *The Ornament of Action: Text and Performance in Restoration Comedy*.

Peter Holland

Holland has remained busy since our interview. His edition of the Arden 3 *Coriolanus* was issued in 2013. It is considered groundbreaking for its innovative introduction that eschews the standard format but manages to cover everything important despite beginning with an extended analysis of four productions of the play from the thirties that resound at points throughout the rest of the introduction. A few years ago, I audited a seminar on *Coriolanus* at a Shakespeare Association of America conference. Holland was the respondent. I counted eleven copies of his edition around the table, brought by the seminarians. It is good to be Peter Holland. Arden must have liked his approach, for Holland has been named a general editor of the forthcoming Arden 4 series along with Zackery Lesser, and Holland's former student Tiffany Stern, both "Talking Books" guests who also came along too late for inclusion in this book.

In addition to continuing to edit *Shakespeare Survey*, number seventy-one is available now, Holland is a general editor with Adrian Poole of a series called Great Shakespeareans. The eighteen volumes, published between 2010 and 2013, look at the Shakespeare-related work of some very influential figures including actors such as Edmund Kean and Judi Dench, directors such as Granville Barker and Peter Hall, filmmakers such as Orson Welles and Akira Kurosawa, writers such as Alexander Pope and Charles Dickens, and thinkers such as Karl Marx and Sigmund Freud. Holland personally edited volume two on actors in the seventeenth and early eighteenth centuries, contributing the chapter on Garrick, and volume eighteen about four innovative directors in the twentieth century, contributing the chapter on Peter Brook. With Bridget Escolme and Farah Karim-Cooper, Holland is co-series editor of Shakespeare in the Theatre, the first books released in 2017. Each volume looks at theatre companies, such as Paul Menzer's book on the American Shakespeare Center in Staunton, Virginia, or the work of single directors, such as Abigail Rokinson-Woodall's on Nicholas Hytner's Shakespeare work. The series is published by Arden.

Received the day I did the final revision on this introduction is *The Oxford Handbook of Shakespeare and Performance*, edited by James C. Bulman. Holland contributed the chapter "Forgetting Performance." Holland explains his subject, "I shall want, in the course of this essay, to trace the ways in which the difficulty posed by the Shakespeare text in performance, especially on stage rather than screen, is the consequence of the tense awareness of forgetting in the act of watching," p. 172. Challenging, yes, but typically Holland writes a multifaceted study of the problem.

Holland was an undergraduate in Cambridge where he stayed to work for 28 years, trying to convince the University that performance was worth studying. He worked with dozens of Cambridge students who went into the professional theatre such as directors Nicholas Hytner and Sam Mendes, actors Simon Russell Beale and Tilda Swinton, and designer Tom Piper. This was followed by an appointment as Director of the Shakespeare Institute and Professor of Shakespeare Studies at the University of Birmingham. Holland gave the annual Shakespeare Lecture at the British Academy in 2000. He is now the McMeel Family Professor of Shakespeare Studies at Notre Dame, which is unusual for being part of the Department of Film, Television, and Theatre. He is now the Academic Director of Actors for the London Stage (formerly ACTER), which is based in Notre Dame.

Need more evidence that Peter is a scholar? If so, the interview should settle your lingering doubts. It originally appeared in *Shakespeare Newsletter*, 53:1, #256, Spring 2003.

•••••••••••••••••••••••••••

MPJ: *Who are the best performance critics?*

Peter Holland: I read, and I want everyone to read, anything and everything written by people like Tony Dawson, Barbara Hodgdon and Bill Worthen (in alphabetical order!). They make us rethink what Shakespeare performance criticism is all about. Dawson's study of *Hamlet*, Hodgdon on *The Shakespeare Trade* and Worthen on *Shakespeare and the Authority of Performance*, for instance, have each made major advances in our work. Dawson's volume is in the Shakespeare in Performance series, one of those exciting series that both present the raw material for theatre research and give us some outstanding analysis as well. There is also *Players of Shakespeare* where actors give us their accounts of Shakespeare roles they have played, and the Arden Shakespeare at Stratford series, also under the benign editorship of Robert Smallwood. And then there is the Cambridge "Shakespeare in Production" editions which annotate the play with details drawn from the whole history of production. Plus all the brilliant work that comes from critics of Shakespeare on film: Russell Jackson, who has done phenomenal archival research to help us understand the history of Shakespeare film, or among the new radicals, Richard Burt and Courtney Lehmann, both of whom always provoke me to think hard, even when I don't agree with a word they say. It is a wonderfully exhilarating time to study Shakespeare in performance with so much brilliant work appearing every year.

Have any books on textual editing been helpful to you?

Well, there are the classics: W. W. Greg on *The Shakespeare First Folio*, Ronald B. McKerrow's *Prolegomena for the Oxford Shakespeare*, C. Hinman's extraordinary *The Printing and Proof-Reading of the First Folio of Shakespeare*, and the Wells/Taylor *Textual Companion*, always fascinating and thoughtful even when it is downright annoying. When I'm editing, I obviously look at their details closely. So often they are brilliantly right, or, if this isn't nonsense, equally brilliantly wrong. It is a chance to be provoked and rethink.

The best way to learn about textual editing (apart from doing it!), is to study the fine editions that great textual critics produce. To take two recent examples, John Jowett's outstanding *Richard III* for Oxford, or Stanley Wells's *King Lear* in the same series, both editing quarto texts with perceptive skill.

Did books help direct your career?

I think it was less a matter of books than people. The first lecture I ever heard as an undergraduate was by Anne Barton, and I went to every lecture she gave from then on. Her work is always so profoundly scholarly, so acutely perceptive, and yet always so unfailingly lucid. Anne was my research supervisor and taught me how to be a scholar and a critic.

Ah, ha! I tricked you into admitting that you are a scholar!

I am proud that some of my work is as widely accessible as all of hers is, and especially that I have given lectures that have been enjoyed equally by high-school students and conference delegates. I was also lucky to be taught as an undergraduate by Brian Vickers, who made me realize what is out there, those things that make engaging the possibilities of the discipline so exciting. I vividly remember Brian coming round to my apartment on a Sunday morning with some extra reading for the week's supervision: not only articles, but reviews in scholarly journals, the kind of writing where scholars talk to each other through their writing. Their teaching was all of a piece with their writing: always scholarly and always original. Books like Anne's *Shakespeare and the Idea of the Play* and Brian's astonishing later achievement in *Shakespeare: The Critical Heritage* stand out for me as formative works.

Perhaps even more important was the fact that my parents took me to theatre all the time. I first went to Stratford when I was nine to see Paul Robeson as Othello and, the same season, to see *A Midsummer Night's Dream* directed by Peter Hall. All my work emerges from the sheer pleasure of watching Shakespeare in performance and trying to understand what happens on stage or on film to create that pleasure. It is, in one sense, the purest self-indulgence; I get paid to do what I want to do anyway: watch Shakespeare in performance and talk about it.

OK, I'm jealous. Which books do you consult frequently?

There are the obvious ones, the books that every Shakespeare critic would acknowledge as crucial to our work: I can't do without Spevack's one-volume Harvard concordance at my elbow, Bullough's *Narrative and Dramatic Sources*, the great complete editions like *Riverside* and *Oxford*, Folio and quarto facsimiles, and all those other reasons I can never see that my desk is made of wood for the stacks of books on it, beside it, enveloping it in the scholar's security blanket.

But we are lucky to live in the time of on-line materials. My editing is profoundly affected by having the *Oxford English Dictionary* online. When I was editing *A Midsummer Night's Dream*, checking an *OED* reference meant reading with a magnifying glass in my compact edition or lifting one of those twenty heavy volumes off the library shelf. Now I can search so much more easily that I search more frequently—and the results are always intriguing, making me realize not only the *OED*'s citations from Shakespeare, but also the semantic possibilities a word could have in the early modern period, the range of meanings that the passage may be playing with. Of course, the on-line corpora that LION, for Literature Online, provides make more extensive searches easy, and reveal the *OED*'s limitations. Here is an example: Coriolanus describes himself as "Like to a lonely dragon." This is the *OED*'s first citation for the word "lonely," but check the word out in the English Drama database and you'll find there are a number of earlier examples.

Who isn't read anymore who should be rediscovered?

I have great admiration for some of the early work in performance criticism like Richard Flatter's *Shakespeare's Producing Hand* which tried (and often failed) to read the First Folio as a kind of evidence for performance practice, or Richard David's *Shakespeare in the Theatre*, not only a collection of reviews, but a thoughtful understanding of how particular kinds of effects might be, ought to be, and have been achieved in productions. We need to go back to such writing and relearn their lessons.

I'm glad you mentioned David. I bought English Shakespeares *because I liked David and wanted more. Which recent books are especially good?*

That's a tough one, but I would like to mention two very recent books that deserve our eager attention. Stephen Orgel's *The Authentic Shakespeare* brings together his essays over many years, writing that is always fresh and original, stimulating and, in the very best sense, radical, sending us back to the roots of texts to understand them anew. I have greatly enjoyed the collection edited by Jonathan Gil Harris and Natasha Korda, *Staged Properties in Early Modern English Drama,* essays that consider props on stage and their complex cultural meanings, changing our perception of the materiality of objects on stage.

Name a Shakespeare book that is just plain fun.

That's easy: Schoenbaum's *Shakespeare's Lives*—his history of Shakespeare biography. I spent a great deal of last year writing the Shakespeare entry for the *New Dictionary of National Biography* (it will be the longest entry in the dictionary, and is due out next year), and I ended up feeling just as stupid as so many of the sad figures Schoenbaum records.

Which non-lit-crit books have you found particularly helpful?

Dozens of them, especially theatre and film biographies and memoirs, those accounts that really make one understand what an actor is doing, like Simon Callow's extraordinary *Charles Laughton: A Difficult Actor*, one actor writing astonishingly perceptively about the work of another. As someone who can't act and can't direct, I rely on such work to tell me how to watch, how to become a good spectator.

Are there any important subjects where the books are out of date, and need to be replaced?

Yes, nothing to do with my own field of study, but I would love to see major new investigations of Shakespeare and art. We have no substantial study since Moelwyn Merchant's *Shakespeare and the Artist*, though there have been steps towards producing catalogues of Shakespeare paintings. I hope the study of Shakespeare and music will come back to the forefront of our attention. One day I will get round to teaching the course on "Shakespeare and Opera." I've wanted to turn my hand to that. One day!

Peter, thanks. It is always fun talking about books with you.

Ann Thompson

Everyone who breaks with tradition creates controversy, and Ann Thompson has broken with tradition. As one of the general editors of the Arden 3 Shakespeare editions and as co-editor of 2006 *Hamlet* with Neil Taylor, Thompson challenged the editorial tradition we all inherited. They are replacing Herald Jenkins's universally acclaimed Arden 2 edition with a two volume, three text *Hamlet* that will make both Quartos and the Folio version fully accessible. For the first time, nearly everyone will be able to afford and experience the multiplicity of *Hamlet* texts.

This has not set well with traditionalists who feel that the general public should always receive the expected conflated texts, understandably love Harold Jenkins, and decried the new edition before it was published. I welcome the opportunities and challenges the new texts present. Thompson and Taylor have been at pains to point out that the replacement is not an attack on Jenkins: Arden is replacing all the plays in the second series. Moreover, one reason for taking this approach is precisely that there seems little point in duplicating what Jenkins did so well. Readers can easily get a Folger edition if they want the play conflated, and Jenkins is readily available from libraries and second hand booksellers. The Arden 3 *Hamlet* second quarto, the main text of the two, was republished in an updated version in 2016. It features twenty-five pages called, "Additions and Reconsiderations." The other volume with the First Quarto and the Folio versions of the play is unchanged.

A glance at Thompson's other publications shows her moving in this direction. There is a previous book on *Hamlet*, also written with Neil Taylor for the series "Writers and their Work." She edited *The Taming of the Shrew* for Cambridge University Press and with Richard Proudfoot and David Scott Kastan is one of the general editors of the *Arden Shakespeare Complete Works* (2000).

Thompson put together two thoughtful volumes on textual work more than a decade apart. An all-star cast of contributors is in the anthology *Which Shakespeare?: A User's Guide to Editions*, 1992, and with Gordon McMullan edited *In Arden: Editing Shakespeare, Essays in Honour of Richard Proudfoot* in 2003. Filled with contributions by Arden 2 and Arden 3 editors, the anthology grapples with the problems facing editors today and offers possible solutions. It is not a stretch the see all of these books paving the road to the 2006 edition of *Hamlet*.

Thompson's research interests are broad. She is the author of *Shakespeare's Chaucer: A Study in Literary Origins*, a book I have been unable to find for years (let me know if you have a spare copy) and wrote with husband John O. Thompson *Shakespeare: Meaning & Metaphor*. With Sasha Roberts, she compiled *Women Reading Shakespeare 1660–1900: An Anthology of Criticism* and with Sylvia Adamson is one of five editors of *Reading Shakespeare's Dramatic Language: A Guide*, the first in an Arden series called "Shakespeare and Language."

Since our interview, Thompson and Neil Taylor edited *Hamlet: A Critical Reader* for the Arden Early Modern Drama Guides. The six chapters by highly respected contributors cover the history of *Hamlet* criticism, current thinking about the play, *Hamlet* and gender, the play in world cinema, the relevance of *Hamlet*, a theatre history of the play by "Talking Books" guest Lois Potter, and resources for the study of the play by Thompson.

Thompson recently retired from King's College, London, where she was a professor of English, head of the English Department, and taught in the M.A. program that King's runs jointly with Shakespeare's Globe Theatre. Upon retirement, Arden published a Festschrift in her honor, *Women Making Shakespeare: Text, Reception and Performance*, edited by Gordon McMullan, Lena Cowen Orlin, and Virginia Mason Vaughan, a book that seems to be a partial fulfillment of Thompson's last comment in our interview. She previously held posts at the University of Liverpool and the University of Surrey Roehampton. This interview originally appeared in *Shakespeare Newsletter*, 53:2, #257, Summer 2003.

••••••••••••••••••••••••••••

MPJ: *Some of our readers are textual novices. Where can they learn about the complexities of textual work?*

Ann Thompson: In the Arden third series, we have tried to make the textual discussion more accessible to non-specialists: readers will find in the Introduction to each play a sample passage of the earliest printed text, and a discussion of what changes the editor has made and why. There are also some useful collections of essays on editing available: I would include *In Arden* as mentioned above, but also *The Renaissance Text*, edited by Andrew Murphy, and *Textual Performances*, edited by Lukas Erne and M. J. Kidnie. All of these contain fairly short essays on a range of issues relating to editing, and both *In Arden* and *Textual Performances* include material on how editing relates to questions of performance.

Whose texts do you especially admire?

It would be invidious to refer to Arden texts here, and I would in any case not want to claim universal excellence for any one series, but in the

Oxford series I especially admire John Jowett's edition of *Richard III*, and in the New Cambridge series Al Braunmuller's edition of *Macbeth*. Both of these combine the best of modern scholarly editing with an awareness of critical and performance issues. I'd also like to put in a word for editions published outside the Anglo-American tradition such as the "synoptic" *Hamlet* prepared (in English) by Jesus Tronch-Perez and the editions of the First and Second Quartos of *Hamlet* prepared (in Italian) by Alessandro Serpieri: these editions are particularly valuable for their detailed commentaries, undertaken from perspectives Anglo-American scholars may find refreshing.

Let me be invidious for you and mention the Arden 3 editions of John Cox's and Eric Rasmussen's Henry VI, part three, *and Jonathan Bate's* Titus Andronicus. *Both impressed me with their thorough thoughtfulness, even when, on occasion, I chose to keep an open mind instead of agreeing with their arguments. Whose books influenced you the most?*

I was trained in traditional scholarship by my Ph.D. supervisor, Richard Proudfoot (with whom I'm now working again on Arden 3), and by the Shakespeare scholars I encountered at the University of Liverpool, Kenneth Muir and Philip Edwards. Having completed my Ph.D. (which became *Shakespeare's Chaucer*) at a time when studies of themes and characters seemed more or less exhausted, I would probably pinpoint works on scenic structure and on language as in some ways the most important early influences—books like Emrys Jones' *Scenic Form in Shakespeare* and Stephen Booth's edition of the *Sonnets*. In the 1970s and 1980s I was excited by the "new" approaches to Shakespeare studies exemplified by Juliet Dusinberre's *Shakespeare and the Nature of Women* and by collections like John Drakakis' *Alternative Shakespeares* and Jonathan Dollimore and Alan Sinfield's *Political Shakespeare*, though I always wanted to keep one foot in the realm of traditional scholarship while exploring what became known as "theoretical" approaches.

That is interesting, since so many people seem to do one or the other. Are there any books that you refer to frequently?

As an editor today, I am lucky to have access to a number of excellent recent works which were not available when I edited my first play in 1984. I would instance Alan C. Dessen and Leslie Thomson's *Dictionary of Stage Directions* (1999), Naseeb Shaheen's *Biblical References in Shakespeare's Plays* (1999), George T. Wright's *Shakespeare's Metrical Art* (1988), N. F. Blake's *A Grammar of Shakespeare's Language* (2002) and Jonathan Hope's *Shakespeare's Grammar* (2003).

For teaching as well as for research purposes, I am glad to be able to draw on the Cambridge Shakespeare in Production series (which includes an excellent recent volume on *The Taming of the Shrew* edited by Elizabeth Schafer) and the Manchester Shakespeare in Performance series (which includes an excellent recent volume on *Othello* by Lois Potter). Both series look at performance choices, but in different ways: the Cambridge volumes provide a text of the play in question with extensive annotation, scene by scene and sometimes line by line, of how it has been performed; the Manchester volumes provide a more discursive performance history, focusing on key productions on stage and screen.

Who should be rediscovered?

I would nominate editors in the eighteenth and nineteenth centuries who edited just one text or a small number of texts, as compared with those who undertook the entire canon. In the case of *Hamlet* I would instance Charles Jennens (1773), Thomas Caldecott (1819) and especially George MacDonald (1885), whose Folio-based edition anticipates the Oxford one by about a century.

Are any non-lit-crit books that you have found particularly enriching in your thinking and writing about Shakespeare and early modern theatre?

I very much enjoyed reading non-literary discussions of metaphor for the book you have been unable to obtain! John and I looked at discussions of metaphor by linguists and philosophers, notably George Lakoff and Mark Johnson (*Metaphors We Live By*), Eva Kittay and Adrienne Lehrer ("Semantic Fields and the Structure of Metaphor"), Group Mu (*Rhétorique de la poésie*), J. F. Ross (*Portraying Analogy*) and Donald Davidson ("What Metaphors Mean"). We hoped to make this material accessible to literary scholars, but we seem not to have succeeded!

Well, not for me, but I'm inter-library-loan challenged.

We noticed that non-literary scholars had been having lots of conferences on metaphor and publishing lots of books, but they always looked at metaphor in everyday language and tended to assume that literary metaphor was something completely separate. We tried applying their theories to Shakespearean metaphor and found that there was actually a great deal we could learn from them.

That's fascinating. I have never been able to get a copy of your Chaucer book, so I'll start with some of those. What are you reading now?

In the line of duty, I've just been reading the typescript of a book of essays on *Shakespeare and the Language of Translation* edited by Ton Hoenselaars, which was commissioned for the "Shakespeare and Language" series and which I'm happy to say has turned out to be very interesting.

Amongst current studies of *Hamlet* I'm reading Lukas Erne's *Shakespeare as Literary Dramatist* which has an original take on the relation between so-called "bad" quartos and the longer texts: he makes a case for Shakespeare as someone who wrote for readers as much as he wrote for the stage.

Are there any important subjects where the books are out of date, and need to be replaced?

Perhaps it is time for some new work on Shakespeare's sources? Editors still use Geoffrey Bullough's *Narrative and Dramatic Sources* as a standard resource, but quite a lot of work has been done in a rather piecemeal way since 1975 and some kind of synthesis or summary would be very useful.

What needs are there for a book that perhaps you don't want to write?

When Sasha Roberts and I did *Women Reading Shakespeare* I had planned to do more work in that area, either on individual women or on phenomena such as women's Shakespeare clubs and reading groups, but I don't seem to have had time to get back to it. Perhaps I will yet—if there is life after *Hamlet*!—but there is plenty of material for other people to research too.

Thanks, Ann. I appreciate you telling us about these great books.

George T. Wright

Silly me. I avoided George T. Wright's book *Shakespeare's Metrical Art* for years because the writing I had seen about metrics and rhetoric is usually in such stilted prose that my brain dulls more that the words enlighten. It was Brian Vickers's frequent use of Wright's work in *"Counterfeiting" Shakespeare: Evidence, Authorship, and John Ford's Funerall Elegye* that straightened me out. Wright shows how iambic pentameter was used by Chaucer and others, reached something of a culmination in Shakespeare, and then takes us up through Milton. Wright's prose flows as freely as the pentameter line, and proves that the design really can be seen in the details. He makes readers so aware of meter that I even noticed Wright slipping into iambic pentameter in his descriptions. This only hints at Wright's insights into other poets, which have been published in two books, *The Poet in the Poem: The Personae of Eliot, Yeats, and Pound* published by the University of California Press and *W. H. Auden* published by Twayne in two editions.

His somewhat autobiographical essay "Troubles of a Professional Meter Reader" is a lot of fun. You will find it in his book *Hearing the Measures: Shakespearean and Other Inflections*. The articles in this book include "Hendiadys and *Hamlet*," which won the MLA's William Riley Parker Prize in 1981, and "The Lyric Present: Simple Present Verbs in English Poems." It won the Parker Prize in 1974. It is an excellent collection.

It is not surprising that *Aimless Life: Poems 1961–1995* is full of metrical fun. There are nearly fifty pages of poetry about higher education and some excellent translations of Catullus.

Among his many awards and prizes are a Guggenheim Fellowship, an NEH Fellowship, two years of a Fulbright lecturing in France and one in Greece, and the Robert Fitzgerald Award in 2003 for lifetime achievement in the study of prosody. Before retiring to Kentucky where he has family, Ted Wright taught at the University of Minnesota for 25 years as Regents Professor of English, and is now Emeritus. This interview first appeared in *Shakespeare Newsletter*, 53:3, #258, Fall 2003.

••••••••••••••••••••••••••••

MPJ: *You already covered some of this in* Troubles of a Professional Meter Reader, *but that is now ten years old. Which of the more recent books on the poetics, prose, and rhetoric of Shakespeare and his contemporaries are outstanding?*

George T. Wright: Russ McDonald's book, *Shakespeare and the Arts of Language* is brilliant, wide-ranging, full of unexpected and valuable insights on every aspect of Shakespeare's language, especially on Shakespeare's ambiguity and the doubleness of his language. The Arden Shakespeare's *Reading Shakespeare's Dramatic Language: A Guide* collects very readable, informative essays on almost every aspect of Shakespeare's language. It is edited by Sylvia Adamson and others. Frank Kermode's book, *Shakespeare's Language*, registers this subtle critic's insights and his reservations, especially about Shakespeare's late style. Not so recent but well worth mentioning is John Porter Houston's *Shakespearean Sentences*, a fine study of Shakespeare's brilliant uses of syntax. I haven't yet caught up with Jonathan Hope's *Shakespeare's Grammar.*

I have. It is as great as reported. Did your teachers and their books have much influence?

It was not so much books as mentors, or poets. Mark Van Doren's yearlong undergraduate course in Shakespeare (the second half actually taught by Raymond Weaver) made me sure I wanted to major in English and teach or write. My graduate study at Columbia, though, soured me on scholarship; the professors seemed remote and devoted to trivia. When, four years later, I went back to graduate school at Berkeley, many professors there were friendly and spirited. I worked with Josephine Miles especially, and found her quantitative studies of style very revealing—in *Eras and Modes in English Poetry* or *Style and Proportion*, for example. I would never do work quite like that, but I liked talking poetry with someone who was a poet herself, who cared about poetic style, and wanted to devise ways of describing and even measuring it. I also studied with (and read for) Willard Farnham and learned something from his wide knowledge and large-minded view of the world—and Shakespeare.

Your interest began with twentieth-century poetry, if your publication history is an indication.

I started as a specialist in modern literature, especially poetry, and taught courses in W. B. Yeats, T. S. Eliot, W. H. Auden, even James Joyce, throughout my teaching life. That included directing dissertations on such disparate authors as Anthony Trollope, Andrew Marvell, William Faulkner, Doris Lessing, Walt Whitman, Gary Snyder, H. D., D. H. Lawrence, and Jean Rhys. But my own major interest was always in poetic style. I wrote a lot of verse, and I memorized a great deal—hundreds of lines of Milton and thousands of Shakespeare, including eventually all the sonnets. When I went to Minnesota, two courses named "Techniques of Poetry" fell into my hands, and I was able to focus on matters like meter, sound effects, diction, imagery, and rhetorical figures. I learned from many books, but certainly Sister Miriam Joseph's *Shakespeare's Use of the Arts of Language* was a mine of information and enlightenment. Teaching of this kind led me and my writing back from the moderns to the Renaissance—to Thomas Wyatt and John Donne, and especially to Shakespeare. But I was fifty-five before I published my first piece on Shakespeare (the hendiadys essay), and sixty-two when *Shakespeare's Metrical Art* was published. I'm closing in now on King Lear's age (not an hour more nor less).

Well, Nuncle, which books influenced you the most, outside of metrics?

Mainly the poets themselves from Shakespeare to Auden; the criticism of Eliot and Auden: Eliot's *Selected Essays* and *On Poetry and Poets*, and Auden's *The Dyer's Hand*; and great prose stylists, especially John Ruskin, Matthew Arnold, Walter Pater, Henry James, and Joyce. Critics and scholars always seemed secondary. In graduate school no older book on Shakespeare seemed to me quite as stunning as, say, Erich Auerbach's *Mimesis: The Representation of Reality in Western Literature*, with its powerful readings of Western landmark texts.

In writing my dissertation on personae in modern poetry I found Robert Langbaum's *The Poetry of Experience* very helpful. We take ideas about personae for granted now, but Langbaum was a perceptive early reader of Robert Browning's dramatic monologues. Richard Ellmann and Hugh Kenner were also continually interesting on modernist poets and Joyce, Ellmann especially with his well-informed books on Yeats (*Yeats: The Man and the Masks* and *The Identity of Yeats*), and his brilliantly researched and skillfully presented biography, *James Joyce*. Kenner's *The Pound Era* was a stylish model for modernist scholars, connecting all the writers and artists and somewhat perversely casting Pound as their vital center. Also, the insights into point of view and narrative distance that I found in Wayne Booth's *The Rhetoric of Fiction* couldn't help being useful to a close reader of poetry.

Do you refer to any books frequently?

Certainly the *Harvard Concordance to Shakespeare* and the *Oxford English Dictionary*, but also the *New Princeton Encyclopedia of Poetry and Poetics*, largely edited by Alex Preminger and Terry Brogan. For the *Sonnets*, I continually go to Stephen Booth's great edition and to Helen Vendler's *The Art of Shakespeare's Sonnets*, two wonderful books by remarkably observant and exhaustive critics. Stephen is especially revealing on patterning—of words, phrases, sounds—that seems casual, accidental, surprising, and only maybe meaningful. Helen, whose criticism of poetry in all periods is without rival in our time for its perceptiveness and penetration, focuses more on the sonnets's deliberate organization of motifs, imagery, ranges of reference, and poetic structures.

Are there any books that deserve more attention than they have received?

One that I never see cited, except by me, is the modest but useful little book on Shakespeare's meter by Delbert Spain, *Shakespeare Sounded Soundly*. Written by an actor largely for actors, it offers practical assistance to anyone trying to cope with the problems of speaking Shakespeare's verse on the stage.

What is the most important book on metrics that you have read?

For metrical scholars, the indispensable book is Terry Brogan's brilliant bibliography, *English Versification, 1570–1980*. It's an extraordinary compilation, done (I think) before Brogan was thirty and when he was still a graduate student. Most entries are annotated, and there are long sensible essays on numerous subjects. Brogan has since left the profession because English departments could not find a place for a specialist in metrics, even for such an exceptional scholar.

What's wrong with this picture? Whose books do you greatly admire?

Too many to mention. Here are a few: Jonas Barish's first-rate book on Jonson's prose style, *Ben Jonson and the Language of Prose Comedy*, and his marvelous one on *The Antitheatrical Prejudice*, with its superb survey of narrow attitudes toward the theater from the Greeks to our own time. Wolfgang Clemen's *English Tragedy before Shakespeare*, excellent for its clear and persuasive studies of exactly what its subtitle promises: *The Development of Dramatic Speech*. M. M. Mahood's *Shakespeare's Wordplay*, the classic on its subject. Graham Bradshaw has a wonderful polemical style; even when I disagree with him I love the fluency and grace with which he argues his points in *Shakespeare's Skepticism* and *Misrepresentations*. I've learned a lot from many other critics, scholars, metrists, and especially editors, who master a craft I entered Shakespeare studies too late to attempt.

I'm also grateful for the many splendid collections of essays available to scholars now, some of essays previously published, like those in the Garland series on individual Shakespeare plays. But essays now are often written explicitly for a collection, which will therefore be less random and more comprehensive. One favorite is *A Companion to Shakespeare*, edited by David Scott Kastan, which not only includes some brilliant essays, but is beautifully printed and produced.

And filled with top contributors. Name a Shakespeare book that is just plain fun.

I second Alan Dessen's nomination of Thurber's "The Macbeth Murder Mystery" as the funniest piece on Shakespeare,[1] but of course it isn't a book. Neither is Laura Bohannan's "Shakespeare in the Bush," but it's certainly fun to read. So, in a different way, is "The Sea and the Mirror," Auden's poetic "Commentary" on *The Tempest*. I've also enjoyed Peter Cummings's poems about Shakespeare, some of which have appeared in *The Shakespeare Newsletter*. For that matter, *The Shakespeare Newsletter* is fun to read.

A man after my own heart, but you can't have it. What books need to be written that perhaps you don't want to write?

Studies of the expressive metrics of Shakespeare's contemporary playwrights. And, despite the books on Shakespeare's language I mentioned earlier, studies of his style, of the larger motions and manners of speeches and scenes, are all too rare nowadays. There's a whole large world of style waiting to be explored by sensitive critics.

Thanks for saying that, Ted. As much as I respect and enjoy Shakespeare's works, we are not doing nearly enough with his contemporaries. Thanks also for taking time to talk about books with me.

Note

1. See the interview with Alan C. Dessen, p. 24.

Jonathan Bate

In a political climate where the writers of the past are often condemned for their limitations, where former "geniuses" are reduced to apologists for old power structures, it was admirably audacious of Jonathan Bate to title one of his books, *The Genius of Shakespeare*. The book is a stimulating investigation of why Shakespeare has so often been called a genius. Bate considers the social forces that needed a National Poet, yes, but also finds balance in the qualities Shakespeare packed into his work, qualities that resonated with successive generations.

Other stimulating works are *Shakespeare: An Illustrated Stage History*, co-edited with Russell Jackson and the CD-ROM resource *Arden Shakespeare: Texts and Sources for Shakespeare Studies*. Bate is something of a *Titus Andronicus* guru, editing the Arden 3 edition, writing the introduction to Julie Taymor's published screenplay of her 2000 film *Titus*, and he wrote a *New York Times* article about the film that was used in the booklet accompanying the DVD. An honest scholar willing to be persuaded, he declared in the Arden that the play was written by Shakespeare alone, a position he later publically corrected.

Bate has twice illuminated Shakespeare's debt to a certain Latin poet. *Shakespeare and Ovid* demonstrates how thoroughly Shakespeare knew Ovid and how thoroughly Ovid influenced Shakespeare. He also edited a useful edition of Arthur Golding's 1567 translation of *Metamorphoses*, which many scholars believe Shakespeare used instead of reading Ovid in Latin.

Two books in part about Romantic writers are *Shakespeare and the English Romantic Imagination* and *Shakespearean Constitutions: Politics, Theatre, Criticism 1730–1830*. The first looks at Shakespeare's influence on several Romantic writers, and at how they knew him. The second is a wide-ranging historical account of Shakespeare's broader place in eighteenth and early nineteenth century cultural life, with a particular emphasis on political history, especially as viewed through the provocative eyes of caricaturists such as James Gillray and George Cruikshank, and on the theatre. A central argument concerns the radicalizing of Shakespeare that took place via the acting of Edmund Kean and the reviewing of early Shakespeare critic William Hazlitt. Bate also wrote a novel about Hazlitt, *The Cure for Love*.

His interest in the Romantic poets has created a new way of viewing them: environmentally. *Romantic Ecology: Wordsworth and the Environmental Tradition* argues, among other things, for a "green" criticism, with Wordsworth's poetry as a starting point. *The Song of the Earth* finds a strong ecological consciousness in a wide range of works from Rousseau to the Romantics to twentieth century poets such as Wallace Stevens, Elizabeth Bishop, and Les Murray. This interest in poetry and ecology continues in two books, *John Clare: Selected Poems* and the U.K. bestseller *John Clare: A Biography*, both published in 2003.

Sir Jonathan Bate

With Eric Rasmussen, Bate is the editor of a book that collects Shakespeare's works and another that mostly does not. *The RSC Shakespeare: The Complete Works* takes the unusual approach of basing all texts of the First Folio, then adds lines from Shakespeare's quarto editions when those lines are not in the Folio. This is contrary to the practice of most editors, who pick what they believe is the best text, Folio or quarto, and conflate from the other texts. The edition includes Shakespeare's poetry and his plays not printed in the Folio to make sure that all works in other "complete" collections of Shakespeare are included. Unfortunately, Palgrave published this in 2007, after our interview, so I could not ask the reasons for the editorial choices in this edition. Even more curious is Palgrave's 2013 companion volume *William Shakespeare and Others: Collaborative Plays*, a deceptive title that seems to indicate that the plays contained therein are in part by Shakespeare. Shakespeare is the co-author of four of these plays and many argue the co-author of another, but he did not write any portion of the other five plays in this volume. What links them all is that Shakespeare at one time or another had been thought to be the author or co-author by someone. The actual collaborate plays in this volume are not in the *RSC Shakespeare*, so in that sense the plays Shakespeare did co-author in this book completes the earlier collection.

After our interview, 2009, came a book I will not describe here, for Bate discusses it near our interview's end. It is called *Soul of the Age: A Biography of the Mind of William Shakespeare*.

Bate's most recent biography is *Ted Hughes: An Unauthorized Life*, a critical sensation. Hughes is known for writing about the outdoors, so this is in line with much of Bate's previous work. He is also General Editor of the impressive *Oxford English Literary History* in thirteen volumes. After many years working on other writers and projects, Bate is returning to Shakespeare. As I revise this introduction, he is completing a book for Princeton University Press called *Shakespeare's Classical Imagination*, an expanded version of his E. H. Gombrich Lectures on Shakespeare and the Classical Tradition.

In addition, Bate has dabbled as a playwright. *Being Shakespeare* is a one-man play written for the notable actor Simon Callow. It played Edinburgh Festival Fringe and had runs in London, New York, Chicago, and Trieste. Bate also consulted on the British Museum's Shakespeare exhibit created for the 2012 Cultural Olympiad.

Jonathan Bate succeeded Philip Edwards as the King Alfred Professor of English Literature at the University of Liverpool, where he also held a Leverhulme Personal Research Professorship. At the time of our interview, he had recently moved to a chair of Shakespeare and Renaissance Literature at the University of Warwick and joined the board of the Royal Shakespeare Company. He has since become provost of Worcester College and professor of English literature at the University of Oxford. Sir Jonathan was honored with a C. B. E. in 2006 and a knighthood in 2014, the youngest person to be honored for contributions to literary scholarship. This interview originally appeared in *Shakespeare Newsletter*, 53:4, #259, Winter 2003/2004.

••••••••••••••••••••••••••••

***MPJ:** Is "green" criticism applicable to Shakespeare?*

Jonathan Bate: Certainly: if by "green" criticism we mean a thinking of humankind's relationship with nature, it is applicable to all periods. Pastoral and anti-pastoral are central to all Shakespeare's genres—I've always been fascinated by the structural similarity between *As You Like It* and *King Lear*.

That's interesting. Has anyone in the past come close to a "green" view of him?

Most "green" criticism—including my own—has focused on more recent literature, and in particular the alienation from nature caused by industrialization, technology and modernity, but older books such as Leo Marx's *The Machine in the Garden*, with its powerful reading of *The Tempest*, are definitely proto-green.

Titus Andronicus *fascinates me. In addition to your excellent edition, are there any really great books on the play?*

I still have time for Jan Kott's chapter on it in *Shakespeare our Contemporary*. Alan Dessen's little book on the play in performance is great on the seminal Peter Brook and Deborah Warner productions (*Shakespeare in Performance: Titus Andronicus*), and there's a fine chapter in Richard Marienstras' important, under-rated book *New Perspectives on the Shakespearean World.* It was originally written in French with a title that translates as "the near and the far"—I don't know why the English version was given such a bland title.

The joys of marketing. As an editor who has also written about the theory of editing, whose editions do you especially admire?

The Wells-Taylor Oxford *Shakespeare* made us rethink editorial practice, return to first principles. But now I have a dream of synthesizing the more radical textual theories of the last twenty years with the older editorial tradition—the edition I most admire for doing that is, strangely enough, Dr. Johnson's (1765). He built on the innovations of his predecessors such as Lewis Theobald (1726), but was ultimately ruled by good sense, accessibility and trust in the Folio.

This amounts to the same question, but for Shakespeare and Ovid. *So much work is being done of Shakespeare and the classical tradition. Whose books should we read?*

As you say, there's so much. My own work took inspiration above all from Leonard Barkan (*The Gods Made Flesh: Metamorphosis and the Pursuit Of Paganism*) and Thomas Greene (*The Light in Troy*), but I've also got a lot of time for younger critics such as Colin Burrow, Heather James and Raphael Lyne. Their work is very well represented in Cambridge University Press's essay collection, *Shakespeare's Ovid*, edited by Tony Taylor.

Whose books helped direct your career?

As an undergraduate I was most influenced by two of my professors, Frank Kermode (especially *The Classic: Literary Images of Permanence and Change*) and Christopher Ricks (especially his essays on poetic allusion, now gathered in *Allusion to the Poets*). As a graduate student I wrestled with Harold Bloom's *Anxiety of Influence: A Theory of Poetry.* In the eighties, like everyone else, I was blown away by Stephen Greenblatt's *Renaissance Self-fashioning.* In the nineties the book that mattered to me most was Robert Pogue Harrison's *Forests: The Shadow of Civilization*, though its chapter on Shakespeare is its one disappointment. Harrison argues that the original "other" against which civilization defines itself is not "woman" or "the racial other," but the very forest which must be cleared in order for civilization (the word that comes from Latin "of the city") to be built. It was thanks to this book that my *Song of the Earth* is a theoretically much more sophisticated work than my little squib *Romantic Ecology.* Harrison's recently published a fascinating sequel, *The Dominion of the Dead*, which pursues a similar line in relation to burial practices—the organic relationship between the human and the humus.

My wife and I took a Stanford Continuing Studies class from Robert on Dante a couple of years ago. I was interested in his book on Dante's La Vita Nuova *called* The Body of Beatrice, *but he kept suggesting I read* Forests, *instead. The subject is obviously dear to him. Are there any books that you refer to frequently?*

We're so obsessed with the latest flash theory we often forget the value of reference works: my current *vade-mecums*—if that plural is possible—are Gordon Williams' amazing *Dictionary of Sexual Language and Imagery in Shakespearean and Stuart Literature*, and Stuart Gillespie's wonderfully judicious and comprehensive *Shakespeare's Books: A Dictionary of Shakespeare Sources*, in the invaluable series of Athlone Shakespeare dictionaries.

Who isn't read anymore who should be rediscovered?

I'm doing a lot of thinking about Shakespeare and intellectual history at the moment. That, together with my interest in the history of the idea of "nature" has sent me back to J. F. Danby, *Shakespeare's Doctrine of Nature*, which I hadn't read since I was an undergraduate. It stands up really well in terms of both contexts such as Hooker and readings of texts such as *Lear*.

Are there any books of the past several years that you think deserve more attention than they have received?

I was really impressed with James P. Bednarz, *Shakespeare and the Poets' War*—a brilliant revisiting of the "poetomachia." His argument doesn't stand up in every particular, but I'm sure he's right that the "poetomachia" extends to a broader range of plays, and involves Shakespeare more centrally, than is often assumed. It can't be a coincidence that John Marston wrote a play called *What You Will*, first performed in 1601. What, YOU, Will??!

What is the most important book on Shakespeare, his times, or early modern theatre you have read?

Impossible question: my cop-out is to say the work of E. K. Chambers—the wealth of material collected in the four volumes of *The Elizabethan Stage* and the two volumes of *William Shakespeare*. As I grow middle-aged and grumpy, I attach more and more importance to facts, at least as a starting-point for speculation.

And Chamber's The Medieval Stage *is not bad, though my question did not reach back that far. Whose books do you greatly admire?*

When starting out I especially admired C. L. Barber's *Shakespeare's Festive Comedy*—for taking the comedies seriously and for its reading of my favorite Shakespeare play, *Henry the Fourth, part one.* It's one of those books I don't dare reread for fear I won't like it so much now.

Name a Shakespeare book that is just plain fun.

Robert Nye's novel, *The Late Mr. Shakespeare.* Written from the point of view of a boy actor looking back from very old age during the Restoration, it covers most of the important "facts and problems" about Shakespeare in a highly inventive way. Having once turned the life of William Hazlitt into a novel myself because I didn't want to write a conventional critical book about him that no-one would read, I'm very interested in the borderline between creative writing and criticism.

Are there any non-lit crit books that you find particularly enriching?

Charles Nicholl's books, for the way they bring the atmosphere of the age alive. *The Reckoning* is terrific not for its proposed solution to the circumstances of Marlowe's death, but because you can smell the river in it. Also the work of Quentin Skinner on the language of political theory in the early modern period, e.g., his *Foundations of Modern Political Thought.* Skinner is one of the very few academics who can claim to have shaped a whole discipline: thanks to him, political theory is no longer the ahistorical procession of "great books" taken out of time, but rather a discipline closely linked to both history and rhetoric, and therefore of enormous relevance to us as Shakespeareans.

What are you reading now?

Roy Porter's last book, *Flesh in the Age of Reason*—had he lived, he would have followed it with a book on culture and medicine in the sixteenth century. It would have been fascinating. Porter's previous book, *Enlightenment,* was about the mind in the eighteenth century; this one tells the other half of the story by examining the body, the "flesh" and the fleshly life. I rather feel in our period that the need is the other way round: recent criticism has endlessly dissected the Renaissance body, but I think it's time we wrote more about the Elizabethan mind.

Are there any books you'd like to mention, but I lacked the wit to ask about?

Schoenbaum's *Shakespeare's Lives* was obviously a big influence on my work on Shakespeare's cultural "afterlife"—

—and on The Genius of Shakespeare. *Are there any important subjects where the books are out of date, and need to be replaced?*

I'll answer by telling you about the book that Penguin has just commissioned me to write: they've had E. M. W. Tillyard's *Elizabethan World Picture* (1943) in print for sixty years and it still sells, despite the assault on it in the 1980s—they want me to do a "Shakespeare's world picture" kind of book to replace it. Lots of sixteenth century intellectual context, but benefiting from the Skinnerian revolution in the historiography of political thought. I'm deep in la Primaudaye's *French Academie* (1586) as we speak.

Ah, thus your comment about the need for more work on the Elizabethan mind. I hope it is so good that you escape the debunkers sixty years hence. What needs are there crying out for a book that perhaps you don't want to write?

The "green" reading of Shakespeare—it would be just too predictable for me to be the person to write it.

Jonathan, thanks for talking books with me.

Lois Potter

Lois Potter is one of our finest performance critics. I saw her at a conference when I was a budding Shakespearean. She made some very sensible comments, so I made a note of her name. I soon saw it everywhere, most often reviewing plays for the *Times Literary Supplement*. Her reviews helped me understand productions I had not seen and articulated my view of shows that I had. I soon discovered her books.

Among those books is the volume on *Twelfth Night* in the Text and Performance series and the excellent *Othello* for the series Shakespeare in Performance. With the Arden 3 emphasis on performance history, it is no surprise that Potter was asked to edit a volume. *The Two Noble Kinsmen* was published in 1997 with an updated edition in 2015. Still on the Shakespearean theme is a Festschrift entitled *Shakespeare: Text and Theatre, Essays for Jay L. Halio* which Potter co-edited with Arthur F. Kinney. Four "Talking Books" guests contributed to this volume: Alan C. Dessen, Roslyn L. Knutson, Ann Thompson, and Virginia Mason Vaughan.

An incomplete list of other books includes: *A Preface to Milton*, editing a schools edition of books III and IV of *Paradise Lost* with John Broadbent, editing *Playing Robin Hood: The Legend as Performance in Five Centuries*, whose title explains the premise, and *Secret Rites and Secret Writing: Royalist Literature 1641–1660*. Potter was the General Editor of the first volume of the series The Revels History of Drama in English. *The Life of William Shakespeare: A Critical Biography* was published well after our interview in 2012 by Basil Blackwell.

Potter was an undergraduate at Bryn Mawr and earned her Ph.D. at Girton College, Cambridge, on a Marshall Scholarship. After many years at the University of Leicester, she became the Ned B. Allen Professor of Renaissance Literature and Drama at the University of Delaware before retiring in 2008. Potter received the ultimate compliment, a Festschrift entitled *Early Modern Drama in Performance*, edited by Darlene Farabee, Mark Netzloff, and Bradley D. Reyner. The book features essays by several "Talking Books" guests, including Alan, Dessen, Virginia Mason Vaughan, and Ann Thompson. This interview originally appeared in *Shakespeare Newsletter*, 54:1, #260, Spring 2004.

••••••••••••••••••••••••••

***MPJ:** How did you come to performance criticism?*

Lois Potter: Oddly enough, I think it was my *first* critical approach, though I didn't know that it was. My parents took me to a high school production of *Twelfth Night* when I was eleven. Before we went, I looked at the first page of the play and, seeing "If music be the food of love, play on," put it down in bewilderment. That evening, a young man walked onto the stage and said, "If music be the food of love, play on," and I understood him perfectly. From then on, I found that reading plays could recreate—or create—the experience of seeing them. When I began to look round the public library to see what other people thought, the books I liked best were those that made me aware of theatrical choices: Harley Granville-Barker's *Prefaces to Shakespeare* and Arthur Colby Sprague's *Shakespeare and the Actors*. I liked A. C. Bradley's *Shakespearean Tragedy* too, because character criticism is often pretty close to theatrical criticism. Sprague was a professor at Bryn Mawr. In my first year there, I got a job reading aloud to him (he had to be careful of his eyes), so we had a very close connection throughout my undergraduate years and I learned about the older "stage history" school, where promptbooks and reviews put together a jigsaw of a past production.

Who is doing the best performance work today?

I like all the usual suspects, but I prefer intelligent reviews—*Shakespeare Survey*, *Shakespeare Quarterly*, the *Times Literary Supplement*. I just read an excellent review of Jonathan Miller's *King Lear* by Geoffrey O'Brien in the *New York Review of Books*. Reviewing is getting better and better: academics usually move from postmodernism to relativism, so they don't attack every director who didn't direct the play according to their reading of it; they see other plays, not just Shakespeare's, so they have a sense of the larger theatrical context. I also like to read actors on acting, as in "The Players of Shakespeare" series (originally edited by Philip Brockbank, then by Russell Jackson and Robert Smallwood). One of the few books that attempts to come to terms with the impure, contingent quality of the theatrical experience is Gary Taylor's *Moment by Moment in Shakespeare* (1985, also published as *To Analyze Delight*). He watched 11 performances of the RSC's *Henry V* (I assume he got free tickets) and found that, although audiences loved it, there was a huge difference between the message they received and the one the director thought he was sending. I'm in search of an aesthetic that can account for the messiness of the theatrical experience.

Did moving from England to America change the kinds of productions you see and write about?

Not a lot. I visit England twice a year in any case. Also, I'm lucky to be in a part of the U.S. that's very active theatrically. Quite apart from New York, both Philadelphia and Washington, D.C., have everything from large, expensive showcases to little upstairs studios. Americans don't appreciate their own regional theatres. But of course there are differences. In many ways, American theatre benefits from the fact that the audience isn't full of A-level students preparing for an exam on the play. Directors have to tell the story clearly and audiences are genuinely surprised at what's happening. For instance, the first scene of *Richard II* is often a bore. When I saw it in California during the Iran-Contra hearings it was electrifying. The audience could relate to two deeply religious people swearing publicly to diametrically opposite things. I love seeing plays in Washington, D.C., because the thought that the same performance might be being watched by someone from Congress or the Supreme Court transforms it for me.

Did books direct your career?

I doubt that anything really directed it; I've had the career of a billiard ball. Most of my publications were the result of someone asking me to write them. But, on the few occasions when I've taken any sort of initiative, it has usually been to say that I'd like to write more about the theatre.

Whose books influenced you the most?

In some ways, productions have been my most important books. I've learned an enormous amount both by watching rehearsals when I was younger, and by trying to understand productions that puzzled me at first, like Peter Brook's *Antony and Cleopatra* (1978) and Steven Pimlott's *Richard II* (2000). I've learned a lot from my ex-colleague Roger Warren, see, e.g., his *Staging Shakespeare's Late Plays*, although we often disagree, and from Ann Thompson and Richard Proudfoot, my editors for the Arden *Two Noble Kinsmen*, who combine textual expertise with a really good sense of the theatre.

I like the way you don't just read books or watch plays, but grapple with them, working with their ideas. Are there any books that you refer to frequently?

The Harbage-Schoenbaum *Annals of English Drama*. I find it fascinating to see what sorts of plays were being produced and perhaps written concurrently with each other. I think the new Stanley Wells collection, *Shakespeare in the Theatre*, will be another starting-point for me. I thought I knew all the good reviews by now, but he found a lot more.

Who should be rediscovered?

The old Shakespeare Variorums have a surprising amount of good theatre criticism. Another writer I have found very useful, because of his theatrical imagination, is Martin Holmes, e.g., *Shakespeare and His Players*, which discusses, for instance, the importance of stage fights and scenes where people have to don armor on stage. A review of *Shakespeare and the Traditions of Comedy* by my Cambridge supervisor Leo Salingar, said that much of his work, "need never to be done again." It used to be everyone's ambition, including mine, to write that kind of magisterial book, but now topicality is everything and it's unfairly neglected.

One of my goals with this column is to show that the current way isn't the only way. I am glad you mentioned Salingar. Whose books do you greatly admire?

Emrys Jones's *Origins of Shakespeare* and, still more, *Scenic Form in Shakespeare*. He offers a different way of analyzing the influence of other dramatists on Shakespeare—not just verbal echoes but echoes of the scenic configurations and rhythms.

Name a Shakespeare book that is just plain fun.

John Gross's anthology, *After Shakespeare*, is an anthology of writing about Shakespeare, not just the usual stuff, and most of it is amazingly good.

Is there anything outside of literary criticism that had a particularly enriching effect on your thinking?

Yes, a lot. When I first saw Tom Stoppard's *Rosencranz and Guildenstern are Dead*, given by Oxford undergraduates at the Edinburgh Festival, it had a critical edge that it probably doesn't have now.

Let's note that this is the very first production. I'm jealous.

Stoppard wrote an exchange between R and G, where one of them impersonates Hamlet and the other, after rattling off the recent ghastly events at Elsinore, asks accusingly, "Now why exactly are you behaving in this extraordinary manner?" It brought the house down in 1966, because a lot of people were still buying T. S. Eliot's argument that Hamlet was dominated by an emotion "in excess of the facts as they appear." It never gets the same kind of laugh when I see it these days. Several fictitious works contain portrayals of Shakespeare that I find convincing: one chapter of John Arden's *Books of Bale*, Peter Whelan's *The School of Night*, and Grace Tiffany's recent novel, *My Father Had a Daughter*, narrated by Judith Shakespeare. Tiffany doesn't give all the facts about Judith's marriage, presumably because they would have made for a downbeat ending, but otherwise this is a remarkably good fusion of scholarship and entertainment. I also like seeing Shakespeare in translation. I've watched *Macbeth* in French, German, Finnish, Japanese, and Chinese, not to mention Verdi's Italian opera. I've worked a bit with Jean-Michel Déprats, a very fine French translator of Shakespeare, and nothing gets you closer to the language than looking at the choices someone has to make in order to retain at least some of the multiple meanings, syntactic eccentricities, rhythms, and registers. It stops you from taking the lines for granted.

Grace Tiffany's new novel has Shakespeare as the protagonist. It is entitled Will, *and Grace tells me it should be out by the time this interview is published. What are you reading now?*

Monstrous Adversary, Alan Nelson's biography of the Earl of Oxford is just the book I've been hoping someone would write, and he was the ideal person to do it. Also Lukas Erne's *Shakespeare as Literary Dramatist*. Erne, like Harry Berger, argues for a Shakespeare whose works can be given the kind of subtle analysis that theatre-based criticism frequently disqualifies because "it wouldn't work in production." I don't see the two as polarized: some productions seem to me to have the same intellectual content, and to deserve the same level of attention, as the subtlest critical text. But people are always telling me that most of what I get out of performances is what I put there myself.

I very much sympathize. Are there any important subjects where the books are out of date, and need to be replaced?

T. W. Baldwin did some great work on Shakespeare's educational background, but he assumed that everyone who studied Latin must have hated it, and many other writers take their cue from him. My own knowledge is much more superficial than Shakespeare's, but I can't believe that he didn't feel the same fascination I do with what happens to an idea when it moves from one language to another. I'd like to convey something of that.

Thanks, Lois. Some of your answers have given me new ways to think about familiar things. There is nothing I find more rewarding.

Andrew Gurr

When most of us think of Andrew Gurr, we think of the best performance research. His books about the history and the physical and social conditions of early modern English theatre, published both before and after our interview, became standard works. Reading *The Shakespearean Stage, 1574–1642, 4e*; *Playgoing in Shakespeare's London, 3e*; *The Shakespearian Playing Companies*; *The Shakespeare Company, 1594–1642*; *Shakespeare's Opposites: The Admirals Company 1594–1625*, and *Staging in Shakespeare's Theatres*, the last written with Mariko Ichikawa, brings readers as close to visiting a Wooden O as we can get without a time machine.

As chief academic advisor to Shakespeare's Globe in London, Gurr helped guide design and other decisions, and was Director of Globe Research until 2002. Out of this came *Rebuilding Shakespeare's Globe* and *The Design of the Globe: Conclusions from the Archaeological Evidence for Shakespeare's Globe Theatre*, the second written with Ronnie Mulryne and Margaret Shewring. Research into the King Men's other theatre, the Blackfriars, led to the essay collection *Moving Shakespeare Indoors: Performing and Repertoire in the Jacobean Playhouse*, edited with Farah Karim-Cooper.

This aspect of Gurr's reputation is so well established that some forget his success as the editor of three Shakespeare texts for Cambridge University Press, *Richard II*, *Henry V*, and *The First Quarto of Henry V*. Three plays by Francis Beaumont and John Fletcher edited by Gurr are *The Knight of the Burning Pestle*, *The Maid's Tragedy*, and *Philaster*. He wrote a small book called *Shakespeare's Hats* for the 64-page Piccoli Libri series of Rome, a survey of the Elizabethan body language as it relates to headgear. He has also written a popular biography of Shakespeare, several study guides, edited two books on East African literature, produced a monograph about postcolonial writers, and co-wrote one on Katherine Mansfield with Clare Hanson.

Born in Leicester, England and raised in New Zealand, Gurr earned his Ph.D. at Cambridge where he studied with Muriel Bradbrook. He is at the University of Reading where he is co-director of the Renaissance Texts Research

Andrew Gurr

Centre. This interview was originally published in *Shakespeare Newsletter*, 54:2/3, #261/262, Summer/Fall 2004.

•••••••••••••••••••••••••••

MPJ: *I'm fascinated by the research that goes into books like* The Shakespearian Playing Companies *and* The Shakespeare Company. *How do you prepare books like these?*

Andrew Gurr: You do need a retentive memory—Chambers's *Elizabethan Stage* has 1,930 pages in its four volumes, much of it key quotations (Chambers was a masterfully accurate transcriber), and G. E. Bentley's continuation has another 2,905 in its seven volumes, *The Jacobean and Caroline Stage*. If to those venerable repositories, you add all the new evidence that has accrued in the last sixty years, you have a lot to hold in mind. And in perspective—our thinking has moved a healthy distance away from Chambers and Bentley, especially since the rethinks of the 1980s. Keeping all that information under control is like shaking a kaleidoscope—each new joggle, resulting from a new discovery or a larger scale of thinking, shifts the details in the picture, and (I hope) justifies setting out the new vision in print. There are so few hard facts we can rely on, and we have to question everything. That means always looking out for the all too often seemingly old-fashioned and pre-theoretical (I've been called that) material, the "hard" information, and then contextualizing it so that it shines (or resonates—

the Elizabethans were hearers more than they were lookers) in the most helpful way. The chief business of research into the Elizabethan drama, as with editing, is a matter of identifying the most useful information and ploughing it into the endless process of contextualizing the plays.

Others have looked at different companies and other facets of early modern theatre history. Who is doing good work in this field?

Roz Knutson does excellent work on the company repertories (*The Repertory of Shakespeare's Company, 1594–1613*, and her articles). Scott McMillin and Sally-Beth MacLean's book on the Queen's Men (*The Queen's Men and their Plays*) was a ground-breaker in showing how thoroughly that company, and by implication most of the others, controlled and shaped its products. There is some particularly good stuff coming out now on the post-duopoly companies, following what Brian Gibbons (*Jacobean City Comedy*), and Sandy Leggatt (*Citizen Comedy in the Age of Shakespeare*) originally laid down, opening out the issues of the city comedy plays of 1598 and after, and the different allegiances that the writers and their companies seem to have maintained with different sections of the London community.

I have asked several people about editing Shakespeare, so let's look at Beaumont and Fletcher. How do you set out editing their texts?

There are some pretty grand questions about the principles on which you can do any edition, starting with who is it for, and do we modernize the spelling or not. I'm not very keen on the dumbing-down process that seems to be a prerequisite for a lot of Shakespeare editions. At least with the non–Shakespeare plays you can assume a market reasonably widely-read and informed about Shakespeare. My first two B & F editions were based on the principle that an old-spelling text gets you closest to the original, a principle I still prefer, unlike most publishers. It entails making fewer changes to the text, of course, and advertising its foreignness. But my third B & F was for the Revels series, which follows the Arden idea and modernizes its texts for non–Shakespeare authors, so I had to revise my principles for that. Otherwise, it's a question of being constantly on the lookout for points that might need a note, whether about changes in language usage, political or other hints implicit in the text, or points about the stage directions and dialogue that might indicate what the original staging was meant to show. Editing demands a maximal awareness of the play's context, both local and more generally. I was doing the B & F editions while I was trying to write the first edition of *The Shakespearean Stage*, a book I was impelled to do largely out of frustration at finding how easy it is to miss the infinite number of small changes that words take on after four centuries when you don't know the local context, and to make facile assumptions that a better knowledge will correct. There was also, of course, the feeling that Chambers and Bentley had left us lost in the trees, and that such a huge wood needed a map giving it a clearer shape.

Whose books helped direct your career?

I loved working with Muriel Bradbrook, because she had so much fascinating evidence in her head and ready to hand out. She could pull you up short by challenging any of those assumptions we so readily make without thinking hard enough to call them into question. Equally, she was firmly set on recovering all we can of the original works and their context, an ambition I still feel some nostalgia for. All of her work, including *The Rise of the Common Player*, which she was writing through the time she supervised my thesis, has stayed with me. Her own first book, written when she was still an undergraduate and won the Harness Prize, was called *Elizabethan Stage Conditions*, a title I'd have loved to be able to use. Otherwise, the chief books I pored over were Chambers and Bentley, not just for the mass of hard information they can throw up, but to get some kick from the frustration they generated by making us wade through it all, like an endless mudflat with no shoreline.

Who influenced you the most?

Apart from Bradbrook, I was taken over very early on by Walter Hodges's *The Globe Restored*. That was a revelation to me, not just for Walter's incredible skill at depicting three-dimensional spaces with his minimal line-drawings, but as really hard-graft detective work, probing the little evidence there is about the early theatres like the Globe and coming out with sound conclusions. More recently I've depended on Sam Schoenbaum's *William Shakespeare: A Documentary Life* for its healthy skepticism, and even more his wonderfully entertaining *Shakespeare's Lives*.

Are there any books that you refer to frequently?

My current favorite is a new one, Ross Duffin's *Shakespeare's Songbook*. It not only has references to all the pop songs of Shakespeare's time that are mentioned in the plays, but the music too, so you can sing along with your reading and editing. And I make good use of most of the essays in the Cox and Kastan *New History of Early English Drama*. They are state of the art, full of information and sharp in challenging the old assumptions. You can't ask for much more than that when you read the essays by Peter Blayney on printing playbooks or Alan Nelson on staging at Cambridge.

Who isn't read anymore who should be rediscovered?

I've long admired Alfred Harbage, and not just for his populist politics.

His *Shakespeare and the Rival Traditions* has now been largely overtaken by deeper delvers who make a much more complicated story than was possible with his thirties-politicized "us and them" approach, but he was a genius at finding vivid signifying details or incidents, and is always a seductive read. And I've always loved going back to Molly Mahood's *Shakespeare's Wordplay*. It's still the best introduction for students starting to read Shakespeare.

Are there any recent books that you think deserve more attention than they have received?

I love the books that bring out facts we'd never bother to find out for ourselves, like Robert B. Graves's *Lighting the Shakespearean Stage*, or those that open up new territories, like Mariko Ichikawa's *Shakespearean Entrances*. Her book makes you think about what might happen in the time actors took to enter or leave the Globe stage—they could get off up to four lines of dialogue before they actually disappeared. Alan Dessen's books are crammed with revelatory thoughts about the original staging, which all too few modern directors make use of. I really prize such points as his comment that the Folio text (unlike most modern editions) has Malvolio make his cross-gartered entry *before* Olivia says her two lines about being madly in love. That generates some marvelous cross-currents in our reception of that moment.

What is the most important book on early modern theatre you have read?

For me personally, it was Walter Hodges's account of the Globe—*The Globe Restored* of 1953—and the riches it promises the studious artisan in that field of work. Beyond that, I think John Orrell's *The Quest for Shakespeare's Globe*, for its meticulous scholarship using areas of expertise that nobody had thought of applying to the question before, is a revelation. If you start with the tangible structure of the early theatre, of course, you very soon get drawn into what it was used for, and so to a fresh approach to the plays. A bit ironically, that basis for study has led me to think recently that the Blackfriars should be rated higher than the Globe. It preceded the Globe, and if they had been able to use it back in 1596, the Globe would probably never have been built. But the Globe has a magic that pulls everyone into its circle, and once inside you need to know about the staging, the original playgoers, the companies, and all of that extra context. So I guess you could say that the idea of the Globe generated all that I have done since in Shakespeare studies.

Andy, that's fascinating. Whose books do you greatly admire?

I truly admire Stephen Orgel's work, above all the essays collected in

Authentic Shakespeare. Stephen not only uses his title as an ironic joke, but makes it a signal (carrot and stick both) of what he's really after. I think he has probably done more than anyone to get us to face up to the major tasks that still challenge us.

I agree. Name a Shakespeare book that is just plain fun.

While I was a student in New Zealand I read a book by that elegant and eloquent Canadian, Logan Pearsall Smith, called *On Reading Shakespeare*. Its first sentence is: "There are many books about Shakespeare, and all of them are mad." That was a self-reflexive statement amply and wittily justified in the rest of the book. And, since I do still find a bit of macabre fun watching the anti–Stratfordians go through their contortions (through more than thirty years I've waited for one of them to take on Sonnet 145, addressed to Anne Hathaway, and I'm still waiting), I'd say Irvin Matus, *Shakespeare in Fact* can provoke quite a few giggles.

It can indeed. Are there any non-lit-crit books that you have found particularly enriching in your thinking and writing about Shakespeare and early modern theatre?

Thomas Kuhn on scientific revolutions (*The Structure of Scientific Revolutions*), and his idea of major paradigm shifts coming when the established concepts get dislodged by the growth of too much contrary evidence, is basic to my thinking. I suppose too that Hayden White on history as fiction (a movie, in my view) has to be borne in mind by anyone trying to write any sort of history or biography. (*Tropics of Discourse: Essays in Cultural Criticism*).

What are you reading now?

A book of essays put together in honor of Brian Gibbons, *Plotting Early Modern London: New Essays on Jacobean City Comedy*, edited by Dieter Mehl, Angela Stock, and Anna-Julia Zwierlein. It has some remarkable revisions of Harbage. Actually, I'm dug really deep into a book called *The Great Game*, about the century of political power struggles between Russia and Britain over Afghanistan that lies behind Kipling's *Kim*. It tells an awful tale of governmental fiddling and people burning, an appallingly lucid story that anticipates the disastrous involvement of the USSR in Afghanistan in the 1980s and now the U.S. in Iraq. It's another story of history repeating itself as farce (Peter Hopkirk, *The Great Game: On Secret Service in High Asia*).

Are there any books you'd like to mention, but I lacked the wit to ask about?

Robert Weimann's *Author's Pen and Actor's Voice* is both a wonderfully level-headed survey of the main concerns about Shakespearean performativity and a rich source of fresh thinking about it.

Good choice. Are there any important subjects where the books are out of date and need to be replaced?

I think that all the editions and series of editions are seriously out of date in their current approach to the presentation of the plays as performable texts. Lukas Erne (*Shakespeare as Literary Dramatist*) is right to argue that the original printed texts were produced knowingly for readers rather than for playgoers, though I think he makes the assumption that Shakespeare himself promoted the publication of his plays too readily—he sold them to the company, which then saw to their publication (or not). We need to rethink the whole process of book production and what drove different authors to get their plays into print.

What book do we need that perhaps you don't want to write?

I'd like to see a book that takes Shakespeare on as an individual who played some very private games with his profession. Why, for instance, did he write "Once more unto the breach, dear friends," which every actor of *Henry V* counts as his most wonderful speech, and make it the prelude to an attack on Harfleur that failed? He cannot have expected his company to stage all the ambivalences about Henry which he wrote into that play, and indeed they did remove that speech and the scaling ladders from the version they staged in 1599. Why, too, did he always write so much more into his histories than the company could use? And what was he doing when he made Giulio Romano, painter of the most famous erotic pictures of all time—the sixteen sexual positions that Aretino turned into sonnets—the singular maker of Hermione's statue? A book on that aspect of the man might do a lot to clarify our thinking about the plays at large.

Andy, you have some great questions there. Thank you. I appreciate you taking time to talk about books with me.

Anthony B. Dawson

Anthony B. Dawson is the co-author of one of the most unusual scholarly books in recent years, if only because of the way it makes its arguments. *The Culture of Playgoing in Shakespeare's England: A Collaborative Debate* is a dialogue between Dawson and Paul Yachnin about the social and political environment that informed playgoing for early modern people, and how going to plays was a part of their lives. The authors have very different perspectives on this, so they structure their book as point/counterpoint. This allows Dawson and Yachnin to clarify their ideas as each tests the perspective of the other. In the end, neither is converted, but their turf is well defined, and problems with both sides are exposed. This is a logical, telescoped extension of the way scholars speak to each other in different books, and an approach that other scholars with other interests should consider.

Dawson's other books address interpretive questions related to Shakespearean performance and dramaturgy. *Indirections: Shakespeare and the Art of Illusion* attempts to define how Shakespeare misdirected the perceptions of readers and theatergoers for artistic ends. *Watching Shakespeare: A Playgoers Guide*, a book written for educated theatre-goers as well as students and scholars, explores choices and problems posed by the performance possibilities of eighteen Shakespeare plays. *Shakespeare in Performance: Hamlet* is a superb survey of important productions on stage and film. Dawson has also written extensively on other early modern playwrights as well as on Shakespeare and performance theory, and on editing and textual theory.

Dawson had not edited many plays prior to our interview, just Marlowe's *Tamburlaine the Great: parts one and two* and Shakespeare's *Troilus and Cressida*. He has since added the Arden 3 edition of *Timon of Athens*, co-edited with Gretchen Minton in two editions, the Oxford World's Classics edition of *Richard II*, co-edited with Philip Yuchnin, and the second quarto of *Hamlet* supplemented with lines from the Folio for the one volume *Norton Shakespeare, 3e*. Dawson also edited discrete online versions of all three *Hamlet* texts that are available to those who purchase the big Norton book. You will find this in the bibliography under the lead General Editor, Stephen Greenblatt. Tony

Anthony B. Dawson

Dawson is a past president of the Shakespeare Association of America, and is Professor Emeritus of English at the University of British Columbia. This interview was originally published in *Shakespeare Newsletter*, 55:1, #264, Spring 2005.

••••••••••••••••••••••••••••

MPJ: *I know that* Tamburlaine *does not present great textual problems, still you have to process the differences between the octavos, choose readings, and understand the background of Marlowe and his plays. Which books, articles, or editions were helpful when preparing your edition?*

Anthony B. Dawson: *Tamburlaine* was a kind of rehearsal for the much more daunting task of editing *Troilus and Cressida* and *Timon of Athens*. I was asked to revise the J. W. Harper edition, not start from scratch; originally, this was meant to entail only a new introduction and some changes to the annotations. However, I ended up doing a lot of work on the text, because I found a number of inconsistencies; I also felt that considerable revision of punctuation was necessary in order to make the text more accessible to modern readers and performers, and I found that the annotations needed a lot of updating and changes. While I did of course consult the 1590 octavo edition and used it as my control text (the other early octavos and quartos all derive from the 1590 edition), I was spared the time-consuming task of a full collation, since the New Mermaids are not full scholarly editions.

For me, the most helpful previous editions (besides Harper's) were those of J. S. Cunningham for the Revels series, and Una Ellis-Fermor's excellent edition from 1930. Other books that I found stimulating were *Two Renaissance Mythmakers: Christopher Marlowe and Ben Jonson* (Selected papers from the English Institute; 1975–76) edited by Alvin Kernan, with splendid essays by a number of critics including Stephen Greenblatt and Michael Goldman, John Bakeless's 1942 classic biographical portrait, *The Tragicall History of Christopher Marlowe,* which put together a wealth of information about Marlowe's short but intense life, and, with a grain of salt, Charles Nichol's provocative study of Marlowe's life and death as a spy, *The Reckoning.* I also focused a fair bit of energy on performance, especially the two major British productions of 1976 and 1992, which informed my interpretation of the play's dynamics.

Troilus and Cressida *is more complicated. Who has enriched your thinking as you struggled with these texts.*

You're right, it is more complicated, one of the trickiest plays in the canon to edit, since the exact relation between the Q and F texts is virtually impossible to settle with any confidence. This means that one faces serious difficulties in establishing a control text, deciding about particular readings, and adjudicating between substantive variants (of which there are more than 500). Besides that, of course, *Troilus and Cressida* is one of the most densely written and abstracted of Shakespeare's plays and thus requires a great deal of careful elucidation in the commentary. I found the whole project immensely satisfying because of the problems the play poses, which I hope I've managed to confront (not necessarily "solve") in an interesting way. No doubt the single most helpful precursor for editors of the play is H. H. Hillebrand's Variorum edition, but I also benefited enormously from earlier editions and commentary by Alice Walker (Cambridge, 1957), G. B. Evans (Riverside, 1974), and Kenneth Palmer (Arden 2, 1982), plus of course David Bevington's recent Arden edition (1998). Among other influential commentators on the text, I'd single out W. W. Greg, especially *The Shakespeare First Folio* (1955), Phillip Williams' articles on the relations between Q and F (in *Studies in Bibliography*). Ernst Honigmann, *The Stability of Shakespeare's Texts* which discusses revision and provenance, Gary Taylor (both in the *Textual Companion* to the Oxford edition and in an important article in *Shakespeare Studies 15* on the texts of the play), and William Godschalk ("The texts of *Troilus and Cressida*" in *Early Modern Literary Studies 1* online). All these scholars spot different crucial features of the text and all contribute ideas about the relation of Q to F. I found myself not entirely agreeing with any on them, but was stimulated by how they made me attend to important detail.

Whose work in the theory of performance scholarship has influenced you?

What I have felt over the past ten years or so is not the influence of a particular person or persons so much as that of a group of people who are engaged in an ongoing and developing conversation—people like (in alpha order):

Barbara Hodgdon, whose *The Shakespeare Trade: Performances and Appropriations* is a brilliant account of both the ideology and pleasure of modern performance, told with Barbara's characteristic wit and verve. Peter Holland, who has done so much for performance criticism, as editor and facilitator as well as critic; of his extensive work, I'd single out *English Shakespeares: Shakespeare on the English Stage in the 1990s*, for me an indispensable remembering of the best of recent Shakespeare performance. Dennis Kennedy, whose *Looking at Shakespeare: A Visual History of Twentieth-Century Performance* is certainly the best book on the visual aspects of performance in the twentieth-century, and one that I found especially helpful for my thinking about the different visual styles of *Hamlet* performance when I was doing the book on that play.

Stephen Orgel has been crucial in helping us see Shakespeare performance in historical perspective; his elegant introductions to the Oxford *Tempest* and *Winter's Tale* and his short but wonderfully rich book on gender and performance, *Impersonations: The Performance of Gender in Shakespeare's England*, are texts that I return to regularly.

Carol Rutter, whose *Enter the Body* captures the delights and ideological occlusions of the body, especially the gendered body, on display in English Shakespeare (a fine follow-up on her earlier book of interviews with Shakespearean actresses, *Clamorous Voices*). Her lovely and pointed writing is for me always a pleasure to read. Bill Worthen, whose lucid and cogently argued work on the *Authority* and *Force* of Shakespearean performance (to cite two of his titles), its uniqueness and its distance from text, is for me a welcome stimulant and often a corrective to my own thinking.

Each of these is wonderful in a different way, each is a joy to read, and each has immeasurably enhanced my own work. Earlier of course, there is the unsurpassable work of Granville-Barker's *Prefaces to Shakespeare*, and the ground-breaking books of John Styan, particularly *The Shakespeare Revolution*.

Has Lukas Erne changed the way you think about performance scholarship?

No. He's added a useful corrective to a view that I never held anyway—i.e., that Shakespeare wrote his plays with *only* performance in mind. I found his book provocative and extremely well researched, but I wasn't always convinced by his arguments—he sometimes falls into the trap of assuming as proven what is in fact a fairly tendentious point, and then using that as a basis for a new argument. And, like many of the performance critics he opposes, he has preserved what I see as a mistaken distinction between literary and performed, often considering the latter in terms that are too narrow (speed, direct action and plot development, etc.). There are aspects of the "literary" that are not only performable, but add immeasurably to the subtlety and scope of performance. Still, there's no doubt that insistence on the literary aspects of Shakespeare is valuable and important, and the timing of Erne's book, which came at a moment when there is a (for me, welcome) turn back to the aesthetic in Shakespeare criticism, has added to its impact.

I have seen some scholarly books from Canadian publishers that have not received much attention, at least in the United States. Are any wrongly neglected?

There's an interesting recent book out from U of Toronto called *Shakespeare in Canada* edited by Diana Brydon and Irena R. Makaryk, with essays by a wide range of Canadian critics (including me) that I think deserves wider circulation than it seems to be getting. One thing that emerges from the collection is that there is a wide variety of valuable, and in a few cases, uniquely Canadian, work being done on Shakespeare in Canada, in performance studies, theory, and criticism. But overall I don't see neglect of Canadian scholarship as a major problem.

Marta Strazinky's chapter on Canadian radio Shakespeare broadcasts is very helpful in the work I'm doing now. Those interested should take a look. Which books influenced you the most?

There's a fair range: certainly Northrop Frye's books—not only those on Shakespeare (*A Natural Perspective* and *Fools of Time*), but his *Anatomy of Criticism* as well; Granville-Barker's *Prefaces to Shakespeare* (the work of a brilliantly innovative theatre practitioner in the early 20th century who was as well a remarkably acute critic of both character and theme), and Bradley's foundational *Shakespearean Tragedy*, of course; Jan Kott's iconoclastic *Shakespeare our Contemporary* made a big mark when I was young, because it brought Shakespeare forcibly into the present and was written with an insouciant, almost journalistic manner, though it perhaps was less an influence and more a brilliant provocation. The single most influential book on Shakespeare for me is probably C. L. Barber's *Shakespeare's Festive Comedy*, one of the finest and most humane books of criticism I know.

In textual matters the work of the so-called "new bibliographers," especially W. W. Greg, has been indispensable of course; even though they have come in for a lot of criticism lately for being too "essentialist" and for searching (in vain) for the ideal text, their work laid the foundation for all the analytic study of texts and provenance that has been conducted since. The work of the revisionists, as declared in the ground-breaking book *The Division of the Kingdoms* (edited by Gary Taylor and Michael Warren), put into practice in the Oxford edition of the *Complete Works* edited by Taylor and Stanley Wells along with the *Textual Companion* thereto, and argued by wonderful scholars such as Ernst Honigmann (*The Stability of Shakespeare's Text*), and Paul Werstine (in a series of excellent, skeptical articles on various aspects of textual theory), has challenged the received ideas of the New Bibliographers, arguing forcibly, for example, that Shakespeare did regularly revise his plays. They thus regard the idea of an "original" text as chimerical and have urged the independence of early texts, which, they say, should not be conflated but considered, and even published separately (as has happened most famously with *King Lear* in the 1987 Wells and Taylor Oxford edition).

There are also some wonderful books in theatre history, such as Andy Gurr's *Shakespearian Stage* and *Playgoing in Shakespeare's London*, Scott McMillin's *Elizabethan Theatre and the Book of Sir Thomas More* and Tiffany Stern's *Rehearsal from Shakespeare to Sheridan*; they combine careful, original scholarship, with deft interpretation in order to fill out our picture of the conditions of early modern playing—the actors, the companies, the theatres, the audiences.

Then there's the work of the new historicists, especially Stephen Greenblatt's *Renaissance Self-fashioning* and Louis Montrose's essays on the relations between early modern texts and their historical contexts (gender, courtly competition, etc.), which helped change the way many of us think about the relation of literature and culture. At around the same time (early and mid-1980s), the work of feminist scholars began to take hold; a key text in this movement was *The Woman's Part*, a volume edited by Carolyn Ruth Swift Lenz, Gayle Greene, and Carol Thomas Neely that made us all realize that gender was a category we needed to pay more attention to. Following that, a number of critics helped expand and map this under-examined territory; of these, the most influential for me were Coppélia Kahn (*Man's Estate*, and as co-editor with Gayle Greene of *Making a Difference: Feminist Literary Criticism*), combining psychoanalysis with an understanding of the politics of gender; Linda Woodbridge, whose wide-ranging, sympathetic and enormously influential survey of the status of, and controversies about, women, *Women and the English Renaissance: Literature and the Nature of Womankind, 1540 to 1620* is a book to which I still frequently return; and Gail Paster, whose *The Body Embarrassed: Drama and the Disciplines of Shame in Early Modern England* changed the way we think about the early modern gendered body.

Finally, my co-author and good friend Paul Yachnin has influenced me in all kinds of ways, not least in his book, *Stage-wrights: Shakespeare, Jonson, Middleton and the Making of Theatrical Value,* a probing and convincing reassessment of the commercial grounding and the relatively "powerless" cultural role of the Elizabethan theatre; but also, often, by helping me figure out what I really think about something.

Are there any books that you refer to frequently?

Huston Diehl's *Staging Reform, Reforming the Stage: Protestantism and Popular Theater in Early Modern England*, which opened up the field of Shakespeare and reformed religion, making a careful and plausible case that the theatre was more closely linked to Protestant ways of thinking than had previously been recognized; Kathy Maus's *Inwardness and Theatre in the English Renaissance*, for me the essential book on early modern subjectivity as it was represented and constructed in the theatre, with brilliant readings of some key plays; Michael Neill's *Issues of Death: Mortality and Identity in English Renaissance Tragedy*, a compelling and beautifully written account of revenge, time and death in Shakespeare and early modern tragedy more generally. These days, anthologies are becoming important locations for new and important work—for me two of the top ones are David Kastan and John Cox's wide-ranging *A New History of Early English Drama*, which features essays by many of the top people in the field, each writing about their particular specialty with insight and originality, and Jim Bulman's *Shakespeare, Theory and Performance*, which helped push performance criticism in a more creative and theoretically savvy direction. I can't let this question go without mentioning the book I no doubt refer to the most, G. B. Evans' wonderful *Riverside* edition of Shakespeare's works, with its splendidly and carefully edited texts, its excellent supporting material and its succinct but penetrating notes and commentary on the text.

The first Riverside *is fifty percent of the reason I became serious about Shakespeare. Who isn't read anymore who should be rediscovered?*

That's a tough question. Derek Traversi maybe? I remember reading *An Approach to Shakespeare* with fascination years ago—I wonder how it would read today; Traversi is a very shrewd analyst of textual and imagistic detail. Certainly Empson, especially *Some Versions of Pastoral*, with that astonishing essay on the double plot. Erich Auerbach's *Mimesis: The Representation of Reality in Western Literature*, an essential account of how literary representation has worked over the centuries; Maynard Mack's *King Lear in Our Time*, no longer of "our time" exactly, but still timely and important, not least for its ethical commitment. And should we be re-reading Tillyard? He's suffered quite a lot of bad press, but it's at least possible that his work deserves a more balanced assessment. L. C. Knights's *Drama and Society in the Age of Jonson* is another fine forgotten book, intelligently blending historical interpretation with close reading long before the new historicists. Joel Fineman's provocative book on visuality and subjectivity in the Sonnets (*Shakespeare's Perjured Eye: The Invention of Poetic Subjectivity in the Sonnets*) might also be ripe for rediscovery.

Are any books of the past several years that you think deserve more attention than they have received?

Well, I'd say that there are a few critic/scholars whom I really admire who don't seem to get as much press as they should—Joel B. Altman, Edward Pechter, and James Siemon, to name a few. Altman's *Tudor Play of Mind: Rhetorical Inquiry and the Development of Elizabethan Drama* on rhetoric and dramatic form, is a classic analysis of the way styles of rhetorical education affected dramatic structure and dialogue. Since that book, he has published a remarkable series of complex essays on *Henry V*, *Othello* and other plays, in which he explores issues of historical interpretation. Pechter is provocative and wonderfully skeptical, and a fine, witty writer, always attuned to the turns and potential lapses of whatever critical paradigm is "hot"—a kind of meta-critic if you will; his *What was Shakespeare?: Renaissance Plays and Changing Critical Practice* gives a fair sample of his sharp-eyed, and sharp-witted method. I think James R. Siemon's excellent *Shakespearean Iconoclasm* is one of the best neglected books of criticism around—clear, penetrating analysis, never flashy or self-promoting, but damn good; he also has a new book out, *Word Against Word: Shakespearean Utterance*, which looks very closely at the verbal texture of Shakespearean utterance and which is on my list of "must read soon."

What is the most important book on Shakespeare, his times, or early modern theatre you have read?

That's a tough one too—I guess Bradley's *Shakespearean Tragedy* for one; although his work, from the late nineteenth century, has been largely repudiated, it can't be dismissed—his attention to character, even if he occasionally takes it too far, is brilliant and responds to what most people like and admire about Shakespeare. He's an astute, theatrically attuned reader, though he's not often given sufficient credit for this latter quality. Then there are the great reference works by E. K. Chambers, Greg's work on the text, and lovely works of criticism such as Barber's *Festive Comedy.* I've already mentioned Greenblatt's *Self-fashioning*, and I could add his *Shakespearean Negotiations: The Circulation of Social Energy in Renaissance England.* Both books, and the "new historicism" that he helped to invent, have been enormously influential.

Whose books do you greatly admire?

Well, those I've already named, certainly, so I'd ask the reader to glance once again over the illustrious people listed above. To those I'd add (alpha order again): Jonathan Bate, a writer of great range and sensitivity—his *The Genius of Shakespeare* is the best popular book on Shakespeare and his *Shakespeare and Ovid* displays his learning and his subtle understanding of literary influence.

Harry Berger, always provocative, an extremely perceptive reader of both texts and painting, committed to the literary as against the performed. While I didn't agree with his counter-performance argument in *Imaginary Audition*, I found it bracing and in some ways (if one accepted his premises, which many performance critics actually did without noticing) dead right.

Lynne Magnusson has drawn attention in quite a new and important way to the play of language in Shakespeare and Renaissance writing more generally. Her *Shakespeare and Social Dialogue* introduced recent work in social linguistics and communication theory to the study of social interaction in Shakespearean drama with surprising and influential results.

Reg Foakes, whose precise and thoughtful writing on Shakespeare in performance has graced the profession for decades; also outstanding are his work as an editor (most decisively his Arden 3 *King Lear*) and the contribution he has made in making available crucially important material for the study of theatrical history such as *Henslowe's Diary* and *Illustrations of the English Stage.*

Stanley Wells, of course. He is the dean of Shakespeare scholarship today, in both performance and textual studies; facilitator, editor, indefatigable advocate, he has contributed more to the field than any single person.

Name a Shakespeare book that is just plain fun.

After Shakespeare compiled (brilliantly) by John Gross. One can roam around in the book, read at random, picking up tidbits from writers of myriad backgrounds as they respond to Shakespeare in marvelously diverse ways.

What are you reading now?

Lots of stuff about *Timon of Athens* of course, but more interestingly,

I'm reading Virgil and working on the way he was read by Shakespeare and other Elizabethan dramatists. I think the relation of these writers to the classical past has been rather neglected lately.

Are there any books you'd like to mention, but I lacked the wit to ask about?

I'm interested in the spate of biographical writing about Shakespeare that has recently taken shape. Stephen Greenblatt's *Will in the World* is just out and I'm eager to read it, to compare it with Katharine Duncan-Jones' fine, irreverent look at *Ungentle Shakespeare*, and soon there will be James Shapiro's book on the year 1599, also focusing on what Shakespeare was up to in that year. So, an area in which we thought we knew what there is to know proves surprisingly fertile. A similar thing has happened with the general topic of Shakespeare and religion, which for a long time was sorely neglected, and is now overcrowded and controversial.

Thanks, Tony. Many of your answers are discoveries for me, and that is one big reason that I do this.

Katherine Duncan-Jones

Before Katherine Duncan-Jones made a splash in the Shakespeare world, she was known for her work on Philip Sidney. Her editions include *Sir Philip Sidney* for the Oxford Authors series reprinted as *Sir Philip Sidney: The Major Works*, and *The Countess of Pembroke's Arcadia: The Old Arcadia*. She also wrote an interesting literary biography, *Sir Philip Sidney: Courtier Poet*.

Duncan-Jones was on the fringe of Shakespeare scholarship, weighing in on Donald Foster's attribution of "A Funerall Elegye" to Shakespeare (she was not convinced) amongst other matters, until she was given the plum assignment of editing the *Sonnets* for Arden 3. Her introduction unflinchingly confronts the sexuality of the poems and makes the case that Shakespeare authorized Thomas Thorpe's publication. While this has been controversial, the edition has received much praise. This was followed by another plum, the Arden 3 *Shakespeare's Poems*, edited with H. R. Woudhuysen, containing the rest of Shakespeare's non-dramatic verse.

The biography *Ungentle Shakespeare: Scenes from His Life* has also been controversial. This is not the gentle swan of Avon found in the Romantic tradition, but a tough business man whose drive to make money shaped his character. The Folio Society published a collection of document facsimiles related Shakespearean in 2004, the very documents Duncan-Jones used when writing her biography. *Shakespeare's Life and World* was published right before our interview. Duncan-Jones gathered the materials and wrote the introductory chapter. Unfortunately, the book was not available at the time of the interview, so I was not able to base any questions on it.

Two follow-up books were published after our interview. *Shakespeare: From Upstart Crow to Sweet Swan: 1592–1623* studies his reputation from the staging of his early plays until the publication of the First Folio and *Portraits of Shakespeare* studies the three portraits that Duncan-Jones claims were acknowledged by Shakespeare's friends to be his likeness, then looks at subsequent uses of Shakespeare's images. There is a lot of food for thought in this book, even though I am skeptical about some of the claims.

Duncan-Jones has published dozens of articles and has been a regular theater reviewer for the *Times Literary Supplement* for over thirty years. She spent one year as the *New Statesman*'s regular theatre critic, which gave her an opportunity to review contemporary plays as well. After many years as a Tutorial Fellow in English at Somerville College, Oxford, Duncan-Jones is now a Senior Research Fellow. Since 1992 she has been Fellow of the Royal Society of Literature. This interview was originally published in *Shakespeare Newsletter*, 55:2, #265, Summer 2005.

••••••••••••••••••••••••••

MPJ: *Since our readership is a mix of Shakespeare scholars and fans, not everyone is familiar with Sidney. Reading your books will give them an excellent start. What did you find most helpful when preparing them?*

Katherine Duncan-Jones: Having been trained in the decipherment of Elizabethan secretary hand when I was a graduate student in the 1960s gave me a huge advantage, as there is a lot of Sidney material in manuscript, including voluminous correspondence and texts of many of his literary works. If only that kind of material survived for Shakespeare! There *are* important Shakespeare records in manuscript, some of which I felt had been rather neglected by previous scholars, such as the 1596 grant of arms to John Shakespeare—but no personal correspondence, and no manuscript texts of his literary works. Of course, when preparing my own biographies of both Sidney and Shakespeare, I also benefited greatly from the work of previous scholars: especially Malcolm Wallace and James Osborn (both American!) in the case of Sidney, and E. K. Chambers and Samuel Schoenbaum, in the case of Shakespeare.

Any thoughts about Sidney's other works?

Sadly, I don't keep up properly with work on Sidney nowadays, but I am delighted by the fact that some of his works, especially his *Defence of Poesy* and the earlier, shorter, version of his romance *Arcadia*, now regularly appear in university courses both in the U.S. and the U.K. This was not the case in the 1960s and 70s, when there were widespread misapprehensions that he was a pampered aristocrat (he got his knighthood only after his major works were completed), and that his style was difficult.

You take such an individual path in your introduction to the sonnets that I wonder if you may have read something that challenged your ideas, or that perhaps stimulated you to go your own way?

I think my "individual path" was determined partly by my own rather independent personality. But equally important was my background reading. Working on Sidney for so many years ensured that I was steeped in Elizabethan poetry of the 1570s and 80s, the period immediately before Shakespeare took off. I used regularly to lecture on Elizabethan sonnets, as well as on Sidney, and when I reached Shakespeare's *Sonnets* it was always apparent to me that they were astonishingly unlike those of the 1580s and early 1590s. This led me to two views which appeared rather radical at that time, though both are now more widely accepted. The first was that many of Shakespeare's sonnets may have been written late, after 1600, being in some cases written or revised quite close in time to their publication in 1609. Secondly, I became convinced that as his collection evolved, perhaps over the course of many years, Shakespeare must have decided consciously to flout the whole Petrarchan/courtly love tradition. Addressing most of his sonnets to a young man, rather than to a chaste and unattainable lady, was an extraordinarily bold thing to do. I also felt that disproportionate attention had been given by previous critics to the relatively small number of sonnets connected to the so-called Dark Lady. Many of the sonnets in that part of the collection suggest that she is no lady, nor is she chaste or remote. The speaker seems to hate her almost as much as he loves her. Sonnet 144, "Two loves I have, of comfort and despair" is the most extreme expression of loathing for the woman, but few suggest much fondness, let alone adoration.

Many who are not convinced the sonnets are autobiographical, including myself, tend to look at other sonnets as justification for believing Shakespeare's are fictional, but your point that they are different than the other extant sonnet sequences is challenging. I need to think about this. Thank you. Are there any sonnet commentaries that were helpful, or that you recommend?

I grew up with the wonderfully annotated editions of the *Sonnets* by W. G. Ingram and Theodore Redpath, and, rather later, Stephen Booth, both of which I greatly admire, even though both omit *A Lover's Complaint* which was appended to the Sonnets in 1609. Helen Vendler's *The Art of Shakespeare's Sonnets*, a text and commentary, came out at the same time as my own Arden edition, and I hugely admire that, as well, though I think it's hard for students, or indeed for any readers, to find their own paths forward from her brilliant, austere, almost algebraic analyses of individual sonnets.

How about Shakespeare biographies? You obviously worked most closely with the records, but you must have looked at someone.

I rather avoided reading other biographies! But I relied heavily on the work of E. K. Chambers's *William Shakespeare: A Study of Facts and Problems* and Samuel Schoenbaum's *William Shakespeare: A Documentary Life* with its wonderfully useful complement *William Shakespeare: Records and Images*. Among more fully written up "literary" biographies, I particularly admire Russell Fraser's two volume life, *Young Shakespeare* and *Shakespeare: The Later Years*.

Since you write a lot of theater criticism, I wonder whose work you find most stimulating or influential?

In addition to such golden oldies as George Bernard Shaw, James Agate and Kenneth Tynan, I admire the theatre reviews of Michael Billington in *The Guardian*, Paul Taylor in *The Independent* and Susannah Clapp in *The Observer*. I always avoid reading other reviews until I have written my own. Once I do read any of these three, I am generally struck by how much more neatly, wittily and concisely they have made points that I felt myself laboring over quite clumsily. I have the luxury of having more time than they do—sometimes nearly a week—and usually more words. But I'm not sure that that's always a good thing! Most recently I've been writing about Kevin Spacey's *Richard II* at London's Old Vic, for which the *TLS* gave me a whacking 1700 words.

Is there one book that really inspired you?

I grew up in a bookish family. But it was at school that I fell in love. A charismatic English teacher, Miss Kate Flint, brought in an old folio edition of Sidney's *Arcadia*, and read aloud a tear-jerking passage from it describing the death of Zelmane, a lovesick girl disguised as a boy. I have adored the Elizabethans ever since.

Whose book influenced you the most?

This really does date me! My constant resource used to be C. S. Lewis's *English Literature in the Sixteenth Century*. This showed that a work of reference could be extremely readable and at times even funny. Lewis's many perverse judgments and textual inaccuracies provoked me to appreciate the importance of accurate texts.

I understand he wrote quotations from memory, cock-sure he had them right. We all know the danger of doing that! Name a Shakespeare book that is just plain fun.

Caryl Brahms and S. J. Simon's novel *No Bed for Bacon*, a powerful, unacknowledged model for the delightful 1999 film *Shakespeare in Love*.

Those looking for sources for that film might also look at Clement Dane's play, Will Shakespeare. *It is overwrought, but there are a few striking parallels to the Tom Stoppard–Marc Norman screenplay. What are you reading now?*

Re-reading Henry James's *What Maisie Knew*. I am a rapid and wide reader, and despite my love for the Elizabethans, most of my reading for relaxation is from the nineteenth and twentieth centuries.

James is fun. Thanks, Katherine. I really appreciate the chance to chat about books with you.

Lukas Erne

Every several years someone writes a book that every Shakespearean has to read. These books challenge the assumptions behind the way we think about Shakespeare and his work and shape future discourse. Such a book is *Shakespeare as Literary Dramatist* by Lukas Erne, important enough to have been published in two editions (2003 and 2013). He argues that Shakespeare intended some of his plays to be published and read, preparing them as literary texts that were then shortened for performance. Even if one is not persuaded by all of Erne's ideas, no one in the field can ignore this book. Long after our interview, this was followed by the companion volume, *Shakespeare and the Book Trade,* which tries to make the same case by finding Shakespeare's printed texts compatible with authors who saw their works through the press.

While these books have captured most of the attention, other titles are also noteworthy. Erne edited *The Limits of Textuality*, the thirteenth in the series "Swiss Papers in English Language and Literature," with Guillemette Bolens. It collects some of the papers given at the International Conference on the Limits of Textuality, at the University of Geneva in 1999. *Textual Performances: The Modern Reproduction of Shakespeare's Drama* was edited with M. J. Kidnie. The thirteen chapters include an all-star cast of contributors such as Leah Marcus, David Bevington, Michael Warren, Ann Thompson, and Ernst Honigmann. The subject is the editing of Shakespeare's plays as editors weigh playhouse research, biography, and printing house practices.

Of special interest to me is *Beyond 'The Spanish Tragedy': A Study of the Works of Thomas Kyd* for the Revels Plays Companion Library. It studies all publications identified as Kyd's up that time, presenting fresh perspectives on the neglected works and extensive treatment of *The Spanish Tragedy*, arguing that parts of the lost play *Don Horatio* were appropriated into the text of *The First Part of Hieronimo*. I hope that Erne and Manchester will consider a second edition. Kyd's caché has not been higher since his death, with a number of anonymous collaborations recently attributed him.

After our interview, Erne published editions of *The First Quarto of Romeo and Juliet* and *Soliman and Perseda*, one of the works attributed to Kyd by

Gregor Sarrazin as early as 1892. He has written *Shakespeare's Modern Collaborators*, a defense of editors in crafting modern editions of Shakespeare, and co-edited *Medieval and Early Modern Authorship* with Guillemette Bolens. This book boasts an impressive group of contributors such as Helen Cooper, Colin Burrow, and future "Talking Books" guest Patrick Cheney. They engage with current debates about the very concept of an "author."

Lukas Erne

Four books are scheduled for publication between now and 2020. *Shakespeare in Geneva: Early Modern English Books (1475–1700) at the Martin Bodmer Foundation: An Introduction and Catalogue*, written with Devani Singh, should be in print by the time you read this, and an edition of *Belvedere, or the Garden of the Muses: An Early Modern Commonplace Book*, edited with Devani Singh, is under contract to Cambridge University Press. Erne is the General Editor of the forthcoming *Early Modern German Shakespeare*. The first volume, with early modern German versions of *Hamlet* and *Romeo and Juliet*, will be edited by Erne with Kareen Seidler. The second volume with early modern German versions of *Titus Andronicus* and *The Taming of the Shrew* will be edited by Erne with Florence Hazrat and Maria Shmygol.

Lukas Erne is Swiss born and educated, with post-graduate work in Oxford as a Berrow Scholar from 1994 to 1997. After teaching at the University of Geneva, he became Professor of English Literature at the University of Neuchâtel. Earn returned to Geneva to take the Chair of English Renaissance Literature. He won the 2002 Calvin and Rose G. Hoffman Prize for the essay, "Biography, Mythography and Criticism: The Life and Works of Christopher Marlowe." This interview was originally published in *Shakespeare Newsletter*, 55:3, #266, Fall 2005.

••••••••••••••••••••••••••••

***MPJ**: You have made quite a splash for such a young man. Who were the teachers, and which books turned your interests in this direction?*

Lukas Erne: I've had a number of stimulating teachers, but there are three who have been particularly important. During the five years I studied at the University of Lausanne, Neil Forsyth—whose recent book on *Paradise Lost*, called *The Satanic Epic*, received a prestigious prize from the Milton Society of America—first made me appreciate many of the great early modern authors I still love and work on today, notably Shakespeare, Marlowe, Donne, and Milton. The "Shakespeare in Performance" trips to Stratford-upon-Avon which he organized led me to write my MA thesis with him on Shakespeare. So he has a lot to answer for. Then, during my years in Oxford in the mid-nineties, I was lucky enough to work with Emrys Jones and D. F. McKenzie—superb teachers and scholars both. McKenzie taught me what pleasure and profit can be derived from textual and bibliographical work. As for Jones, even though the doctorate he supervised was on Kyd, I realize retrospectively that he has taught me more than anyone else about Shakespeare. I never discussed the argument of *Shakespeare as Literary Dramatist* with either Jones or McKenzie, but it was no doubt the experience of working simultaneously with the two that turned my interest in this direction.

The long bibliography and extensive notes in Shakespeare as Literary Dramatist *almost make this interview superfluous, but let's pretend someone is not going to read everything and wants to see the key texts that helped your research. Where should they begin?*

A number of articles and books paved the way to specific parts of my argument, so they might be a good place to start: Peter Blayney's "The Publication of Playbooks," in John D. Cox and David Scott Kastan's *A New History of Early English Drama* made me reconsider the early publication history of Shakespeare's playbooks; Andrew Gurr's New Cambridge edition of Q1 *Henry V* and his "Maximal and Minimal Texts" article in *Shakespeare Survey* were important for their conjunction of insights from stage history and textual studies. Richard Dutton's "The Birth of the Author," in Cedric Brown and Arthur Marotti's *Texts and Cultural Change in Early Modern England*, influenced my thinking about Shakespeare as a dramatic author; and Stephen Orgel's "The Authentic Shakespeare" and "Acting Scripts, Performing Texts," both now available in *The Authentic Shakespeare*, helped me recognize the importance of the "bad quartos" for my argument. Giorgio Melchiori's essay in *The "Hamlet" First Published (Q1, 1603) Origins, Forms, Intertextualities* preceded me in thinking of Shakespeare as a literary dramatist; Laurie Maguire *Shakespearean Suspect Texts: The 'Bad' Quartos and Their Contexts* and two *Shakespeare Quarterly* essays, of 1990 ("Narratives about printed Shakespearean texts: 'Foul Papers' and 'Bad Quartos'"), and 1999 ("A Century of 'Bad' Shakespeare Quartos") by Paul Werstine were important for their revisionary thinking about the "bad quartos"; other articles by Werstine and William Long convinced me of the importance of the extant manuscript playbooks. Brian Vickers's edition of *English Renaissance Literary Criticism* helped me understand that there is nothing anachronistic about the concept of Shakespearean dramatic authorship, and his incisive review essay of the Wells and Taylor *Textual Companion* in *The Review of English Studies*, contributed to my sense that many of the Shakespeare texts we have been studying are very different from the plays as they were performed by Shakespeare and his fellow players.

A number of studies have had a more diffuse but perhaps equally important influence, for instance the *Textual Companion* I just mentioned, which I find to be a prodigious achievement, despite my occasional disagreements; Richard Helgerson's *Self-Crowned Laureates: Spenser, Jonson, Milton and the Literary System* helped me think about Shakespeare's place in the "literary system" of his time; Harry Berger's *Imaginary Audition: Shakespeare on Stage and Page* with its enabling articulation of a specifically readerly response to plays; and Arthur Marotti's *Manuscript, Print, and the English Renaissance Lyric* contains an incisive study of the process of legitimizing of printed lyric poetry.

I have noticed that even those who hate *the Oxford* Complete Works, *and that word is not too strong for some people, have to contend with the completeness, thoughtfulness, and frequent good judgement of the* Textual Companion. *After nearly three decades it is still the place most of us turn first.*[1] *What have you read since publication that supports or perhaps argues with your thesis?*

I've been very fortunate with the quality of the response to my book. Many of the reviews I've come across have been genuinely helpful, not only expressing appreciation but also raising questions which call for further reflection and investigation. On top of the reviews, there was the 2004 conference at the University of Lancaster, "The Return of the Author in Shakespeare Studies," organized by Richard Wilson, at which the book was incisively discussed by many participants. Plus, and this has been a source of continued enjoyment, I've been receiving many emails, some from scholars I greatly admire, some from people I'd never heard of, and a few of these emails led to prolonged exchanges from which I've learnt a lot. The total response has been so multi-faceted that it would be unfair to single out one aspect or one scholar here, but I will obviously want to make my contribution to the continuation of the dialogue.

I noticed that you cite some books with German titles. The work that I see is usually on my side of the language barrier. Are there any books those of us stuck with English should know about, anything that really should be translated for a wider audience?

There is a lot of material in German that deserves the attention of Shakespeareans, beginning with seventeenth-century adaptations of Shakespeare plays by itinerant players, some of which have never been translated. As for modern scholarship, if I had to designate a candidate for translation, I would recommend Part IV of the *Shakespeare-Handbuch*, edited by Ina Schabert. Parts I to III (about the period, the man, and the work) are useful without breaking new ground, but the last part, about the Shakespeare reception, provides an excellent survey, with comprehensive historical and geographical coverage, including the reception in music and the visual arts.

I read your book on Thomas Kyd over the Christmas break, and like it very much. It is fascinating, learned, yet accessible. Some of our readers are not professional Shakespeareans, so please forgive a deliberately ignorant question or two. What is the standard text of Kyd's work, and which of the readily available texts do you recommend?

The edition of *The Works of Thomas Kyd* by Frederick S. Boas remains standard, but it is hopelessly outdated. It is really pre–New Bibliography, and ignores all rigorous principles of scholarly editing, as Greg pointed out in a review as early as 1901. The best edition of *The Spanish Tragedy* is still that by Philip Edwards in the Revels series, though it too is coming of age. Among the more recent and more lightly annotated editions, I would recommend J. R. Mulryne's in the New Mermaids series and David Bevington's in the Revels Student series.

I've been looking for an excuse to publicly thank Philip Edwards and his wife. They befriended me at the first conference I attended. I did not know anybody and felt out of place the way shy people do. They talked to me during breaks, always returned kindness for my ignorance, and helped me feel I belonged. I shall always be grateful to them. Where do you think discourse on Kyd will go next?

The Spanish Tragedy will remain the key text, but I am convinced that much is to be gained from looking at the play in the context of Kyd's other works, in particular *The First Part of Hieronimo* and what it preserves of the otherwise lost *Don Horatio*. Reading *The Spanish Tragedy* without awareness of the other play with which it originally formed a diptych is a bit like reading the second parts of *Henry IV* or *Tamburlaine* without awareness of the first.

Are there any books of the past five years that you think deserve more attention than they have received?

Yes, there is one that comes to mind immediately, a reference work, arguably the most important reference work since the *Short-Title Catalogue*. I'm thinking of Steven May's three-volume *Bibliography and First-line Index of English Verse, 1559–1603*. It may end up transforming important parts of English early modern studies if we fully exploit its potential. So far, I've only come across one review, but it's a very useful review, and easy to access, too, in the on-line journal *Early Modern Literary Studies*, by Douglas Bruster.

What are the most important books on Shakespeare's literary qualities?

There is a small number of outstanding books all of which explain to me an important aspect of how Shakespeare's dramatic artefacts work: George T. Wright's *Shakespeare's Metrical Art* and Brian Vickers's *The Artistry of Shakespeare's Prose* are key for the artistry of Shakespeare's language; they are also nicely complementary, Wright teaching us how Shakespeare used meter, Vickers how he used prose. Emrys Jones's *Scenic Form in Shakespeare* is the best book on Shakespeare's scenic organization, but it is essential reading for much else, too, such as Shakespeare's adaptation and transformation of his own earlier work, his dramatization of time, and his use of a two-part structure. David Bevington's *Action Is Eloquence: Shakespeare's Language of Gesture*, finally, is for me the key study of Shakespeare's stagecraft. No one would want Shakespeare studies to be confined to an investigation of the works' artistry, but I am convinced that our enjoyment of and engagement with Shakespeare would be much impoverished without the scholars who fully alert us to this artistry.

Whose books do you greatly admire?

Well, there are many scholars whose books I admire, but if I have to single out one of them, I'll go for Ernst Honigmann. It's hard to think of a Shakespearean who has made us rethink so many key issues, textual, biographical, and critical. For instance, *Shakespeare: The Lost Years* is the foundational text for much recent revisionary work on Shakespeare and religion, and *The Stability of Shakespeare's Text* did much to stimulate thinking about Shakespeare and revision. Incidentally, Honigmann also argued against the mistaken consensus of Shakespeare's alleged indifference (or opposition) to the print publication of his playtexts, and he did so even before I was born.

Name a Shakespeare book that is fun.

Let me recommend one which you may never have heard of—*A Few*

Words About William Shakespeare's Plays (1780), by my fellow—Swiss Ulrich Bräker, a peasant who worked hard all day, and read and wrote about Shakespeare by night. Bräker is a wonderfully enthusiastic and surprisingly shrewd reader, considering his lack of formal education. Readers of your column may want to know that his short book has been translated into English by Derek Bowman.

Excellent. Are there any books you'd like to mention, but I lacked the wit to ask about?

Patrick Cheney is doing important work which reminds us that Shakespeare, throughout his career, was both a dramatist and a poet, and was thought of and published as a dramatist and a poet. *Shakespeare, National Poet-Playwright* and his forthcoming book *Shakespeare's Literary Authorship* show that this is a distinctive form of authorship that can be traced back all the way to Ovid. Heminge and Condell did us a great service by producing the First Folio in 1623 with almost all of Shakespeare's plays, but our view of Shakespeare still hasn't fully recovered from their exclusion of the poems. Patrick Cheney is also editing *The Cambridge Companion to Shakespeare's Poetry*, which promises to be more than a state-of-the-art survey, for it really advances what seems to me a compelling argument, which is that when studying Shakespeare's poetry, we need to look not only at the poems but also at the plays.

What needs are there crying out for a book that perhaps you don't want to write?

It's not a book I wouldn't *want* to write but which only one person *can* write. The person is Peter Blayney and the book is the history of the Stationers' Company and the printers of London, 1501–1616. He's been working on it for some time, and it will no doubt make a real difference once it's published.[2]

And I am looking forward to it. Thanks, Lukas. Our conversation has been an education, and I appreciate that.

Notes

1. It has since been superseded by *The New Oxford Shakespeare Authorship Companion* edited by Gary Taylor and Gabriel Egan.
2. The book has since been published.

R. A. Foakes

All Shakespeareans owe a debt to R. A. Foakes. In his edition of *Henslowe's Diary* (with R. T. Rickert, 1961, revised alone, 2002), he made available one of the most important documents of the early modern English theater, then published an edition without the commentary but in facsimile as *The Henslowe Papers* in two volumes (1977). Much of the work done by historians of the English theatre is made possible because Henslowe's records are now easily accessible. Less well-known, but also vital, is *Illustrations of the English Stage, 1580–1642*, which goes way beyond the Globe images we have seen again and again, conveniently putting between two covers what survives of the visual record of early modern theater. There are more than eighty illustrations with commentary describing what we know and what may be deduced about these images.

While these books show a strong interest in early performance, Foakes has also published on cultural matters. *Hamlet Versus Lear: Cultural Politics and Shakespeare's Art* considers the reasons for the changing critical standing of these plays. *Shakespeare and Violence* connects current concerns about violence to the way Shakespeare used it in his storytelling, and also shows the evolution of Shakespeare's treatments of violence as his career progressed.

An incomplete list of his other books include the Arden 2 editions of *Henry VIII* and *The Comedy of Errors*, the Arden 3 *King Lear*, Penguin editions of *Much Ado About Nothing* and *Troilus and Cressida*, and the Cambridge University Press *A Midsummer Night's Dream*. His 1966 Methuen edition of Thomas Middleton's *The Revenger's Tragedy* was revised in 1996. The 1978 survey *Marston and Tourneur* was about Shakespeare's contemporary playwrights John Marston and Cyril Tourneur for Longman's Writers & Their Work series. *The Columbia Dictionary of Quotations from Shakespeare*, was edited with second wife Mary Foakes, and two books are sufficiently classic that they were reprinted in 2004 by Routledge (*Shakespeare: From the Dark Comedies to the Last Plays: from Satire to Celebration*, originally published by the University of Virginia Press in 1971, and *Coleridge on Shakespeare: The Text of the Lectures 1811–12*, originally published by Wayne State University Press in 1989). Foakes also

R. A. Foakes

edited the selection *Coleridge's Criticism of Shakespeare* and the two volumes of *Coleridge's Lectures on Literature* for the *Collected Coleridge*. The lectures are mostly about Shakespeare. Foakes has written a few other books more directly about the Romantics as well.

The night before revising this introduction, I found an important article by Foakes that is more than sixty years old. "The Players Passion: Some Notes on Elizabethan Psychology and Action" demonstrates that early modern audiences believe good actors mirrored real behavior, but bad actors parodied it. Foakes further suggests that the good actors developed a performance style that expressed, "greater extremes of passion" than that employed by modern actors, though due to cultural differences this style, what was so impressive then would seem too formal and even silly now. This became so commonplace in Shakespeare studies that I have seen stated many times over the intervening years. The basic idea has had nuance added in recent years, but the basic idea is still there.

Foakes received the ultimate compliment, a *Festschrift*, entitled *Shakespeare Performed: Essays in Honor of R. A. Foakes*, edited by Grace Ioppolo. The essays study ways that Shakespeare was performed in his time and in ours. It is a book that, like its honoree, strives to show that the theatrical and the literary are not separate, but closely related. From 1956–60, Foakes wrote the annual book review column in *Shakespeare Survey*. He received his Ph.D. from the University of Birmingham and was one of the original Fellows at the Shakespeare Institute in Stratford-upon-Avon. Foakes had a Harkness Fellowship at Yale University and taught at a number of schools in England and North America, including the University of Toronto and UCLA, where he was Professor Emeritus until his death at the age of ninety in 2013. This interview was originally published in *Shakespeare Newsletter*, 55: 4, #267, Winter 2005/2006.

••••••••••••••••••••••••••

MPJ: *I love* Henslowe's Diary. *After years of reading about it and seeing quotes from it, I have finally read it in context. One of its delights are the careful and learned notes and glosses that, of necessity, take us back to older bibliographical approaches usually neglected these days. How did you go about finding all the facts and figures, and which books were helpful?*

R. A. Foakes: I was really building on the amazing advances made by W. W. Greg and E. K. Chambers. The "New Bibliography" of their time has been much criticized recently, but they laid the groundwork for modern scholarship. *The Elizabethan Stage* contains a mine of information about playhouses and plays, often crowded into footnotes, while Greg provided the first bibliography of the drama of Shakespeare's age in his magisterial *A Bibliography of the English Printed Drama to the Restoration*, and, in Malone Society reprints, a treasure-house of editions of rare plays. I also had the benefit of studying palaeography with C. J. Sisson, who fostered a sense of excitement in studying manuscripts. His beautifully written *Lost Plays of Shakespeare's Age* deserves status as a classic work. It brings to life entertainingly two lost plays by major dramatists, including Chapman, Webster and Ford, that were written in relation to lawsuits, as well as the only known texts of jigs.

I finally found a copy the last time I was in London. Great book. Let's ask a similar question for Illustrations of the English Stage. *So much there is not found in the books commonly in our home libraries. How did you locate all of these images?*

My *Illustrations* book took years to complete, and locating some of the images was especially time-consuming. Only a detail of the map of Paris Garden, for instance, which pinpoints the location of the Swan theatre, had been previously reproduced, except in a not very clear detail by Richard Hosley. It took time to discover that the map was no longer where he found it, in the care of the Southwark Diocesan Board of Education, but had been placed on deposit in the Greater London Record Office. I was especially pleased to find and reproduce the image of John Green in costume as the actor playing Nobody in the anonymous play *No-Body and Some-Body*. A footnote in Chambers *Elizabethan Stage* led me to this, the only drawing of a known actor in costume, which had never been reproduced in English or American publications. Tracking images and getting them newly photographed involved much travel and endless correspondence, before the days of email. Many of the illustrations had been reproduced in frontispieces of editions or books on the stage, but, as in working on Henslowe, I was bothered by the lack of a book that would gather all the information together.

The Revenger's Tragedy *is such an interesting play. Which books have shaped the discussion about it?*

The Revenger's Tragedy intrigues me as a great masterpiece of its kind. The question of its kind, however, remains a fascinating one, and unresolved. Since I edited the play there has been some challenging critical debate about it, as by Jonathan Dollimore, who saw the play as a radical critique of the ruling ideology in *Radical Tragedy*, and by Wendy Griswold, who argued in *Renaissance Revivals* that it supported a nationalistic conservatism. Macdonald P. Jackson's facsimile edition and account of the authorship problem in *The Revenger's Tragedy Attributed to Middleton* is essential reading. John Kerrigan's *Revenge Tragedy from Aeschylus to Armageddon* is a splendid survey, and has an interesting chapter on humor and self-reference, arguing that ambivalence about revenge develops a "comic tonality" in such plays, but the jury is still out on the function of the comic elements in *The Revenger's Tragedy* and the plays of Marston.

You have been involved in many editions as well as critical books. What makes a good critical edition, and why do we need so many new editions?

Working on a critical edition is challenging and satisfying. There is always something new to be found, as we can only understand Shakespeare in relation to our own time, and there is no better way to know a text thoroughly than to edit it. In recent decades there have been great advances in presenting texts. In Arden 2, completed only in the 1980s, stage history and the theatrical aspects of plays were usually dealt with in a more or less brief appendix to a critical introduction. In growing disappointment with such treatment, I sought in my edition of *A Midsummer Night's Dream* for the Cambridge Shakespeare to bring the stage into focus by dividing my introduction into two parts, "the play in the mind" and "the play on the stage." This seemed innovatory at the time, 1985, but now the Oxford, the Cambridge, and Arden 3 editions have all put great emphasis on stage productions and, more recently, film versions. Another important change has been the shift in commentaries from authoritarian explanations that allow for no alternatives, as exemplified by a gloss to the line in *King Lear*, "And my poor fool is hanged," that reads simply "i.e., Cordelia." Now glosses are more likely to suggest possible meanings that permit the reader to choose.

There are, of course, many student editions available, but the major editions, such as those I mentioned, all demand that the editor rethink everything about the play. A good critical edition enables the user to see the play, as it were, freshly in close-up, and really gain an intimacy with it. A good critical edition can be more helpful and instructive than a heap of books of criticism.

It may be a blind-spot of mine, but I tend not to read Coleridge, or Auden, or any well-known poet on Shakespeare, finding in the little I have read that they tend to reveal far more about their preferences than about Shakespeare. It is different, of course, if I am studying the poet, but to use a parallel example, I do not find the condescension of Eliot helpful when I am reading Massinger. Am I wrong about this? What does Coleridge offer students of Shakespeare?

I think Coleridge changed fundamentally the ways in which Shakespeare was understood, and was the first great "modern" critic. When he grew up in the late eighteenth century, Dr. Johnson was still a dominating force in Shakespeare criticism, a critic who applied a concept of regularity to the plays, as if they should have been written according to external criteria, rules he assumed Shakespeare, conceived as an uneducated child of nature, often ignored. Coleridge rejected the idea of rules and dramatic unities and developed a criticism based on the idea of organic unity, to be found within Shakespeare's orchestration of each play. He redefined the vocabulary of critical terms, and invented "practical criticism," the close scrutiny of the text and its imagery, which became so important in the twentieth century. He also was innovative in pursuing what he called "a psychological rather than a historical" mode of reasoning in discussing the plays—the term "psychological" was new, and at one point he apologized to his audience for using it. Coleridge's criticism is fragmentary, but seminal, and worth mining for insights that still resonate, such as his famous comments on Iago as embodying "the motive-hunting of motiveless malignity," and on Hamlet as "continually resolving to do, yet doing nothing but resolve."

Thank you. That is very helpful. Which books helped direct your career?

I loved theatre when I was young, having ready access to the Birmingham Repertory Theatre and the Royal Shakespeare Theatre in Stratford-on-Avon. So my first publications were provoked by the inadequacies of imagery criticism, as practiced by Caroline Spurgeon in *Shakespeare's Imagery and what it tells us* and Wolfgang Clemen in *The Development of Shakespeare's Imagery*. They were only interested in poetic imagery and treated plays as poems with scant regard for the stage. They provoked my first critical writings, which argued that stage images such as the blood in

Macbeth were as important as poetic imagery for understanding the plays. This seems obvious enough now, but most criticism in the 1950s and 1960s pretty much ignored the stage. As to positive influences, rather than any one book, I believe working on *Shakespeare Survey* in its early years influenced me, as a new annual in which Allardyce Nicoll sought to connect literary and theatre criticism with theatre history and reviews of current productions.

Are there any books that you refer to frequently?

Raymond Williams's *Modern Tragedy*, which anticipated and influenced the deconstruction of traditional views carried further by Jonathan Dollimore and others. Also A. D. Nuttall, who has contributed towards a formal theory of tragedy in *A New Mimesis* and *Why Does Tragedy Give Pleasure?*, offering a critique of Aristotle's concept of catharsis in specific relation to Shakespeare. Postmodern criticism of Shakespeare has been mainly concerned with dismantling various notions of authority, and investigating contradictions or faultlines in the plays, and has little interest in value or aesthetics. Perhaps Nuttall's turn will come.

Are there any books of the past ten years that you think deserve more attention than they have received?

A difficult one: I don't know how to measure importance. Critical fashions change, and all of us need to keep in mind what actually went on during the early modern period, hence a book I keep by me is *English Professional Theatre, 1530–1660*, edited by Glynne Wickham, Herbert Berry and William Ingram, a compilation of documentary records. But ever since working on Henslowe I have returned to the documents that provide us with vital basic information, which I think we need to keep in mind. In this context a book that deserves to be better known is Julian Bowsher's *The Rose Theatre: An Archaeological Discovery*. This analysis of findings at the site of the Rose is very suggestive in relation to the staging of plays at the Fortune and Globe, for example in the positioning of stage posts.

Whose books do you admire?

I admire writers who can captivate by their style and involve the reader, e.g., Stephen Booth's fine *King Lear, Macbeth, Indefinition and Tragedy*, which subtly destabilizes traditional readings of the plays. Stephen Greenblatt's *Shakespearean Negotiations* is a pleasure to read because he writes so well and the anecdotes with which his chapters begin are intriguing, although I am quite unpersuaded by his rejection of any idea of artistic completeness, and his emphasis on the marginal and fragmentary in Shakespeare's plays. Another book that is a delight to read is M. M. Mahood's *Bit*

Parts in Shakespeare's Plays. This commentary on all those minor characters, mostly unnamed, gentlemen, ladies, sentries, messengers, and so on, who have a few lines or intervene in some way in the plays, shows how much they contribute to the action, and focuses attention on a neglected aspect of Shakespeare's dramaturgy.

I am a Molly Mahood fan. This is a wonderful and under-read book. Name a Shakespeare book that is just plain fun.

Terry Hawkes, *That Shakespeherian Rag: essays on a critical process*, ingenious, very clever, and offers intriguing perspectives on the prejudices of some older critics. His essay "Telmah," on John Dover Wilson's classic study *What Happens in Hamlet*, brilliantly demonstrates how his reading of the play was affected by events in 1917 during World War 1—by his disagreement with W. W. Greg, who published an essay on the dumb-show and the play within the play in November 1917, and by the news of the outbreak of the Bolshevik revolution in Russia at the same time. The book serves as a reminder to all of us that our critical views are not simply neutral, but have ideological implications.

Are there any important subjects where the books are out of date, and need to be replaced?

I have been bringing myself up to date with performance criticism, which is very prominent now, and has sparked several series on plays in performance. I am intrigued by what seems to be a gap between theory, as exemplified in the writings of W. B. Worthen and others, and practice, as seen in the critiques of actual productions by Peter Holland, Carol Rutter and others. Theoretical critics seem anxious to escape from the texts of Shakespeare's plays, since they are interested in "performativity" (a term I find hard to grasp) and what Worthen in *Shakespeare and the Force of Modern Performance* calls "fashioning texts into behaviour," or what the actors do with a play. Hence they tend to despise what they regard as conventional or traditional productions, and find exciting innovatory reinventions that may have little connection with the canonical texts. Those critics who are more concerned with analyzing mainstream stagings of plays seem to be operating on a different wavelength. There are some intriguing issues that emerge, e.g., is it possible to establish the boundaries between a Shakespeare play, an adaptation of it that is based on the text, and a reworking that effectively rewrites it?

What need is there for books that perhaps you don't want to write?

We seem to have lost touch with aesthetics, which is discounted by current theories, and I would like to see a revival of interest in the formal properties of the plays. A. D. Nuttall, as mentioned earlier, has made a start with his books on tragedy. But we don't seem to have advanced much beyond the claims made for form based on scenic units that were advanced in such works as *Scenic Form in Shakespeare* by Emrys Jones and *Shakespearean Design* by Mark Rose. Also character criticism has more or less disappeared (the chapter on it in the *Shakespeare: An Oxford Guide* begins with the heading "the rise and fall of Shakespearean character criticism"), and I think is due for a revival. If it comes, it will be in a different kind from the psychological analysis, often in Freudian terms, that Coleridge began to develop, and which flourished through much of the twentieth century.

Are there any books you'd like to mention, but I lacked the wit to ask about?

Andrew Cunningham and Ole Peter Grell, *The Four Horsemen of the Apocalypse*, subtitled *Religion, War, Famine and Death in Reformation Europe*. It provides a splendidly illustrated European setting for the age of Shakespeare, and explicates the ways in which the recurrent crises of the period from 1500 onwards were interpreted in apocalyptic terms.

Thanks, Reg. I really appreciate you consenting to be my guest in this column.

Virginia Mason Vaughan

Virginia Mason Vaughan saved me from making a fool of myself. A few years ago, I had my paper for a Shakespeare Association of America (SAA) seminar well in hand. I had read scads of learned articles and books, examined a key prompt book, and viewed several film versions of *Othello*, including several viewings of the one I was writing about. The paper was ninety percent written. I deliberately saved Vaughan's *Othello: A Contextual History* for last because I had heard how brilliant it is. When I finally read the book, I realized it is so brilliant that it made most of my argument far better than I had, and refuted one of my points decisively. Everything in my paper was redundant or wrong, and while that was a problem as far as the seminar was concerned (the leader kindly allowed me to become the respondent, instead), I was grateful to be set straight. The way Vaughan historicizes this play and its afterlife are unmatched.

She wrote on her faculty website, "I want to understand how English people came to think of themselves as 'white' as opposed to the peoples of darker pigmentation they were encountering in Africa and the New World."[1] Other books on *Othello* are *Othello: New Perspectives*, edited with Kent Cartwright and *Othello: An Annotated Bibliography*, compiled with Margaret Lael Mikesell. *Performing Blackness on English Stages, 1500–1800*, continues Vaughan's exploration of Shakespeare's black characters, with particular attention to the ways in which Aaron and Othello—along with many non–Shakespearean Moors—were constructed, performed, and perceived.

Other works take this concern for race and imperialism beyond *Othello*. These include an anthology co-edited with John Gillies, *Playing the Globe: Genre and Geography in English Renaissance Drama* and books with her husband, Columbia University historian Alden T. Vaughan, who shares those interests. Together they wrote *Shakespeare's Caliban: A Cultural History* about the character's origins and manifestations in different times and media, edited the collection, *Critical Essays on Shakespeare's The Tempest* for the series Critical Essays on British Literature, and in a different sense they are editors of the Arden 3 *Tempest* in two editions, the first in 1999 and the second after our interview in 2011. The pair recently edited and contributed to the excellent anthology *The Tempest: A Critical Reader*. On her own, Vaughan wrote a superb performance history, *Shakespeare in Performance: The Tempest*.

Virginia Mason Vaughan

Recent attention is still on the theme of imperialism, and some would say the mixing of races, in *Antony and Cleopatra*. Vaughan edited the text for the third edition of the *Norton Shakespeare*, and followed this up with *Antony and Cleopatra: Language and Writing*. About this book, Vaughan wrote, "This book is very important to me. It almost wrote itself. I poured into it all the things I had learned in 40 years of teaching Shakespeare to undergraduates. In this book I tried to do justice to all the fabulous, inquisitive students I've encountered over the years. The voice is different, because I wanted student readers to feel I was speaking directly to them."[2]

This all is related to colonialism, of course, and the United States is the former colony where the Vaughans live. They were guest-curators of a 2007 exhibit for the Folger Shakespeare Library's seventy-fifth anniversary, "Shakespeare in American Life." The Folger published the catalog of the show that year, compiled and edited by the Vaughans. That research provided a start for their excellent *Shakespeare in America*, part of the Oxford Shakespeare Topics series, in 2012.

There are two books that are less obviously related to race and imperialism, but show an awareness of the less powerful people in a society. Vaughan's revised dissertation was published as *The Drama as Propaganda: A Study of The Troublesome Raigne of King John* for the series Salzburg Studies in English Literature in 1974. It begins her interest in historical contexts, this time for the anonymous play that many say is a source for *King John*. Her monograph argues that unlike Shakespeare's ambiguous treatment of John and his relationship to the church, *The Troublesome Raigne* "exemplifies the popularization of political propaganda in the stage" (20). It is now available from Edwin Mellen Press, and published under the name Virginia Mason Carr. *Women Making Shakespeare: Text, Reception and Performance* is a Festschrift for Ann Thompson containing essays recognizing contributions by women to Shakespeare publishing, performance, and education. It is co-edited with Gordon McMullan and Lena Cowen Orlin. Forthcoming from Arden in 2019 is *Shakespeare and the Gods*, written to provide both a classical and early modern context for the gods Shakespeare alludes to most frequently and suggestively.

Vaughan grew up just a few blocks from where I lived at the time of our interview, in the shadow of Stanford University. She graduated from the University of Michigan and is now Professor Emerita at Clark University in Worcester, Massachusetts. This interview was originally published in *Shakespeare Newsletter*, 56: 1, #268, Spring/Summer 2006.

••••••••••••••••••••••••••••

MPJ: *Your edition of* The Tempest *is almost a mini-variorum, one of the most comprehensive editions of any play I have seen in the Arden series. Your thirteen pages of works cited are daunting. Whose books and articles added the most to your view of the play?*

Virginia Mason Vaughan: We found Nigel Wood's volume on *The Tempest* from the Theory in Practice series very thought provoking, especially in regards to the play's political implications as a whole, not just in terms of colonialism. David Kastan's essay on the play's Old World origins, which we first heard as a paper delivered at SAA, was also influential and we included it in our *Critical Essays on* "The Tempest." But the greatest debt was probably to our predecessors. We were awed at the thought of following in the footsteps of Frank Kermode, whose 1954 Arden 2 edition was pathbreaking, especially in its recognition of the play's New World ramifications. In his Oxford edition, Stephen Orgel frequently took issue with Kermode, but his introduction, too, was magisterial. We tried to steer between the Scylla of eighteenth and nineteenth-century criticism, making Prospero a benign figure of the Enlightenment, and the Charybdis of some late twentieth-century criticism, which makes him a petty tyrant.

It has been seven years since publication.[3] *Have any books or articles come along that extend your work in new directions, or add new dimensions to your argument?*

The Tempest continues to generate a mass of critical material and literary offshoots. Christine Dymkowski's edition for Cambridge's Shakespeare in Production series provides a wealth of information about performance history; David Lindley's edition and his monograph on *The Tempest* in the Shakespeare at Stratford series also complement what we did. David is an expert on early modern music, and his analysis of the play's songs and sound effects is fascinating. Chantal Zabus's work on appropriations of *The Tempest* in *Tempests After Shakespeare* covers a very wide canvas, across the globe with all the major characters. In addition, the anthology *"The Tempest" and its Travels*, edited by Peter Hulme and William Sherman, offers a variety of interesting perspectives. As the title implies, this anthology places *The Tempest* in a global context, both within the trans-Atlantic world of 1610–11 and in adaptations and appropriations from creative artists around the world ever since.

The only thing I don't like about Othello: A Contextual History *is the lack of a works cited separate from the footnotes. The index indicated a heavier than average dependence on Julie Hankey, Marvin Rosenberg, and Peter Stallybrass. Why were the works of these three so helpful?*

M. C. Riggio's *Choice* review chided me for the same thing, and I've resolved never again to publish without a bibliography! I found Julie Hankey's performance edition in the Shakespeare in Production series from Cambridge (which came out in a second, improved version in 2005) helpful because it took the play moment-by-moment, offering specific information on how each scene had been performed over time. That's invaluable when you're trying to reconstruct historical performances. Rosenberg was a pioneer in theatre history studies, and although *The Masks of Othello* now seems dated—especially his efforts to track down the "perfect" Othello or Iago—the historical overview he provides is very helpful. Peter Stallybrass's article, "Patriarchal Territories: The Body Enclosed," in *Rewriting the Renaissance: The Discourses of Sexual Difference in Early Modern Europe* was influential for its concepts as opposed to providing specific information. Unlike Hankey and Rosenberg, Peter viewed the characters as constructed from a series of discursive frameworks, especially patriarchal, circulating in the early modern period. He offered me a different way of thinking about Othello and Desdemona.

Were others as helpful to the way you think about the play, even if they are not indexed as often?

The first section of the book, which situates *Othello* within the context of its own time, was influenced by readings in new historicism, especially Stephen Greenblatt's *Renaissance Self-fashioning*, but also by Phyllis Rackin's *Stages of History: Shakespeares English Chronicles*, and Jean Howard's essay, "The New Historicism in Renaissance Studies." I read widely in primary texts published during the time of production (1603–1604) to see what discourses were circulating that might have shaped Shakespeare's thinking. That's why "Contextual" is in the title.

My thinking about performance in the book's second section was influenced by Bernard Beckerman's *Shakespeare at the Globe, 1599–1609* and posthumous *Theatrical Presentation: Performer, Audience and Act,* edited by Gloria Brim Beckerman and William Coco. Bernie taught me about the dynamic flow of performance and the impossibility of pinning down any one moment as the "meaning" of a play. Robert Hapgood's *Shakespeare The Theatre-Poet* also looks closely at how the character of Othello is layered through language. It is old news now, but in the early 1990s theatre historians were less likely to think in terms of contexts and to explore the ways in which a particular historical moment could change the shape of the play.

What have you learned about Othello *since writing this book, and if you read it somewhere, where?*

I have a chapter on Othello in *Performing Blackness*. There I place Shakespeare's tragedy within the context of blackface performances in contemporary plays. My ideas about Othello keep changing, but this chapter was shaped in many ways by the African-Anglo actor Hugh Quarshie's 1999 lecture, "Second Thoughts About 'Othello.'" Quarshie looks at *Othello* from a black actor's viewpoint; he finds the Moor's emotional deterioration and violent rage to be racist and impossible to perform as written. The essays in *Othello: New Essays by Black Writers*, edited by Mythili Kaul, also forced me to re-think the play's racial dynamics. The African-American contributors to this anthology sometimes expressed contradictory views of Shakespeare's tragedy, with one describing it as being as demeaning to blacks as nineteenth-century minstrel shows and others trying to understand Othello as a black man trying to succeed in a white culture. Lois Potter's volume on *Othello* in Manchester's Shakespeare in Performance series describes the important productions since my book was published, such as the Shakespeare Theatre of Washington's "photo-negative" production with an all black cast and Patrick Stewart as Othello.

My work has always been eclectic. Historical contexts are my stock and trade, but I always try to treat the plays as scripts for performance, both at the moment of production and in theatres and on film. I am also interested in the construction of gender. My chapter in *Othello: A Contextual History* on husbands and wives was shaped by the pioneer work of feminist critics such as Irene Dash's *Wooing, Wedding, and Power*, which taught me to pay attention to the cuts made in women's roles, Carol Thomas Neely's *Broken Nuptials in Shakespeare's Plays*, which helped make me into an "Emilia critic," and Linda Woodbridge's *Women and the English Renaissance: Literature and the Nature of Womankind, 1540–1620*, which provided contexts concerning early modern gender ideology.

At the same time, I have never abandoned my early training in close reading. The text remains primary in my work, and I am pleased that there seems to be renewed interest in Shakespeare's language and in the drama's aesthetic properties. I'm thinking of the work of Russ MacDonald's *Shakespeare and the Arts of Language*, Ann and John O. Thompson's *Shakespeare, Meaning and Metaphor*, Lynne Magnusson's *Shakespeare and Social Dialogue: Dramatic Language and Elizabethan Letters*, and George T. Wright's *Shakespeare's Metrical Art*, among others. Incidentally, I've just bought a 2005 reprint of Sister Miriam Joseph's 1947 *Shakespeare's Use of the Arts of Language*—that shows you that her analysis of early modern grammar and rhetoric is timeless.

One of the things I like about Performing Blackness on English Stages *is the way it will get thoughtful readers to consider the source and limits of their own racial attitudes. Are there any books that have enriched your thinking about this?*

Not exactly. In 1994 Alden and I participated in a conference at the Omohundro Institute for Early American History and Culture at Williamsburg, Virginia, on the topic, "Constructing Race: Differentiating Peoples in the Early Modern World." The goal was to trace cultural attitudes and practices that flourished in early America to their origins in the Old World. The Institute brought together historians, not just of early America but of early modern England, Spain, and Africa. They were joined by literary scholars like myself, Emily C. Bartels, and Mary Floyd-Wilson. The results of the conference were published in the January 1997 issue of the *William and Mary Quarterly*. The conversations we had in Williamsburg plus my work on the essay that Alden and I contributed, "Before Othello: Elizabethan Representations of Sub-Saharan Africans," made me realize how large and how important this topic is. Race is such a complex, often contradictory, concept, and it seemed clear that in order to eradicate racism in our own world, we need to understand the ways in which it was constructed in the early modern period.

Some of the myths about "others" are still commonplace today. Another joy of the book is discovering a number of plays outside of the usual canon that have black characters, or with white characters in disguise as black. Which do you think are ready for rediscovery not only because of their ethnic interest, but as worthwhile plays?

I've been campaigning for a new edition of *Lust's Dominion, or the Lascivious Queen* (first acted in 1600) in Arden's new early modern drama series, a play possibly written by Thomas Dekker and others, because it will provide an invaluable context for *Othello* and because it has interest in its own right, both for the representation of an aristocratic and charismatic black Moor and for its depiction of Spain at a time when England was at war. At the other end of the book's chronology, I'd like to see a good edition of Edward Young's *The Revenge* (1721). Young's tragedy was extremely popular throughout the eighteenth century, and though it strikes us as melodramatic today, its depiction of Zanga, the Iago-like villainous Moor, is truly amazing.

Whose books helped direct your career?

Several books helped me early on, especially as a newly-minted Ph.D. teaching for the first time. C. L. Barber's *Shakespeare's Festive Comedy* and Northrop Frye's *Fables of Identity: Studies in Poetic Mythology* and *A Natural Perspective: The Development of Shakespearean Comedy & Romance* offered me the broad perspective on dramatic structure and form that I desperately needed. I also found Mark Rose's *Shakespearean Design* wonderfully helpful for showing a scene's trajectory in ways that were accessible to students. I borrowed his concept of the scenic arc and frequently distribute schematic hand-outs in class.

Which books influenced you the most?

Although I resist being pigeonholed as a new historicist, I certainly was influenced by the work of Stephen Greenblatt, especially *Shakespearian Negotiations* and *Learning to Curse: Essays in Early Modern Culture.* Jean Howard's *The Stage and Social Struggle in Early Modern England* showed me that historicist scholarship needn't abandon enjoyment of literature for its own sake.

One need not be a new historicist to historicize, though some reviewers do not seem to realize that. Are there any books that you refer to frequently?

Alan Dessen and Leslie Thomson's *A Dictionary of Stage Directions in English Drama, 1580–1642* is an invaluable resource for performance-oriented criticism. I also frequently refer to Schoenbaum-Harbage's *Annals of English Drama*, which is incredibly handy just to settle a date or find the acting company that performed a particular play. Jonathan Hope's *Shakespeare's Grammar* wasn't available when we were doing our edition of *The Tempest*, alas. We used E. A. Abbott's *A Shakespearian Grammar* to discuss the changes in grammatical practice from Shakespeare's day to ours, but we longed for a more current authority.

What are you reading now?

I'm reading or—in some cases re-reading—books on Shakespeare in America, including Michael Bristol's *Shakespeare's America; America's Shakespeare*, Kim Sturgess' *Shakespeare and the American Nation*, Esther Cloudman Dunn's *Shakespeare in America*, and Helene Wickham Koon's

How Shakespeare Won the West: Players and Performances in America's Gold Rush, 1849–1865. As you can see, I read on a need-to-know basis, and fortunately for me, the needs keep changing.

Who isn't read anymore who should be rediscovered?

Since I'm thinking about Shakespeare in America these days, I have rediscovered Charles Shattuck's two volumes on *Shakespeare on the American Stage*. Shattuck pioneered the study of Shakespeare on the American stage, and his overview covers all the bases. Moving from America back to the early modern period, I'd love it if David Bevington's *From Mankind to Marlowe: Growth of Structure in the Popular Drama of Tudor England* were more readily available. It is a magisterial examination of the ways in which the early modern theatre grew out of medieval practices, but most people now think of David simply as an indefatigable editor.

He is also that. Do any books of the past decade deserve more attention than they have received?

At the risk of immodesty, I think the anthology I co-edited with John Gillies, *Playing the Globe*, should have gotten more attention. Contributors like Barbara Sebek, Linda McJannet and Rhonda Lemke Sanford have gone on to publish their own books on geographic constructions in the early modern period. This was cutting edge work when it was published in 1995. William C. Carroll's *Fat King, Lean Beggar: Representations of Poverty in the Age of Shakespeare* opens a window into the early modern underworld of beggars and masterless men. Joyce Green MacDonald's *Women and Race in Early Modern Texts* also deserved more attention than it received. MacDonald moves from discussions of race in the early modern period to look at Restoration texts as well, particularly Aphra Behn's *Oroonoko* (1688). Seeing changes in racial constructions over time strikes me as terribly important, so I did the same thing in *Performing Blackness*. The economics of publishing are partly to blame; hardbacks are so expensive now, yet publishers are very reluctant to issue monographs in paperback. It's a sort of Catch-22.

It is, and limiting for independent scholars without inter-library privileges. What is the most important book on Shakespeare himself that you have read?

I've read the major biographies by Park Honan, Katherine Duncan-Jones, and Stephen Greenblatt, but to my mind the most valuable book in this area is James Shapiro's *1599: A Year in the Life of William Shakespeare*. Without promising more than he can deliver, Jim offers a window into Shakespeare's world. It would be impossible to do this for the entire life, but what he does with one year is simply amazing.

And those at the 2006 Shakespeare Association of America conference could buy it on the last day for five bucks, autographed. It is now on my coffee table and will soon be in my alleged mind. Name a Shakespeare book that is just plain fun.

Sam Schoenbaum's *Shakespeare's Lives* is a wonderfully entertaining survey of the uses and abuses of Shakespeare's biography. Barbara Hodgdon's *The Shakespeare Trade* also provides many laughs at the uses and abuses of Shakespeare within popular culture. Gary Taylor's *Reinventing Shakespeare: A Cultural History from the Restoration to the Present* structures his chapters to suit the time period discussed; Victorian Shakespeare is presented in the style of a Victorian novel, while post-modern Shakespeare is fragmented, and so forth.

Are any non-lit-crit books that you have found particularly enriching?

The obvious answer is the work of historians, including, of course, Alden T. Vaughan, especially *Roots of American Racism: Essays on the Colonial Experience*. From his earliest work on the interactions between Native Americans and English colonists, Alden has tried to understand early modern England's construction of itself and the others it confronted in Africa and the New World. As he worked on the essays collected in *Roots,* I learned a good deal about what could be gleaned from non-literary as well as literary texts circulating in England. My work on blackface performance was also influenced by recent histories of America's minstrel shows, particularly Eric Lott's *Love and Theft: Blackface Minstrelsy and the American Working Class.* I am looking forward to reading Natalie Zemon Davis' new biography of Leo Africanus, *Trickster Travels: A Sixteenth-Century Muslim Between Worlds.*[4]

Are there any important subjects where the books are out of date, and need to be replaced?

I doubt if one person could do it, but E. K. Chambers' *Elizabethan Stage* and G. E. Bentley's *Jacobean and Caroline Stage* should be updated. The amount of information Chambers and Bentley compiled is truly amazing, and it's so convenient to look up the name of an actor or a theatre. At the same time, scholars like William Ingram, Alan H. Nelson, Alan Dessen, and Andrew Gurr have unearthed lots of new information and interpreted the evidence somewhat differently. We've also learned a good deal from excavations at the Rose and the Globe in London and from original stage practices productions at the new Globe and the Blackfriars Theatre in Staunton, Virginia. We need a compilation of what we now know about the theatre and theatrical practices.

What needs are there crying out for a book that perhaps you don't want to write?

I wish Peter Blayney would condense all he knows about early modern printing into one handy volume.[5]

Let's hope it's a paperback. Thanks, Ginger. You have suggested a number of new books to me, and I appreciate that.

Notes

1. This has been taken down since Vaughan's retirement.
2. Email dated 30 November 2015. This has been slightly edited for the context of this book, with Vaughan's approval.
3. This was prior to the second edition.
4. This was published in 2006.
5. This was published in two handy volumes in 2013.

MacDonald P. Jackson

Attributions are common. Convincing attributions are rare. That fact makes MacDonald P. Jackson one of the few important attribution scholars of our time. For decades and in dozens of books and articles, he has presented evidence that lends or denies credence to many attributions. Because his work is informed by previous scholarship and is rigorous and statistical, it stands up to scrutiny. Some who challenge him do not do so with the same rigor. They simply declare he cannot be right theoretically and so avoid confronting the evidence Jackson and others have amassed.

Among Jackson's works in attribution are the 1965 pamphlet *Shakespeare's A Lover's Complaint: its date and authenticity*, which made the case for Shakespeare's authorship of the poem, followed decades later and after our interview by *Determining the Shakespeare Canon: Arden of Faversham & "A Lover's Complaint"* in 2014. In the latter part of the book, Jackson defends "A Lover's Complaint" from evidence and arguments that undermined its canonization since his pamphlet was published. The book shows that Jackson has moved well beyond his comments in our interview. Jackson also made the case that scene eight of *Arden of Faversham* was Shakespeare's back in the nineteen-fifties, and in this book adds stylometric evidence by subsequent scholars and new findings of his own to attribute more scenes to Shakespeare. Published in 2017, *The New Oxford Shakespeare Complete Works*, edited by Gary Taylor and others, is the first complete works to include the play, crediting scenes four through nine to Shakespeare. Jackson had a hand in this inclusion as a member of the attribution board for the *New Oxford* text, but note that works were only added when the opinion of the board was unanimous. He also contributed three essays to the book that replaced Oxford's *Textual Companion*, *The New Oxford Shakespeare Authorship Companion*, edited by Taylor and Gabriel Egan. These are, "Shakespeare, *Arden of Faversham*, and *A Lover's Complaint*: A Review of Reviews," "Supplementary Lexical Test for *Arden of Faversham*," and "One-Horse Races: Some Recent Studies," which reveals weaknesses in recent counter attributions.

A long association with the works of Thomas Middleton began with *Studies in Attribution: Middleton and Shakespeare*, a book written to establish Mid-

MacDonald P. Jackson

dleton's dramatic canon. Jackson found further evidence of Middleton's hand in *Timon of Athens* and gave Middleton two plays in the Shakespeare apocrypha, *The Puritan, or the Widow of Watling Street* and *A Yorkshire Tragedy* (1608). His *The Revenger's Tragedy: Attributed to Thomas Middleton: A Facsimile of the 1607/8 Quarto* was the first edition to get Middleton's name on the title page of that great play. Jackson is also an associate general editor to General Editor Gary Taylor of *The Collected Works of Thomas Middleton*, for which he again edited *The Revenger's Tragedy* and contributed to this edition's companion volume *Thomas Middleton and Early Modern Textual Culture*, edited by Taylor and John Laranino. These were published simultaneously shortly after our interviewed appeared, though Jackson's work on these volumes was completed beforehand.

One edition is controversial, and should be. Jackson notoriously helped Gary Taylor add parts of George Wilkins's novel, *The Painful Adventures of Pericles Prince of Tyre* (1608), to the edition of the play in the Oxford *Complete Works* (1986). *Defining Shakespeare: Pericles as Test Case* comes as close to proving that the first two acts of that play were written by Wilkins as current tools allow. He more conventionally co-edited with Michael Neill *The Selected Plays of John Marston* for the series Plays by Renaissance and Restoration Dramatists. Jackson was added to the team editing *The Works of John Webster* beginning with the second volume, joining David Gunby and David Carnegie after the passing of Antony Hammond. This comprehensive, old-spelling edition rethinks the Webster canon, uses current editing theory, and will probably replace the standard edition by F. L. Lucas for decades to come. The third volume was published shortly after our interview in 2007.

For seven years (1984–91) Jackson wrote the annual review of editions and textual studies for *Shakespeare Survey*. He was honored with a Festschrift, *Words That Count: Essays on Early Modern Authorship in Honor of MacDonald P. Jackson*, edited by Brian Boyd.

Out of the early modern era is another fine contribution to attribution studies, *Who Wrote "The Night Before Christmas"?: Analyzing the Clement Clarke Moore vs. Henry Livingston Question*. The poem is traditionally attributed to Clement Clarke Moore (1779–1863), who included it in his complete works, but has often been claimed for Henry Livingston (1748–1828). Jackson uses his stylometric and other tests to determine the authorship of this famous poem. Sorry. No spoiler alert here.

Jackson is Emeritus Professor and Honorary Research Fellow at the University of Auckland, where he enrolled as an undergraduate in 1956. His time there was interrupted for an Oxford B.Litt. He then returned to Auckland as a lecturer in 1964 and stayed, though with some absences for prestigious fellowships and visiting professorships. He is now Emeritus Professor of English at the University of Auckland. This interview was originally published in *Shakespeare Newsletter*, 56: 2, #269, Fall 2006.

••••••••••••••••••••••••••••

MPJ: *I have failed to find a "how to" book for attribution studies. What I know is mostly learned by reading examples of people doing it.*

MacDonald P. Jackson: Harold Love's *Attributing Authorship: An Introduction* is a lively introduction to the whole field, and it includes a sophisticated discussion of the nature of "authorship." Narrowing the focus to our period, in *Shakespeare Co-Author: A Historical Study of Five Collaborative Plays*, Brian Vickers gives a thorough and judicious account of the evidence accumulated over the years for collaboration in *Titus Andronicus*, *Timon of Athens*, *Pericles*, *Henry VIII*, and *The Two Noble Kinsmen*. That book introduces scholars to most of the main approaches and practitioners, as, while focusing on *Pericles*, does *Defining Shakespeare*. And of course Gary Taylor's "The Canon and Chronology of Shakespeare's Plays" in the Oxford *William Shakespeare: A Textual Companion*, assessed previous scholarship. Jonathan Hope's important *The Authorship of Shakespeare's Plays: A Socio-Linguistic Study* has a full bibliography.

Samuel Schoenbaum's *Internal Evidence and Elizabethan Dramatic Authorship* was a comprehensive survey, but its mocking skepticism minimized the accomplishments of such pioneers as E. H. C. Oliphant and H. Dugdale Sykes. Oliphant, a Melbourne man, is my hero. He was next to infallible in detecting Middleton's hand. His *The Plays of Beaumont and Fletcher: An Attempt to Determine their Respective Shares and the Shares of Others* included neat descriptions of the dramatic verse styles of the various candidates and laid the foundation for later research.

Both David J. Lake in *The Canon of Thomas Middleton's Plays* and I (in *Studies in Attribution*) adopted and extended Cyrus Hoy's methods in his series of articles in *Studies in Bibliography* (1956–62) on the "Beaumont and Fletcher" plays. Roger V. Holdsworth's "Middleton and Shakespeare: The Case for Middleton's Hand in *Timon of Athens*," a 1982 Ph.D. thesis which Vickers was unable to consult, is a model of its kind and completely compelling.

There is a set of texts you use in your work, commonly called LION. What is it, and how does it assist in attribution studies.

LION (condensed from Literature Online) is an electronic database, available to subscribing institutions, that contains most English drama and poetry and a fair amount of prose. Virtually all early modern plays, masques, and entertainments are included. The texts are searchable. The site has instructions for using LION. I've made copious use of it, not only for attribution work but also in editing, as a kind of adjunct to the *Oxford English Dictionary* (*OED*). One can check whether a strange spelling in a Webster text can be paralleled elsewhere or is likely to be a misprint. One can find, or fail to find, precedents for odd linguistic usages. One can elucidate obscure allusions by discovering them in other contexts.

LION texts are in the original spelling of their early appearances in print. In order to carry out searches effectively, you need to be aware of the range of spellings that a word may have in the relevant period. You need to know also that searches will not find phrases that straddle a line division, such as "to suffer/The Slings and Arrowes," unless you use the proximity function and key in, say, "suffer" NEAR "Slings" (but uncapitalized "slings" will also work). Another thing to know is that the Shakespeare play texts derive from the First Folio, never from quartos. Practice with LION improves performance.

You used this for Defining Shakespeare, *and other studies. Do any recent attributions convince you?*

Gary Taylor has demonstrated in "Thomas Middleton, Thomas Dekker, and *The Bloody Banquet*" that Lake and I were too pusillanimous about accepting Oliphant's ascription of *The Bloody Banquet* to Dekker and Middleton, and he has made a convincing smaller adjustment to our conclusions in "Middleton and Rowley—and Heywood: *The Old Law* and New Attribution Technologies." The case for Ford's authorship of *A Funeral Elegy*, made by G. D. Monsarrrat, "*A Funeral Elegy*: Ford, W.S., and Shakespeare," and Brian Vickers, in *"Counterfeiting" Shakespeare: Evidence, Authorship, and John Ford's "Funerall Elegye"* strikes me as pretty compelling, as it struck you, Mike.

Yes, it did. Who else is doing good work in attribution?

Some of the most significant is by Marina Tarlinskaja, who analyses verse according to the Russian linguistic-statistical method as explained in her *Shakespeare's Verse: Iambic Pentameter and the Poet's Idiosyncracies*. She has meticulously been investigating *Edward III*, *Sir Thomas More*, and other doubtful plays. Her findings, not yet published, tend to confirm that Shakespeare contributed to *Edward III* (at least 1.2, 2.1, 2.2, 4.4) and wrote Hand D's scene in *More*.[1] Hugh Craig of the University of Newcastle in Australia has developed a mode of stylometric testing that seems statistically sound: he has articles forthcoming on the Additions to *The Spanish Tragedy* and on "A Lover's Complaint."

In the past few years there has been a surge of scholarship suggesting that Shakespeare did not write "A Lover's Complaint," even in your own Festschrift, though stated there with inerrant kindness. Who has raised these doubts, and how do you respond?

Hugh Craig doesn't think it is Shakespeare's. Nor does Brian Vickers, who, in *The Times Literary Supplement*, December 5, 2003, argued that the poem is by John Davies of Hereford, and whose book on the subject will be published soon. Nor do Marina Tarlinskaja or Ward Elliott and Robert Valenza, who, as you know, argued against the attribution in *Words That Count*. But I do, though with some qualms. There have been excellent scholars on both sides of the debate about the authenticity of "A Lover's Complaint." And, whereas different kinds of testing all lead to the same conclusion about *Pericles*, they're in conflict over "A Lover's Complaint." Yet the poem was published as Shakespeare's in the 1609 Quarto of his *Sonnets*, and, as the commentary to Colin Burrow's splendid edition of Shakespeare's *Complete Sonnets and Poems* (Oxford 2002) demonstrates, the links between the sonnets and the complaint are legion.

I have not heard you say that Shakespeare collaborated on Arden of Faversham, *but you seem to think that he did. Certainly the evidence you have presented seems sound, and it keeps accumulating. Do you recommend a particular edition of the play? How can readers learn more about the play and the evidence of Shakespeare's authorship?*

Martin Wine's Revels edition of 1973 is scholarly and has the fullest discussion of authorship. As it happens, I have a long article coming out in the Fall 2006 *Shakespeare Quarterly*, in which I set out evidence that Shakespeare wrote the Quarrel Scene between Mosby and Alice (scene 8 in Wine's edition). My footnotes refer readers to criticism on the play—there has been a lot. I think, currently, that Shakespeare contributed to *Arden*, not that he was solely responsible.

My main reason for resisting Shakespeare's participation is probably not valid: genre. The play is such an atypical subject for Shakespeare that it does not "feel" right to me. To give into this is to ignore all evidence for the sake of my feeling, which would be pretty arrogant, but it is tempting. Do you know what I mean?

I do indeed. But Shakespeare's earliest plays cover a range of genres. He never wrote another Plautine farce like *The Comedy of Errors* or Senecan tragedy of blood like *Titus Andronicus*, the latter a work of collaboration, as I take *Arden* to be.

That is an interesting point, and come to think of it, Shakespeare probably wrote the riot scene in Sir Thomas More *and there are similar scenes in* Coriolanus, *but he did not write a play like* More. *OK, I think I get it. Let's discuss two of the writers whose works you have edited. You co-edited what will certainly become the standard edition of John Webster for many decades. What did you read while preparing these volumes?*

Apart from essential works of reference (*OED*, above all) and all earlier editions, several books have come in for heavy use. Charles R. Forker's comprehensive and superb *Skull Beneath the Skin: The Achievement of John Webster* is the one indispensable scholarly and critical account. No editor of Webster could afford to neglect R. W. Dent's *John Webster's Borrowing*. Dent itemizes Webster numerous plunderings and shows how he adapts and refines his sources. David Carnegie always mounts productions of the plays as we edit them, and these give us fresh insights into the scripts—the comings and goings of characters, what they do, and whom they address. We have supplemented the stage directions of the original quartos to a much greater extent than previous editors, and Alan C. Dessen and Leslie Thompson's *A Dictionary of Stage Directions in English Drama, 1580–1642* has been a valuable aid to formulating them.

But all kinds of books are grist to an editor's mill. For instance, Webster wrote a pageant, *Monuments of Honor*, for the ceremony in which the Merchant Taylor John Gore was made Lord Mayor of London in 1624; so Matthew Davies and Ann Saunders's *The History of the Merchant Taylors' Company*, became of interest as a source of information for our commentary.

About the Middleton Collected Works, I expect that even if it proves to be controversial, as Gary Taylor's projects sometimes do, it will probably become the standard Middleton for much of the twenty-first century. Who shaped your own approach to Middleton and his texts?

Richard Hindry Barker's *Thomas Middleton* is an unpretentious book, but the author had an intimate acquaintance with his subject and knew why Middleton was important, and his appendix on the canon was a useful starting point for my and Lake's investigations. What more than anything else aroused my interest in Middleton was the controversy, summarized by Barker, over whether he or Cyril Tourneur had composed *The Revenger's Tragedy*.

Which is now tucked into the Middleton canon. The collection will create some buzz, at least amongst the sort of people who read SNL.

Yes, the whole project has grown into a massive one, to which over sixty scholars have contributed. Pretty well everything that has ever been written about Middleton is described or listed somewhere in those two books, and Middleton's output is so diverse that they constitute a compendium on early modern literary culture. There's a website: http://english.fsu.edu/library/gtaylor/intro1/htm.

Did books help direct your career?

Actually, no critical or scholarly book set me on the path to becoming a Shakespearean as surely as Laurence Olivier's film of *Hamlet* (1948), which I first saw when I was fifteen. But as an undergraduate I was introduced to the textual problems of *Hamlet* and *King Lear*, and began reading everything on Shakespearean textual studies. W. W. Greg's *The Shakespeare First Folio* and Fredson Bowers's *Textual and Literary Criticism* were constant companions, and I admired the trenchant thought and expression of Alice Walker's *Textual Problems of the First Folio*. I pored over G. I. Duthie's old-spelling edition of *King Lear*, an inspiring model, though even then I disagreed with many of his conclusions, which he revised in his modern-spelling edition of 1960. Another inspiration was J. K. Walton's groundbreaking *The Copy for the Folio Text of "Richard III": with a Note on the Copy for the Folio Text of King Lear*, praised by Greg. Walton had left the University of Auckland English Department for Dublin a year or two before I arrived there as a student. He became one of my predecessors as textual reviewer for *Shakespeare Survey* (1966–8), and his important but neglected *The Quarto Copy for the First Folio of Shakespeare* builds on his earlier book, which had a provocative appendix on *King Lear*. C. F. Tucker Brooke's edition of *The Shakespeare Apocrypha* and Kenneth Muir's *Shakespeare as Collaborator* helped interest me in attribution.

The Brooke being a collection of apocryphal plays with introductions, and Muir's book a survey of previous attributions, analyzed with Kenneth's customary good sense and supplemented with new evidence of his own. Which books influenced you the most?

When I was a student, G. Wilson Knight had replaced Bradley as the dominant Shakespeare critic, or rather, as he styled it, "interpreter," with books such as *The Wheel of Fire: Interpretations of Shakespearian Tragedy*, which, despite the subtitle, included an essay on *Measure for Measure*, *The Crown of Life*, which revalued the late plays, and *The Shakespearian Tempest*, which traced through the canon the symbolic opposites, music and tempest. Knight approached drama and poetry as though they were holy scripture, and his eloquence was infectious. He was alert to a play's poetic texture and atmosphere, its patterns of imagery. But my own sense of Shakespeare was most accurately reflected in, and nourished by, Harley Granville-Barker's *Prefaces to Shakespeare*. Granville-Barker was, of course, a playwright, producer, and scholar, and his commentaries were everywhere grounded in his feeling for the theatre. Perhaps I got most of all from Arden and Cambridge New Shakespeare editions of individual plays. For literary criticism generally, William Empson's *Seven Types of Ambiguity* was a key work, because it teased out, more persistently than anybody had ever done before, the multiple meanings and associations that animate poetic texts—he revealed, and made one alert to, what was going on in poetry to make it so richly satisfying. And, like others of my generation, I absorbed F. R. Leavis, L. C. Knights, and the *Scrutiny* critics, as well as the American New Critics, Allen Tate, Cleanth Brooks, Robert Penn Warren, and company.

Who isn't read anymore who should be rediscovered?

I know Russ McDonald and Frank Kermode have recently written well on Shakespeare's language, but every critic ought to have read Wolfgang Clemen's *The Development of Shakespeare's Imagery* and M. M. (Molly) Mahood's *Shakespeare's Wordplay*. It used to be a truism that Shakespeare's achievement as dramatist is inseparable from his achievement as a poet. Those two books help explain why. Alfred Hart's *Stolne and Surreptitious Copies: A Comparative Study of Shakespeare's Bad Quartos* stands as a challenge to much modern textual scholarship. It amasses a huge pile of evidence in favor of the theory of "memorial reconstruction."

Are there any books of the past twenty years that you think deserve more attention than they have received?

One favorite of mine is Mahood's *Bit Parts in Shakespeare's Plays* for its acute awareness of theatrical values. Anyone who has seen a good production of *Much Ado About Nothing* knows that Verges has a comic presence out of all proportion to the number of lines he speaks. But Mahood analyses the impact on audiences even of spear-carriers. Another instructive book that is seldom cited is Harriett Hawkins's corrective to much critical folly, *The Devil's Party: Critical Counter-interpretations of Shakespearian Drama.* It was a product of her stint as reviewer of critical studies for *Shakespeare Survey* (1980–82) and raises all sorts of basic questions about the nature of Shakespeare's plays and how critical accounts of them can be judged.

Whose books do you greatly admire?

I could compile a long list of names, including those of previous contributors to your column or persons mentioned by them. But I'll put on my textual critic's hat. For what A. E. Housman called "the application of thought to textual criticism" as a discipline, G. Thomas Tanselle has been unrivalled—in his books and in his long survey articles in *Studies in Bibliography.* All theorists about editing should read them. His short *A Rationale of Textual Criticism* would be a good one to start with. Tanselle's distinction between "documents," "texts," and "works" brings clarity and order to lot of muddled thinking. Also, I hugely admire Harold Jenkins's Arden 2 *Hamlet*, "a noble achievement," as George Walton Williams called it, whatever reservations one may have about the textual hypotheses on which it's based.

That is a matter that continues to be debated with the recent publication of Arden 3, and the retiring of Jenkins's edition from print. Name a Shakespeare book that is just plain fun.

Am I the first to answer *A Shakespeare Merriment*, edited by Samuel Schoenbaum's wife Marilyn? It contains several comic classics. The account in it by Wolcott Gibbs of a school production of *A Midsummer Night's Dream* in which he played Puck is a masterpiece.

You are the first to mention it. Gibbs was a popular New Yorker *writer and the piece first appeared in that magazine. Are there any non-lit-crit books that you have found particularly enriching in your thinking and writing about Shakespeare and others?*

I read a lot of poetry of all periods, and also write about it as reviewer, critic, and literary historian. I suspect that helps me appreciate Shakespeare as *poetic* dramatist and the special qualities of his sonnets. My teaching and writing about Shakespeare on screen have been informed by James Monaco's *How to Read a Film*. For attribution studies, I was introduced to statistical techniques by Russell Langley, *Practical Statistics for Non-Mathematical People*.

Sounds like a book I need. What are you reading now?

I recently finished Stephen Greenblatt's *Will in the World: How Shakespeare Became Shakespeare*. Although, or maybe because, it relies on a lot of imaginative guess-work, I found it stimulating. I like the idea that Shakespeare's whole career was, to a significant extent, driven by an urge to recover the status his father lost upon the collapse of the family fortunes when William was thirteen. And Greenblatt is always sensitive to the qualities of the plays. At the moment I'm rereading Vladimir Nabokov's dazzling novel *Pale Fire*, and my colleague Brian Boyd's remarkable book on it: *Nabokov's "Pale Fire": The Magic of Artistic Discovery*.

Brian Boyd being the editor of your Festschrift. Nabokov wrote Lolita *while living here in Ashland, Oregon, which seems to come up whenever the local paper publishes an article about literature. They describe him as writing the book during breaks from chasing butterflies through Lithia Park. Are there any books you'd like to mention, but I lacked the wit to ask about?*

I'm surprised that some of the most brilliant emendations of *The Oxford Shakespeare: The Complete Works* have been ignored by later editors—Gary Taylor's "acorn" for "accord" in *Troilus and Cressida*, 1.3.236, for example, a single-letter change that anyone who has learned from Clemen and Mahood, say, can recognize as obviously right.

Perhaps this is a chance to tell you about a book that was written in the 1960s but never published: Charles Hobday's *Shakespeare's Mind*. Hobday, an English journalist and poet who died last year, published several articles on Shakespeare, notably in *Shakespeare Quarterly*, a fine study of the most famous of Shakespeare's "image clusters" (dogs, flattery, sweets, melting, and so on)—multiple associations of words, images, and ideas that recur from play to play. His fascinating book follows Edward A. Armstrong's *Shakespeare's Imagination* in identifying and exploring many such clusters, and he demonstrates their significance for interpretation, editing, and attribution. Hobday was the victim of skeptical referees in the 60s and seems to have lost heart. But, although in many respects out of date, his work, written with flair, is still so valuable that I encouraged Hobday's literary executor, the poet Fred Beake, to donate the manuscript to the library of the Shakespeare Institute in Stratford-upon-Avon.[2]

I hope that he does. Thanks, Mac, for your fascinating comments about these books.

Notes

1. This play is in the bibliography under Anthony Munday.
2. Hobday's papers were received by the Shakespeare Institute in September 2005. The collection is described here: http://calmview.bham.ac.uk/Record.aspx?src=CalmView.Catalog&id=XMS208&pos=4

Samuel Crowl

Samuel Crowl helped me learn a valuable lesson, though he does not realize it. I was in his seminar on filmed Shakespeare at the 2002 Shakespeare Association of America (SAA) conference in Minneapolis, my first SAA seminar. My paper had what I hoped was an insightful comment about the use of vertical space on stage compared with the limits of the cinematic frame. Sam kindly commented on this, and left room for me to amplify beyond my comments in the paper. An awkward silence followed. I had put it all in the paper and had nothing more to say. Lesson: put it all in the paper, yes, but then do some more thinking and find another insight or a telling example for the discussion. This has since served me well. Thank you, Sam.

Readers also learn from Sam Crowl. His first book, *Shakespeare Observed: Studies in Performance on Stage and Screen* teaches that film and stage production sometimes influence one another, and looks closely at the crosscurrents between Kenneth Branagh's two productions of *Henry V*, on stage (1984) and film (1989). *Shakespeare at the Cineplex: The Kenneth Branagh Era* surveys the many Shakespeare films that followed *Henry V*, teaching us that Branagh's approach to filming Shakespeare has influenced others who made literary and historical feature films in the 1990s, and views the new crop of Shakespeare films in light of modern financing and production practices. *The Films of Kenneth Branagh* studies Branagh's career as a film director, finding unities in films as diverse as the thriller *Dead Again* and *Hamlet*. His *Shakespeare on Film: A Norton Guide* was published shortly after our interview in 2008 to coincide with the release of the second edition of *The Norton Shakespeare*. The "Screen Adaptations" series of books concluded with *Shakespeare's Hamlet: The Relationship Between the Text and Film*, considers many *Hamlet* films, but concentrates on those by Olivier and Branagh.

In addition to these books, Sam has contributed chapters to several anthologies including *Shakespeare and the Moving Image*, edited by Anthony Davies and Stanley Wells, *The Cambridge Companion to Shakespeare on Film*, edited by Russell Jackson, and *Spectacular Shakespeare: Critical Theory and Popular Cinema*, edited by Courtney Lehmann and Lisa S. Starks. Crowl is

Trustee Professor of English at Ohio University, where he began teaching in 1970, and has been honored many times for distinguished teaching. This interview was originally published in *Shakespeare Newsletter*, 56:3, #270, Winter 2006/2007.

••••••••••••••••••••••••••••

MPJ: *You are a brave man, Sam Crowl. It is fashionable to Branagh-bash. You not only wrote a book about him, but say some pretty nice things. In a critical era where so much scholarship on Branagh and Shakespeare films is highly judgmental, you go out of your way to be fair. What's up with that?*

Samuel Crowl: One of Shakespeare's qualities as an artist I try to emulate is his generosity. I prefer writing about works of art that I admire. Hatchet jobs are easy; sympathetic engagement is more risky. Too much contemporary criticism and theory assumes the critic knows more than the artist. I've tried to tip my hat to the artist in an attempt to restore some balance to the enterprise. Branagh is certainly the key figure in the revival of the Shakespeare film in our time, and I've tried to understand the way he blends elements of Hollywood film populism with a deep veneration for Shakespeare's language to provide new avenues of approach to the Shakespeare film.

Samuel Crowl

Since I'm talking to you, I want to ask about films as well as books. In addition to his Shakespeare movies, which films should SNL *readers see to better understand Branagh's Shakespeare work?*

Though it is not often noted, Branagh's Shakespeare films are as indebted to Zeffirelli as they are to Olivier and Welles. He clearly admires the passionate Italian rhythm of Zeffirelli's film style. Notice how important Patrick Doyle's neo-operatic scores are to Branagh's Shakespeare films. Branagh grew up watching popular Hollywood films on television and elements in films as disparate as *Gone with the Wind*, *The Magnificent Seven*, and *Dr. Zhivago* find their way into his Shakespeare films. It is obvious that he watched a number of Vietnam War films—*Platoon*, *Hamburger Hill*, and *Full Metal Jacket* as he was preparing to make his film of *Henry V*. And all the Astaire-Rogers films when he was thinking about making a musical comedy version of *Love's Labour's Lost*. Among his own films, it's obvious that *In the Bleak Midwinter* is clearly meant as a companion piece to his epic *Hamlet,* and I find his *Mary Shelley's Frankenstein*, the film that received his most damaging and dismissive reviews, most deserving of further scrutiny, especially to understand Branagh's film style and the way in which he repeatedly risks all on the romantic excess of a single shot or the relentless energy of a single sequence. See the birth of the Creature for a powerful example.

Who can we read for a contrary view of Branagh?

Courtney Lehmann, in her fine *Shakespeare Remains* clearly engages in a lover's quarrel with Branagh and his Shakespeare films. For other critical responses see Donald Hedrick on *Henry V* (in *Shakespeare, the Movie*, Lynda Boose and Richard Burt, eds.), H. R. Coursen on *Hamlet* (*Shakespeare: The Two Traditions*), Ramona Wray and Gayle Holste on his *Love's Labour's Lost* (in separate essays in *Literature/Film Quarterly*), and Michael Anderegg on the populism of Branagh's *Much Ado About Nothing* (*Cinematic Shakespeare*). Branagh's one Shakespeare film generally applauded by those who write about his work is *In the Bleak Midwinter,* a film never intended to reach a mass audience.

Whereas, I am critical of the film's formula storytelling. Shakespeare at the Cineplex, *I love the incongruity of that title, explores fairly recent films that mostly received the full Hollywood marketing treatment, but there have been some movie, television, and video productions released during this period that did not. Will you please tell us which of these you think are most interesting?*

Well, *Cineplex* did discuss Christine Edzard's *As You Like It* and *The Children's Midsummer Night's Dream* and Adrian Noble's *A Midsummer Night's Dream*, three films which were released on screen only in England and with almost no advance publicity or marketing campaign. The only other Shakespeare movies of the period were the three slasher versions of *Titus Andronicus* directed by Christopher Dunne, Richard Griffin, and Lorn Richey. There were a number of television versions of the plays released during the last fifteen years where the best were those that had begun life as successful stage productions at either the Royal Shakespeare Company or National Theatre. My favorites are Richard Eyre's production of *King Lear* with Ian Holm, Timothy West, and Michael Bryant and Greg Doran's *Macbeth* with Antony Sher and Harriet Walter. Both productions were initially conceived in small playing spaces which, as H. R. Coursen rightly perceives, makes the translation to the intimacy of the television screen easier to achieve. There also have been a rash of Shakespeare spin-offs set in landscapes as various as Oregon, Pennsylvania, South Carolina and Elizabethan London. The most interesting of these films, for me and my students, have been Gus Van Sant's *My Own Private Idaho*—contemporary retelling of the Hal-Falstaff story (with a strong visual nod to Orson Welles's *Chimes at Midnight*) set in contemporary Portland, Gil Junger's *10 Things I Hate About You*—a version of *Taming of the Shrew* re-imagined as a high school teen flick, Billy Morrissette's *Scotland, PA*—where Joe Macbeth and his wife Pat are conceived as hamburger flippers who murder the restaurant's owner (Norm Duncan) in a vat of hot oil intended for making French fries, and John Madden's *Shakespeare in Love*, only the second Shakespeare film to win the Academy Award for Best Picture.

Olivier's Hamlet *being the first. Whose books on Shakespeare films do you learn the most from, or challenge you the most?*

I have had the rare privilege of growing up (and old) with the field. I published my first essay on a Shakespeare film in 1976 ("Chain Reaction: A Study of Roman Polanski's *Macbeth*,") with only a novice's sense of the genre's tradition and then, as if by magic, the next year saw the publication of Jack Jorgens's *Shakespeare on Film*. Jorgens made the first attempt to develop a taxonomy for the Shakespeare film and then proceeded to write a series of intelligent and illuminating new critical essays on seventeen major Shakespeare films released between 1935 and 1971. Jorgens is still where I start when thinking about the form and structure of the Shakespeare film and those individual films that made up the great international phase (roughly 1944–1968) in the history of the genre including work by Olivier, Welles, Kurosawa, Kozintsev, Mankiewicz, and Zeffirelli. At about the same time, Kenneth Rothwell and Bernice Kliman, began *The Shakespeare on Film Newsletter* (1976–92), now incorporated into *Shakespeare Bulletin*, which became an invaluable resource for information about Shakespeare films and the availability of 16 mm prints, as well as an outlet for essays and reviews on both film and television productions of the plays. Rothwell then went on to produce his monumental annotated compendium of Shakespeare films, *Shakespeare on Screen*, and eventually his definitive history of the genre, *A History of Shakespeare on Screen*. Rothwell and Jorgens are the natural starting place for those interested in the genre.

Shakespeare on film has attracted a wide range of critical approaches and sensibilities. I have learned the most from the work of H. R. Coursen, Anthony Davies, Barbara Hodgdon, Russell Jackson, Douglas Lanier, Courtney Lehmann, Mark Thornton Burnett, Michael Anderegg, and Judith Buchanan. The critic whose work I most admire and who repeatedly challenges me to revisit my own thinking about Shakespeare on film is Peter S. Donaldson. His *Shakespearean Films/Shakespearean Directors*, to my mind, the single most exciting critical work in the field; Donaldson's essay on Olivier's *Hamlet* is a brilliant account of the relationship of the film's form and content to crucial events in Olivier's life. Reading it always sends my students back to the film with new eyes: the mark of criticism at its best.

You mention that Ken Rothwell and Jack Jorgens are the natural starting place to read about Shakespeare films. Which films should newcomers begin with?

For me, the genre's range—and its problems and potential—are staked out in Laurence Olivier's *Henry V*, Orson Welles's *Othello*, and Franco Zeffirelli's *Romeo and Juliet*. Jack Jorgens places Shakespeare films into three categories: the theatrical, the filmic (or poetic), and the realistic. Of course these categories often overlap but they are a useful place to begin an understanding of the genre. Olivier's *Henry V* is an example of the theatrical model; Welles's *Othello*, the filmic, and Zeffirelli's *Romeo and Juliet*, the realistic. Most subsequent Shakespeare films tend to be indebted to one of these three models.

You were trained in philosophy at Hamilton College and English at Indiana University. Here you are doing a combination of English and film. How did you teach yourself what you needed to know about film to do your work?

Mike, you are right to understand that all of the leaders of the field were educated as Shakespeareans. My hunch is that none of us (Jorgens, Rothwell, Hodgdon, Donaldson, Coursen, Anderegg) ever had a film course as an undergraduate or graduate student. There were no film courses at Hamilton when I was there. The same was true at Indiana in the early 1960s, but film was in the air if not in the curriculum. We feasted on Akira Kurosawa, Satyajit Ray and the Europeans: Bergman, Fellini, Antonioni, Godard, Truffaut, Resnais, as well as their English counterparts: Tony Richardson, Lindsay Anderson, Karl Reisz. And, of course, the great Americans John Ford, Howard Hawks, Billy Wilder, and Orson Welles. We loved Shakespeare and we loved film. Most of our professors were skeptical about film as an art to rival literature and openly hostile to Shakespeare on film. Even those who enjoyed Shakespeare on stage did not think that the study of Shakespeare in performance was appropriate in the English department.

You went to Theater History for that. So when we came to write about Shakespeare on stage or screen, once our teaching careers had begun, we were largely on our own and self-taught.

I created my first course in Shakespeare on film at Ohio University in 1972. The course attracted an eclectic mix of undergraduates (primarily English, theater, journalism, and communications majors) and several graduate students from the School of Film. I taught them Shakespeare and they (particularly those film grad students) taught me film.

Which Shakespeare films taught you the most about the genre?

Well, paradoxically I think I learned the most initially from the foreign language Shakespeare films, especially Akira Kurosawa's *Throne of Blood* and Grigori Kozintsev's *Hamlet* because I was liberated from the text to concentrate exclusively on the visual story-telling and both films use powerful visual images that echo Shakespeare's key verbal images at work in *Macbeth* and *Hamlet.* Most Shakespeare on film scholars of my generation admit to having a "conversion film" that opened up the power of Shakespeare on screen for them. For Kenneth Rothwell, for example, the film was Zeffirelli's *Romeo and Juliet.* For me, it was Welles's *Chimes at Midnight.* Any sequence from *Chimes* provides a vivid lesson in the art of filmmaking: from screenplay to camera work to the composition of the frame to editing to film score.

For me, it was Olivier's Richard III. *It is not his best film, but I was in a place in my life where I was ready for what it had to give. There are still a few holdouts who do not believe that Shakespeare films are a worthwhile pursuit of academics. How do you answer them?*

When they are finally gone, I will miss them. Healthy opposition always helps in the creation of a new field of scholarly and critical exploration. When Shakespeare on film scholars first started giving papers and appearing on panels at SAA and Modern Language Association meetings we were often met with small and adversarial audiences. Now such panels are eagerly received and have to be scheduled in the largest rooms at the conference. Established scholars like C. L. Barber, George Walton Williams, Ann Jennalie Cook, and David Bevington were instrumental in helping get Shakespeare on stage and film on the agenda at the annual SAA meetings.

The entire postmodern critical movement has been very helpful in opening up new avenues of exploration in the world of literature. English scholars are far more eclectic now than they were in the nineteen-fifties and early sixties when the old historicism and new criticism held sway as the reigning critical methods. In the past forty years film has been recognized as an important art form and is regularly taught in colleges and universities. Literary scholars now consider a variety of "texts," not just the canonical ones included in the *Norton Anthology*. Film is certainly one of those texts and thus it is no surprise that Literature and Film courses have sprung up in the English curriculum across the country. Film was attracted to Shakespeare from its beginnings and the two have had a long, distinguished, if sometimes rocky, relationship. The major hurdle skeptics have to cross is understanding that film is an independent art form and, to be successful, has to absorb Shakespeare on its own terms. The fidelity model doesn't work when translating literature (whether the form be the epic poem, the drama, or the novel) into film which means that literary scholars have to understand what the filmmaker tried to achieve with his or her approach to the source material. What we need is a DVD collection of the great filmed versions of Shakespeare to function something like the First Folio. I echo and amend what Heminge and Condell said in its preface: "See them, therefore; and again, and again. And if you do not like them, surely you are in some manifest danger, not to understand them."[1]

Very good. Whose books influenced you the most?

I join many of your previous contributors to this feature in citing C. L. Barber's *Shakespeare's Festive Comedy* as a book that pointed Shakespeare studies in a new direction, away from the new criticism's exclusive focus on the text, to exciting new ways of seeing the text in relationship with social custom and ritual. It is also beautifully written, and I have tried to use it as a model for my own prose. Other books that seized my imagination in graduate school included William Empson's *Some Versions of Pastoral*, G. Wilson Knight's *The Wheel of Fire*, Northrop Frye's *Anatomy of Criticism* and *A Natural Perspective*, Jan Kott's *Shakespeare our Contemporary*, and Norman Rabkin's *Shakespeare and the Common Understanding*. I was attracted to each of these authors because they had strong personal voices and often placed the Shakespearean text in a broader social, political, or cultural context. As a graduate student I found the new criticism to be a tool that worked well for the lyric poem but didn't unlock all of Shakespeare's artistic energies or those of many of the great novelists I was reading. I wanted a more expansive critical methodology and Barber and Frye and Kott pointed the way. I was also always attracted to what poets had to say about Shakespeare from Coleridge and Keats to Eliot and Auden and Auden's essay on the *Henry IV* plays, "The Prince's Dog," collected in *The Dyer's Hand* remains a favorite.

Those are obviously all early influences. Whose books do you most admire among your contemporaries?

Stephen Greenblatt has had a huge impact on Shakespeare studies in our time, and I am among the many admirers of *Shakespearean Negotiations* even though I find talking with the living Shakespeare more interesting than trying to contact the dead one! What Greenblatt and his fellow new historicists have taught me is the importance of cultural and political context even when dealing with contemporary film and stage productions of Shakespeare. Janet Adelman's *Suffocating Mothers* had a great impact on my thinking about the plays and her work repeatedly enters into my talking about the tragedies in the classroom. I also have incorporated much of Phyllis Rackin's *Stages of History* and Rackin and Jean Howard's *Engendering a Nation* into the way I teach the history plays. All of these books addressed one of the central concerns of Shakespeare scholarship in the past thirty years: gender. The great feminist critics of our time made reading Shakespeare fresh again by making the female voice and body (and its silencing or absence) central to the history plays and the tragedies disturbing critical assumptions about Shakespeare much as film was doing in performance studies. Stephen Orgel's *Impersonations* extended the discussion of gender into new territory especially as it played out in Shakespeare's transvestite theater.

Are there any books that you refer to frequently?

In my own field of performance criticism it is impossible to escape the work of H. R. Coursen. At last count he had published something like eight books devoted to contemporary Shakespeare performances on stage, film, and television. He's literally written about everything, and pulls no punches in delivering his opinions and insights. I have found his work a good place to gather energy for writing along with the aforementioned work of Rothwell and Jorgens. I often turn to some of the volumes in the Shakespeare in Performance series published by the Manchester University Press, particularly those by James C. Bulman (*The Merchant of Venice*), Bernice W. Kliman (*Macbeth*), Jay L. Halio (*A Midsummer Night's Dream*), Scott McMillan (*1 Henry IV*), Barbara Hodgdon (*2 Henry IV*), Alexander Leggatt (*King Lear*), Anthony B. Dawson (*Hamlet*), and Miriam Gilbert (*Love's Labour's Lost*).

I got to know Miriam at your Shakespeare seminar. Who isn't read anymore who should be rediscovered?

G. Wilson Knight, Robert Heilman, and Maynard Mack. I am also quite fond of a little Shakespeare book written years ago by Stanley Edgar Hyman, *Iago: Some Approaches to the Illusion of His Motivation*. Hyman, the most eclectic of critics, views Iago from multiple perspectives: theater history (as a stage villain); Christian doctrine (as a Satan figure); Burkean symbolic action (as an image of the artist); psychoanalytic theory (as a latent homosexual); and intellectual history (as a Machiavel). The book is a healthy exercise in employing extra-literary sources in a judicious and jargon-free manner.

Are there any books of the past twenty years that you think deserve more attention than they have received?

I'm surprised that I don't see more mention in the critical literature of C. L. Barber and Richard P. Wheeler's *The Whole Journey: Shakespeare's Power of Development*. I find it an intelligent, generous, and satisfying treatment of finding Shakespeare's life in his art and his art in his life.

What is the most important book on Shakespeare and the early modern theatre?

James Shapiro's *1599: A Year in the Life of William Shakespeare* is the richest account of its kind I have read. By examining a single crucial year in Shakespeare's life, Shapiro is able to mix historical, political, cultural, biographical, and literary material to tell the story of Shakespeare's move from The Theatre to The Globe and his turn from writing the great comedies and histories to the tragedies and *Hamlet*. It's a book for all readers.

Name a Shakespeare book that is just plain fun.

Richard Eyre's *National Service*. A reflective and sensitive account of being at the center of one of the world's greatest theaters for ten years, culminating in his direction of *King Lear*, starring a trio of English actors nurtured by the repertory system: Ian Holm, Timothy West, and Michael Bryant in 1997.

What books need to be written that you aren't going to write?

We need a good critical history of the Royal Shakespeare Company from the Hall years through the reign of Adrian Noble written by a performance critic of the caliber of Peter Holland. We need individual monographs of the Shakespeare work done by the great British modernist directors: Peter Brook, Peter Hall, Trevor Nunn, Adrian Noble, Michael Bogdanov, Richard Eyre, Declan Donnellen, and Deborah Warner.

That is a superb idea. What are you reading now?

Ian Holm's *Acting My Life*. As mentioned above, Holm is one of those actors whose career has been made possible by the flowering of the repertory company ideal in England in the last forty years of the twentieth century. His career is interesting because he has had as much success in films (generally playing supporting roles) as he has had on stage.

The bookstall at the Chicago Shakespeare Theater is named for you. Tell us how that happened.

A roommate of mine at Hamilton College, Stuart Scott, went on to become the CEO and later Chairman of the largest real estate management firm in the world: Jones Lang LaSalle, with headquarters in Chicago and London. JLL was the firm that supervised the building of the stunning new home of the Chicago Shakespeare Theater on Navy Pier. Stuart and his wife Anne made a substantial gift to the fund raising campaign for the theater. Later, they were approached about having the theater bookstall named in their honor. They declined, but suggested that it be named for me because of my work in Shakespeare in performance. The CST readily agreed and so it came to pass. I am proud to have been so honored but also embarrassed as I did so little to deserve it except to have had a generous college roommate. I'm especially touched as several former students work for the CST and tell me of their pride in sharing a space with their old prof.

Let me add that the Samuel Crowl Bookstall is unique in my experience for having a selection of second hand books of interest to Shakespeareans. They charged too much for a reprint Arthur Huntington Nason's biography of James Shirley there, but I am glad to have it. SNL *readers will want to check out CST and the bookstall when in Chicago. Thanks, Sam, for talking to me about books and films.*

Always a pleasure talking with you about things Shakespearean, Mike.

Note

1. John Heminge, and Henrie Condell, "To the Great Variety of Readers," in *The Norton Facsimile: The First Folio of Shakespeare*, Charlton Hinman, ed. (W. W. Norton & Company, 1968), p. 7.

Barbara A. Mowat

Barbara A. Mowat was one of those rare Shakespeareans who is better known for her editing, essays, and academic posts, than for the books she has written. There is *The Dramaturgy of Shakespeare's Romances*, in which she illuminated these plays with close readings and analysis of how the plays are constructed with reference to Greek romances. Mowat later edited the *Titus Andronicus* quarto with Thomas Berger for the Malone Society. She has also written essays in major journals and chapters in several of the books that you probably have on your shelves. She even had a hand in the New Variorum Shakespeare editions as a member of the MLA New Variorum Committee (1988–1996), and committee chair (1996–2002).

Perhaps most visibly, Mowat and Paul Werstine are the editors of The New Folger Library Shakespeare published by Simon and Schuster, which are widely used in classrooms. All the Folger plays are under revision for print and as e-books as our interview was being prepared with more titles added as I revise this introduction. The digital editions are available through the Folger website.

Mowat greatly influenced Shakespeare studies as an editor. She was Associate Editor (1968–1978) then Co-editor (1979–1983) of the *Southern Humanities Review*, the editor of *Shakespeare Quarterly* (1985–1997), then served as its Executive Editor, and later as Consulting Editor. Her impact on the Shakespeare world was also felt in her positions as Director of Research, and since 2009, Director of Research Emertia for the Folger Shakespeare Library, and is a past chair of The Folger Institute. This highly selective, Shakespeare-centric introduction does a disservice to Mowatt's early, more humanities-wide career, and to the many professorships, fellowships, and committee memberships that she held, and the many guest lectures Mowat gave over the past fifty years. Late in the process of preparing this interview for book publication, I received word that Mowat passed away on November 24, 2017. The outpouring of love on social media for Barbara Mowat by mutual friends and members of her family was impressive, with many people writing about the ways their lives were improved by knowing her. This interview was originally published in *Shakespeare Newsletter*, 57:1, #271, Spring/Summer 2007.

••••••••••••••••••••••••••••

Barbara A. Mowat

MPJ: *What does the Folger Director of Research do?*

Barbara A. Mowat: The title "Director of Research" means that I head the Folger's Research Division. My particular roles within this Division include chairing the Folger Institute, serving as Executive Editor of *Shakespeare Quarterly,* and editing the Folger Shakespeare editions. As the director of the division, I serve as one of the Senior Directors of the Library.

Which books do Folger users find the most useful? Is there anything surprising or unique to the Folger Library?

The Folger archives are so extensive that it is impossible to single out books of most use to Folger readers. The Folger's rare-book archives contain printings in every imaginable field of early modern thought and writing, and readers come from around the world to pore over these materials. For Shakespeareans, perhaps the most indispensable holdings are the Folios, First (1623) through Fourth (1685), the quartos, and the Shakespeare editions from 1709 to the present (and in countless languages). The 1594 *Titus* quarto is unique to the Folger, as is a copy of the Second Folio censored by the Spanish inquisition.

Readers will find the folios under Mr. William Shakespeares Histories, Comedies, & Tragedies: Published according to the True Original Copies *in the bibliography, which is the title on the title pages of all four folios. Since these have the same title, it is necessary to describe then as First Folio, etc., to dis-*

tinguish which folio is meant, and this is the way these books are distinguished in the bibliography. I did not know about the copy of the Second Folio you mentioned. What did the Inquisition censor in the copy?

Most interestingly for me, they excised all of *Measure for Measure*—razored it (or otherwise slickly removed it) from the book. They censored (with heavy ink, so that the words are totally obliterated) words and phrases in *The Tempest* and in other plays ("leaky as an vnstanched wench" is gone, for example), and *Henry VIII*'s closing paean to the future Queen Elizabeth is completely marked out.

That does not surprise me. Is this Folio enlightening about Shakespeare's supposed Catholic leanings?

It's easy to see that the censors disapproved of bawdy or blasphemous language, and that they hated the apotheosizing of Elizabeth I, but the only censoring that strikes me as directly related to Roman Catholicism is the excision of *Measure for Measure.* When I first looked at the evidence of this mutilation of the Folio, I suddenly realized how the Church might have abhorred this play, with its depiction of a layman masquerading as a friar, especially a friar who has "confessed" Claudio and who visits prisons to "instruct" prisoners about their spiritual condition. And the play's final image of a man dressed as a friar seeking the hand of "a votarist of Saint Clare" could have been seen as bringing to life onstage the all-too-common salacious image of sexual liaisons between priests and nuns. This Folio may suggest, then, that either the author of *Measure for Measure* was far removed in his beliefs and sensitivities from those of Roman Catholic censors in seventeenth-century Spain or, more simply, that he was not a Roman Catholic.

Very reasonable. As you suggest, one of the great things about the Folger is the almost one-stop-shopping for quartos and folios, a great asset for collating editors. How useful is this now? Has it been done to death, as I have heard suggested?

The Folger's reading rooms are almost always home to editors preparing a scholarly edition of one or more of Shakespeare's plays—either a variorum edition or an Oxford, Arden, or Cambridge single-volume edition. (One summer, we had three editions of *King John* being edited in our reading rooms.) This means that the Folios, quartos, eighteenth-, nineteenth-, and twentieth-century editions, Edward Capell's notes (1779–1783), and editions with important marginalia are constantly in demand. Since editors of scholarly or variorum editions of a Shakespeare play never simply reprint the collations of previous editors, collation will not be "done to death" as long as the plays continue to be edited.

Good to hear. The work you and Paul Werstine do for the Folger editions seems daunting. Whole squads of scholars do this job in some series, but the two of you turn them out on your own. Which resources have been most helpful to you?

Our most important resources have been the Hinman facsimile of the First Folio and the facsimiles of the relevant quartos. (The Folger has the early printings, but, in order to conserve them, we take them off the shelves in the vault only when something is unclear in a facsimile.) Two additional resources that we have drawn on extensively from the very beginning are the *Oxford English Dictionary* and the *American Heritage Dictionary*—in book form for the first years of the project and now in digital form on our computers.

Other books that we could not do without are the Geneva Bible (1560), Ovid's *Metamorphoses,* Naseeb Shaheen's *Biblical References in Shakespeare's Plays*, and Ross Duffin's *Shakespeare's Songbook* (Norton, 2004). Shaheen's *Biblical References* is indispensable for tracing seeming allusions and quotations from the Bible, and, since Shaheen demonstrates that Shakespeare draws biblical language most often from the Geneva Bible, we also want a copy of the Geneva ready to hand whenever we're writing glosses. The Golding translation of Ovid's *Metamorphoses* is also an important reference—most often for the *Sonnets* and the narrative poems, but for many of the plays as well; and *Shakespeare's Songbook* is essential for editing any play that contains a song, since Duffin's account of each song quoted or alluded to is exhaustive and definitive.

Our ready-reference shelf includes, among many other books, R. W. Dent's *Shakespeare's Proverbial Language*, Gordon Williams's *A Dictionary of Sexual Language and Imagery in Shakespearean and Stuart Literature*, and Charlton Hinman's *The Printing and Proof-Reading of the First Folio of Shakespeare*, along with Gregory Crane's very helpful website, The Perseus Digital Library for texts of classical works and information about classical civilization.

Beyond these basic references, George T. Wright's work on Shakespeare's language is immensely helpful, especially his *Shakespeare's Metrical Art*. Wright understands better than anyone I know the way meter works onstage, and his insights into the way Shakespeare transitioned back and forth between poetry and prose in dramatic dialogue is a godsend for an editor struggling with how to print these transitional lines. Finally, a relatively new work, David and Ben Crystal's *Shakespeare's Words: A Glossary and Language Companion,* is a book we consult often, especially for its panels of "politeness phrases," "discourse markers," and other collections of terms where small distinctions can matter, and where rephrasing in modern English is awkward.

I need a Geneva Bible in my home library, but current editions are too expensive.

I, too, have been looking for a facsimile of the 1560 Geneva for my home library, and have been discouraged by the prices. But Amazon has announced the availability in October of a *Geneva Bible: 1560 Edition* for under $50.00. They don't say who edited it or who is publishing it, but I'm waiting eagerly for these details, so you might want to stay on the look-out.

I looked it up when the information became available. The Bible is edited by Lloyd E. Berry. Thanks for the tip. You have written a number of articles and chapters about editing Shakespeare's texts. This began in the late eighties. What turned your interest to textual criticism?

I have been fascinated with textual criticism since my graduate school days with Fredson Bowers, though my work with him did not include textual studies. Then, in the mid–1980s, Mary Beth Rose invited me to contribute to a collection of essays on textual scholarship, and shortly after this came an invitation to take part in Ann Thomson's editing seminar at the 1991 International Shakespeare World Congress. These invitations provided the occasions for my first two articles about Shakespeare texts—one tracing the transformation of the *Hamlet* text through the centuries, the other analyzing Nicholas Rowe's influence on Shakespeare editing. When Paul Werstine and I began editing Shakespeare's plays for the Folger (the first six were published in 1992), my theoretical interest became very practical. Because Paul was trained as a textual scholar, he initially edited the playtexts while I prepared the glosses and much of the front and back matter. After a couple of years, though, we each grew tired of this division of labor, and we began sharing all aspects of the work. At this point, my interest in textual matters increased, and I found myself thinking and writing more and more often about texts and the history of the texts.

Who is writing most helpfully about textual editing?

Eric Rasmussen's annual essay in *Shakespeare Survey* (1999–2011), in which he comments on the year's work in textual studies, is always helpful. And I don't think I'm alone in turning often to the work of Paul Werstine, which began with analyses of Folio and quarto compositors, but which now extends into broad areas of textual scholarship. Two essays he first published in *Shakespeare Quarterly* ("The Textual Mystery of *Hamlet*," and "Narratives about Printed Shakespeare Texts: 'Foul Papers' and 'Bad' Quartos,") are among *SQ*'s most frequently cited essays, and both have been reprinted in important anthologies; and two chapters of the many he has written in book collections ("Shakespeare," in *Scholarly Editing: A Guide to Research*, and "Plays in Manuscript" in *A New History of Early English Drama*), are significant reference works in themselves. And I know I'm not the only one looking forward to his book on the surviving pre–1640 dramatic manuscripts. For the first time, the texts of these manuscripts are getting the kind of attention editors pay to Shakespeare's early printed texts. In his book, Werstine is extending the work of the New Bibliographers as he describes in inclusive terms the features of each of the playhouse manuscripts, and as he focuses on what the words "foul papers" meant for Shakespeare's contemporaries. We have been waiting a long time for this book.

Guessing from your published articles and lectures, you seem to have worked on The Tempest *as much as any other text, and more than most. What draws you to it?*

One thing I really love about *The Tempest* is that it is such a book-based play. Its intertextuality is remarkable, with the text incorporating narratives from the distant past, such as Greek Romance and the *Argonautica* by Apollonius Rhodius in the third century, B.C.E., all the way through travel tales and letters from Shakespeare's own time. Further, within the fiction of the play, books are also important, with Prospero's library and his conjuring book presented as central to his magic. I'm also fascinated by the play's structure, especially the disjunction between the play's narrative (which covers 24 years) and the action it dramatizes (which takes place in a few hours). And then there's its relationship to Ben Jonson's *Alchemist.* The first performance of this play was almost simultaneous with that of *The Tempest*—we're not even sure which play preceded the other. Each centers on a form of magic—one is a near celebration of spirit magic, the other a reduction of alchemy to a con-game—and they share interesting structural details: each takes place during a few hours of fictional time, and each keeps offstage the source of its magic power—Prospero's book and the alchemist's "laboratory." This odd relationship is one that Tim (F. H.) Mares and I had agreed to explore together. Tim's untimely death left that project still on the shelf, but, like so much about *The Tempest,* it still calls to me.

I hope you can take it up. Who should we read on this play?

I recommend the work of Peter Hulme and William Sherman, among others. Hulme and Sherman have co-authored two books on the play, *The Tempest and its Travels*, and *The Tempest* for the Norton Critical Editions, and Hulme has written not only the influential post-colonial essay "'Nymphs and Reapers Heavily Vanish': The Discursive Con-texts of *The Tempest*," which he co-authored in 1985 with Francis Barker, but also such essays as "Hurricane in the Caribbees: The Constitution of the Discourse of English Colonialism" and "Stormy Weather: Misreading the Postcolonialist Tempest." I also highly recommend Auden's "The Sea and the

Mirror," a wonderful commentary on the play in the form of a collection of poems and a long prose-poem.

You also gave some recent lectures on Shakespeare's reading, a subject we have seldom covered in this column. What have you discovered?

I'm finding that it is possible to trace the ways certain books—for example, the Bible and its marginalia and indices, specific novella, Roman plays, and Italian epics—inform Shakespeare's plays and provide significant clues to how he worked to transform such materials into vibrant dramatic scripts. While I'm also finding that Shakespeare was, as some have long suspected, very bookish, I'm also learning that, when he selected popular fictions or chronicles to dramatize, he read very efficiently. For example, as a busy playwright, he tended to use English translations of foreign works when such translations were available. This says nothing about his ability to read foreign languages; it says only that, for him to work through French or Italian or Latin versions once an English translation became available would apparently have been an unnecessary use of valuable time. Interestingly, the appearance of an English translation of an important work was sometimes followed quickly by the work's becoming an intertext for a play. I suspect, for example, that it is no coincidence that in 1598 Richard Bernard's admirable English translation of Terence's plays was published and that shortly after that Shakespeare turned to Terence's *Hecyra (The Mother-in-law)* as an intertext for *All's Well that Ends Well.* I'm also learning that Shakespeare followed some predictable paths in his converting of popular fictions into dramatic scripts, signaling to the audience the presence of a well-known fiction before he transforms it in unpredictable ways.

Which books influenced you the most?

I would put at the head of the list Madeleine Doran's *Endeavors of Art: A Study of Form in Elizabethan Drama*, to which I was introduced soon after I began graduate study. Her way of looking at art—and especially the transition from the art of the middle ages to that of Shakespeare's day—and her way of placing Shakespeare's plays within the narrative, romance-genre context of that transition, influenced my early study of Shakespeare enormously, drawing me toward Shakespeare's dramatic form and its antecedents. I was especially intrigued by her characterization of all of Shakespeare's plays as having romance/tragicomedy at their core, and her linking of Shakespeare's dramaturgy to romance narrative and to the early dramatic romances. Equally influential was G. L. Kittredge's *Sixteen Plays of Shakespeare,* with its incomparable glossorial notes. I was taught (by Bowers, through Kittredge's notes) to center my study in the language of the plays—and specifically in the language as it meant when it was written, and as it captured and revealed culture, theology, and philosophy.

Are there any books that you refer to frequently?

Books that I return to again and again, no matter what Shakespeare project I'm engaged in, are Robert Burton's *Anatomy of Melancholy* (1621), filled as it is with discussions that help explain Shakespeare's language about the humors, the parts of the body and their relationship to each other, the spirits, love, beauty, and evil, to name only a few areas in which Burton is helpful; Montaigne's *Essais* (1580), an earlier book which in a way picks up where Burton leaves off, providing insight into sixteenth-century modes of thinking about, for example, friendship, belief, cultures, and thinking itself; Susanne Langer's *Feeling and Form: A Theory of Art*, which presents a theory of art based on her important *Philosophy in a New Key*: A *Study in the Symbolism of Reason, Rite, and Art*, applying the larger concept of the symbol to such topics as "The Great Literary Forms," "The Dramatic Illusion," and the major dramatic genres of comedy and tragedy; Thomas Greene's *The Light in Troy: Imitation and Discovery in Renaissance Poetry*, the best book I know about the way earlier writers used yet earlier texts; and Keir Elam's *The Semiotics of Theatre and Drama, 2e*, which continues to teach me about how drama means on the stage.

Who should be rediscovered?

I'm not sure how much Kenneth Burke is read today, but he remains at the top of my list of philosophers whose perceptions and insights are invaluable for a Shakespearean. I particularly like *Counter-Statement*. This collection of essays contains two to which I return often: "The Psychology of Form" and "Lexicon Rhetoricae." In these essays, Burke analyzes the literary (which for him includes the dramatic) as a specifically temporal form that provides for the audience a curve leading from initial expectation, to intermediate frustration, to final satisfaction. Burke analyzes how such a curve is created through progressive forms (syllogistic and qualitative), conventional forms (especially generic forms), and repetitive and minor forms. As I examine the way Shakespeare crafts his dramatic texts, I try always to keep in mind Burke's statement that "the drama, more than any other form, must never lose sight of its audience: here the failure to satisfy … is most disastrous." It seems obvious to me that Shakespeare, as the consummate man of the theater, would always have been alert to this potential disaster.

Are there any more recent books that you think deserve more attention than they have received?

I find Bert O. States's *The Pleasure of the Play* a wonderful book that should be better known. States analyzes the complex interactions between the play and its audience in terms of the implications of Aristotle's comments on the drama. I have found especially useful States's claim that the primary law of drama is that "the interest and pleasure of the audience arise from the gap between the predictable and the unexpected." States uses Sophocles' crafting of *Oedipus Rex* from the already well-known story of Oedipus to explore a master dramatist's creation of the pleasurable gap between the predictable and the surprising. I find States's discoveries wonderfully applicable to Shakespeare's work, with familiar stories that he makes unpredictable.

Any other non-lit-crit books that you have found particularly enriching in your thinking and writing about Shakespeare and early modern theatre?

Paul Ricouer's writings—especially *Time and Narrative*—always send me back to Shakespeare with new questions and new insights. The same is true for Maurice Merleau-Ponty's *Phenomenology of Perception* and his *Signs*.

What is it about these that illuminate Shakespeare for you?

It's not so much that they directly illuminate Shakespeare, as that they lead me to ask larger questions about time and how it functions in drama and in the theater, about the work of narrative in Shakespeare and in the fictions he reads, about the phenomenology of perception, and about systems of signs and symbols in relationship to drama and theater.

What book needs to exist that perhaps you don't want to write?

Someone should write about conjuring books in sixteenth and seventeenth century England. A few years ago, I published a piece on a conjuring book that the Folger owns—a manuscript from the 1580s—linking it to Prospero's book of magic. Any number of people have expressed an interest in the larger topic the essay introduces, encouraging me to write a book about these fascinating documents. Since I'm very unlikely to get around to this, I hope someone else will take it on. It's a great topic.

Thanks, Barbara. I really appreciate the thoughtful and philosophical ideas in your answers.

James Shapiro

One of the most popular Shakespeare books of the new century is James Shapiro's *1599: A Year in the Life of William Shakespeare*. It is a brilliant idea for a book. Not only does he have a subtitle shorter than the main title, Shapiro earned the respect of most Shakespeareans by going into depth about something that can be known: what Shakespeare and his company did that year. Shapiro eschews many of the layers of speculation that mar most Shakespeare biographies. He is the first author interviewed in this column to have his work turned into an audio book, for *A Year in the Life* is available as both abridged and unabridged audio books. The 2015 follow-up volume *The Year of Lear: Shakespeare in 1606* is previewed in our interview.

Shapiro's *Shakespeare and the Jews* was very well received for the way he contextualized Shylock in particular, but really all Jewish characters in early modern literature, by documenting the social and cultural place of Jews in England at that time and shows the means that Shakespeare's play reflects this in some rather knowing ways. Afield geographically, but not intellectually, is *Oberammergau: The Troubling Story of the World's Most Famous Passion Play.* Oberammergau is the name of a German village that has regularly staged a particular anti–Semitic passion play since 1634. It has been treated as propaganda by anti–Semites, but also used by Jewish groups to further their causes. Shapiro presents the history of the play and the sometimes-deadly tug-of-war that has been waged over it.

Rival Playwrights: Marlowe, Jonson, Shakespeare examines the influence these writers had on one another. Shapiro smartly structures the book with the chapters, "Marlowe and Jonson," "Shakespeare and Marlowe," and "Jonson and Shakespeare," capturing every combination. Not satisfied to study influence only in the traditional sense, he considers some non-traditional crosscurrents between these authors, and brings in other playwrights as needed. Unfortunately, we were not able to discuss it because I was unable to get a review copy, nor was I able to get a review copy of *The Columbia Anthology of British Poetry* edited with Carl Woodring, an introductory textbook that includes over 200 pages of poetry from the sixteenth to the middle of the seventeenth century.

James Shapiro (Mary Cregan).

Since our interview, Shapiro has published the aforementioned book on *King Lear* and the well-received *Contested Will: The Shakespeare Authorship Controversy*. This book does not turn over many stones, but some of those that are turned present powerful reasons to reject the rejecters of Shakespeare's authorship. It was published by Simon & Schuster in 2010, and followed by the edited volume *Shakespeare in America: An Anthology from the Revolution to Now*, published by the Library of America in 2014. Shapiro also wrote and presented a three-part BBC documentary on Shakespeare's Jacobean years, *The King and the Playwright: A Jacobean History*, broadcast in 2012.

Dr. Shapiro is professor of English and comparative literature at Columbia University. This interview was originally published in *Shakespeare Newsletter*, 57:2, #272, Fall 2007.

•••••••••••••••••••••••••••••

MPJ: *I fear that we are going to be deluged in books with titles like,* 1606: Shakespeare's Dark Year, *and* Forgiveness Forever: Shakespeare in 1611. *I'm going to blame you. No, actually, I'll welcome any* good *book about Shakespeare and his company. Let's help any bandwagon writers do it well. Which books and other resources were especially helpful as you researched 1599?*

James Shapiro: Funny you should mention 1606—the book I'll be writing after the one on the authorship controversy will be about that very year (though I don't subscribe to Shakespeare's "dark years" or Shakespeare "in the heights" or "in the depths," as biographers once put it). Because I remain deeply committed to writing about important moments in an artist's creative life (rather than a cradle-to-grave biography that must invent what's lost or missing), I'll be turning to the Jacobean Shakespeare, and 1606 is an unusually exciting and well-documented year. I don't expect to have that book written and published until 2016.[1] The research takes a brutal amount of time. And I'll be a bit distracted now that Sam Mendes has optioned *1599*. If a planned 4-part television series on the book comes off, I'll be very pleased—and I suspect you'll see a spate of year-in-the-life books after that.[2] Some, I hear, are already in the works.

As for books and resources that I found helpful, it's pretty simple: I do my best to read everything written in or about a given year, as I did with *1599*. The best archival collections, or at least the ones I've found most useful, are the obvious ones: the Folger, the Huntington, and the British Libraries, though by the time I've finished my research I might end up visiting a score of libraries or archives.

A possible description of the book is that you historicize Shakespeare's work that year. How did you go about doing this?

When I began research on *1599* at the Huntington Library in the late 1980s, it was the heyday of New Historicism—by which I mean that Shakespeareans would rush to the archives, find a telling anecdote or two, rush back to their computers, then write up and publish an essay in short order. That's a slight exaggeration, of course, but it certainly felt like that. Disappointed with a lot of that scholarship, I was determined to get as far beyond the anecdotal as possible. The trick is to cast a very wide net. Of course, there are some invaluable sources—state papers foreign and domestic, R. A. Foakes and R. T. Rickert's 1961 edition of Henslowe's *Diary*, Norman E. McClure's 1939 two-volume collection of John Chamberlain's letters, Adrian Prockter and Robert Taylor's *The A to Z of Elizabethan London*, and John Stow's 1598 *Survey of London*—without which *1599* would have been a far less interesting book.

I cannot read or see The Merchant of Venice *and* The Jew of Malta *in the same way after reading* Shakespeare and the Jews *due to the way you historicize Jews in early modern England, and explore the clichés believed about them. We all know a few things, such as the expelling of Jewish people from England, converts who stayed, and Jews passing as non-Jews, but you have a lot that is not mentioned in most articles and books about these plays. Where did you find this context?*

I had wanted to write about Jews in early modern England when in graduate school, and was told by someone—not my mentor, David Bevington, though I have forgotten who warned me off—that there were no Jews in Shakespeare's England and therefore no Jewish questions worth pursuing. After writing my first book, *Rival Playwrights: Marlowe, Shakespeare, Jonson*, which grew out of my dissertation, I turned to this question and was fortunate to have waited, because historians like David Katz had begun to open the field of early modern English Jewry in his *Philo-Semitism and the Readmission of the Jews to England* and *Sabbath and Sectarianism in Seventeenth-Century England*, while more theoretical scholars in related disciplines were raising questions about national, racial, and religious identity that made it possible for me to ask new questions—and offer some partial answers. My work is always grounded in the archives and I've been fortunate to stumble upon some interesting material.

Oberammergau *would usually be outside of* SNL*'s purview, but it is right in line with* Shakespeare and the Jews, *since the play performed there is considered anti–Semitic and has been used as propaganda. Can you comment on the passion play, and what it tells us?*

Shakespeare and the Jews reached a larger audience than I expected and made me want to reach an even broader one in the books that followed. The Oberammergau Passion Play, performed in a Bavarian village since the early seventeenth century, a play Hitler praised for showing the "muck and mire of Jewry," suited my interests in Renaissance drama and anti–Semitism perfectly. And nobody had come along and made use of the extensive archives in both the U.S. and Germany. It was a more controversial subject than I realized—and I was sued after its publication in Germany, charged with defaming a convicted and dead Nazi who had reportedly been instrumental in packing off the only Jew in Oberammergau to Dachau. Yes, in Germany you can be sued for defaming the dead, and yes, such suits can be very expensive.

Ouch. One of the things you consider in this book is censorship—and it is interesting that the book provoked legal action which is a kind of post-censorship and warning to others to censor themselves. I have a friend, the husband of a well-known Shakespearean and the sweetest man I know. He is Jewish. He finds watching Merchant *too painful and will not see it again. While he is against censorship in principle, he wishes that people would stop performing the play. Will you please comment on this?*

I look at it in a different way. Think of the play as a canary in the coal mine. Anti-Jewish or anti–Semitic sentiment within our culture don't disappear when we stop staging this play. On the contrary: it's through productions that we can actually measure the intensity of such feelings. Sticking one's head in the sand, or calling for it to be censored, is not a wise response. I had the chance to work closely last year (2007) on a brilliant production of the play, directed in NYC by Darko Trejnak, with F. Murray Abraham as Shylock, and the experience confirmed for me the importance of staging, and restaging, the remarkable, and painful, play.

I suspect it was more painful in early modern England than we realize. I repeatedly read that a Christian audience would applaud Shylock's forced conversion, but I doubt it is so simple. England in Shakespeare's time was a nation of forced conversions: to Protestant from Catholic, and that was just the latest round. I imagine that some members of the audience would approve, but others would squirm. It surely hit home for many, especially if a relative had been put to death. Whose books helped direct your career?

The book that first set me on my career path was Bernard Spivack's *Shakespeare and the Allegory of Evil*, which I read as an undergraduate. It offered an outstanding model of how to provide an historical context for something readers didn't grasp well enough, in this case Iago's motiveless malignity.

Which books influenced you the most?

In truth, what I've learned about Shakespeare (rather than about his life and times) I learned in the theater, not in the library, beginning with scores of productions in the late 1970s and early 1980s in London and Stratford-upon-Avon. I have learned more about *Richard III* seeing it performed by Anthony Sher (1984), Ian McKellen (1990), and Simon Russell Beale (1992) than I have from anything I've read.

Some are suspicious of statements like that, but these are teams of people (actors, directors, etc.) offering an interpretation after working closely with the texts, more closely than many teachers do. They may sometimes lack scholarly resources and discipline, but I honor them. Who isn't read anymore who should be rediscovered?

There's a tendency these days to turn to the latest editions or compilations. But there's a great deal out there—much of it from the eighteenth and nineteenth centuries, gathering dust on library shelves or in used bookstores, that is worth a second look. In my current work on the authorship controversy, for example, I've taken a good deal of pleasure reading Delia Bacon (*The Philosophy of the Plays of Shakespeare Unfolded*, from 1857) and J. T. Looney (*'Shakespeare' Identified in Edward de Vere the Seventeenth Earl of Oxford* from 1920)—advocates, respectively, of Francis Bacon's and the Earl of Oxford's claims—not because I accept their conclusions, but because these works tell me a great deal that I otherwise didn't know about how Shakespeare has been read and understood, or in this case, misunderstood. Shakespeare scholarship didn't begin in 1960 and we miss out on a lot by not going back to older, "outdated" work.

Thank you. That is one of the points of "Talking Books." Are there any books of the past few years that deserve more attention than they have received?

If I were giving away Shakespeare books as holiday gifts, I'd order a bunch of copies of Michael Dobson and Stanley Wells's one-volume *Oxford Companion to Shakespeare*. I don't know if it has received the attention it deserves; I do know that I keep it at my elbow and find myself consulting it at least once a week.

Is there a book most of us do not know about but should?

You can probably tell by now that I'm promiscuous in my reading. Favorites don't stay favorites for long and I try to see things from as many perspectives as possible—so I can't think of a single author, or title, or critical approach, that I would consider most important or dominant in my thinking. That having been said, there are books I come upon and value greatly, the most recent of which I've just read in proofs and had a chance to review: Charles Nicholl's *The Lodger: Shakespeare on Silver Street* restores my faith, in the wake of so many recent Shakespeare biographies, that there's a lot more still to be said, and discovered, about Shakespeare's personal and professional world. Nicholl is unsurpassed as an archival scholar—and tells a very good story, too.

Yes, Jonathan Bate told me, "You can smell the river," about another of Nicholl's books, which is a wonderful way of stating what Nicholl does. Name a Shakespeare book that is just plain fun.

In all honesty, I don't read Shakespeare books for fun or pleasure—that's what novels are for. As for a critical book that was sheer pleasure to read—it'll be out soon, by year's end, I suspect—Alan Stewart's *Shakespeare's Letters*—which completely changed my way of reading *Henry the Fourth* as well as *Hamlet*. The conventions governing how letters were written, delivered, and read in early modern England were radically different than they are today—and Stewart's historicizing of the scores of letters delivered or read aloud in Shakespeare's plays is just dazzling.[3]

What are you reading now?

I'm reading a lot of the work that anticipates Brian Vickers's arguments about Shakespeare as co-author. That includes Frederick Gard Fleay's *Shakespeare Manual* from 1876, J. M. Robertson's *The Shakespeare Canon* from 1922–1923, and especially E. K. Chambers's 1924 British Academy lecture on *The Disintegration of Shakespeare*. I'm especially interested in how the reluctance to accept the fact that especially early and late in his career Shakespeare collaborated with other playwrights has unintentionally supported the views of those who believe somebody else—some overlooked Elizabethan aristocrat working in isolation, perhaps—must have written the plays.

Thanks, Jim. I really appreciate you consenting to be my guest in this column.

My pleasure. Great questions, Mike, and a very enjoyable exchange.

Notes

1. *The Year of Lear: Shakespeare in 1606* was published by Simon and Schuster in 2015.
2. The series was not made.
3. This was published in 2008.

Michael Hattaway

Michael Hattaway wears so many scholarly hats that he needs two hat racks. As a textual editor, his books include four volumes for the New Cambridge Shakespeare: the three *Henry VI* plays and two editions of *As You Like It*. His two non–Shakespearean editions are Francis Beaumont's *The Knight of the Burning Pestle*, again in two editions, and Ben Jonson's *The New Inn*.

Hattaway also edits readers. *A Companion to English Renaissance Literature and Culture* from 2000 is a huge book covering a huge number of topics, with chapters on cultural contexts such as rhetoric, race, and early modern ecology, to name just three. It was revised and released as two volumes in 2010. There are also two Cambridge Companions. *The Cambridge Companion to Shakespeare's History Plays* takes a contextual overview then looks at all eleven of Shakespeare's history plays—eleven because *Edward III* is boldly grouped with the first tetralogy. There are also glances at the plays with historical Roman and English characters from other genres, such as *Coriolanus* and *King Lear*. Most of the contributors to *The Cambridge Companion to English Renaissance Drama, 2e*, edited with A. R. Braunmuller, do a fine job of considering the work of Christopher Marlowe, Thomas Dekker, Ben Jonson, John and Thomas Heywood, and others, without neglecting Shakespeare. They contextualize the culture for which early modern drama was written.

Renaissance and Reformations: An Introduction to Early Modern English Literature is a monograph that explains how early modern writers constructed their present and their history, described people and places, explored godliness, and considers the processes that words took to get from writers to audiences.

Hattaway referees the *Hamlet* volume in the excellent "The Critics Debate" series, which studies critical approaches and issues in the play through most of the twentieth-century. The book thrives on the instability of the *Hamlet* texts, finding in them a metaphor for the dozens of *Hamlets* in different critical approaches.

In addition, Hattaway has done impressive work as a performance critic. *Elizabethan Popular Theatre: Plays in Performance* is a primer on how plays were put on in early modern England, culminating in a close look at five plays of the era. His Shakespeare editions all include performance histories, and so does *Shakespeare in the New Europe*, co-edited with Boika Sokolova and Derek Roper. The book looks at the crosscurrents between Eastern Europe and Shakespeare since the fall of the Iron Curtain. Hattaway's essay in this collection surveys performances of Shakespeare's history plays in Britain since World War II, looking at several things including what is gained and lost when the plays are produced as cycles. He has written two interesting film articles. His essay "'I've processed my guilt': Shakespeare, Branagh, and the Movies," blisters Kenneth Branagh's film *Much Ado About Nothing* by showing how badly it misses Shakespeare's subtext. Hattaway more generally looks at films made from Shakespeare's comedies in "The comedies on film," and considers reasons it is so difficult to translate these plays into films. These are sophisticated film criticism.

Michael Hattaway

After our interview, Hattaway delivered the annual British Academy Shakespeare Lecture in 2010 called "Shakespeare and the Fairies," but printed in *Shakespeare Survey 65* as "'Enter Celia, the Fairy Queen, in her Night Attire': Shakespeare and the Fairies." He gave the opening keynote address at the European Shakespeare Research Association conference in Worcester in 2015, entitled "Lands, Realms, Women, and Texts: Possession, Entitlement, and Occupation in Shakespearean Texts and Contemporary European politics," which was recently published in *Cahiers élisabéthains*. Hattaway has published other articles in *Cahiers élisabéthains*, and elsewhere.

Michael Hattaway is Emeritus at the University of Sheffield and currently is a Distinguished Research Fellow at New York University in London. This interview was delayed as he tiptoed through the Folger working on various projects, including a monograph on the way Renaissance dramatists use language to define their culture. He lives in Berkshire, where his free time is spent picking up the hats that overflow those racks. This interview was originally published in *Shakespeare Newsletter*, 57:3, #273, Winter 2007/2008.

••••••••••••••••••••••••••

MPJ: *I learned more about* As You Like It *from your introduction than from any other source not written by Shakespeare, or in a curious way, Thomas Lodge.*[1] *Who informed your ideas about the play?*

Michael Hattaway: When I was an undergraduate in Wellington, New Zealand, I spent far too much of my time acting and then, while a postgrad at Cambridge, suffered a kind of revulsion against that sort of thing. It was being invited to teach at the University of Birmingham Shakespeare Summer School in Stratford-upon-Avon by a wonderful teacher, critic, and human being, Gareth Lloyd Evans, that rekindled my enthusiasm for performance, and then at the University of Kent, with Reg Foakes, my boss and now my friend. I directed some student productions, including *AYL*. In those years Jonathan Miller was invited to give the University's Eliot Lectures: they generated Miller's *Subsequent Performances*, which I think is still the best book on performance on both stage and screen. I have also learnt a huge amount about performance and gender theory from the writings of Barbara Hodgdon ("Sexual Disguise and the Theatre of Gender"), Phyllis Rackin ("Androgyny, Mimesis, and the Marriage of the Boy Heroine"), and Carol Rutter (*Enter the Body: Women and Representation on Shakespeare's Stage*)—all of whom relate theory to performance actualities.

Has there been anything published on the play since your edition that you wish you could have used?

I am in the fortunate position of being able to prepare a new edition. This will enable me to take account of Cynthia Marshall's Shakespeare in Production edition, Robert Smallwood's account of performances at Stratford (*Shakespeare at Stratford: As You Like It*), the huge contribution made by Juliet Dusinberre's Arden 3 edition of the play (although I will be taking courteous issue with some of her findings), and also of Tiffany Stern's pioneering work. Stern is one of those scholars who assembles familiar material and excitingly re-categorizes it. Her *Making Shakespeare: from Stage to Page* forces us to think hard about the different kinds of manuscript that must have been assembled for the printing of a play, and the title of her article "Was *Totus mundus agit histrionem* Ever the Motto of the Globe Theatre?" provokes the answer, "Almost certainly not!"

Tiffany Stern is one of the indispensible early mod scholars. As time goes by, I grow more fascinated by chronicle plays. Is there a book that gives readers a good overview of chronicle plays, not just Shakespeare's, but the chronicle movement, if I can all it that?

Warren Chernaik has just brought out a lively and admirable introduction to Shakespeare's histories (*The Cambridge Introduction to Shakespeare's History Plays*) that mingles historical criticism and theatre history. Phyllis Rackin, *Stages of History: Shakespeare's English Chronicles* and Larry S. Champion, *The Noise of Threatening Drum: Dramatic Strategy and Political Ideology in Shakespeare and the English Chronicle Plays* are useful synoptic surveys that do not try to homogenize the plays—as previous critics used to do.

You wrote in 1990 that the case both for and against Shakespeare's sole authorship of Henry VI, part one *has yet to be proved. Do you still feel this way, and how have the issues evolved since you wrote your introduction?*

I am more than ever convinced that neither side can prove a case. First, I think that those brilliant young men, Christopher Marlowe, William Shakespeare, George Peele, Richard Greene, Thomas Lodge, and Thomas Nashe must have known one another well, and that a fair amount of improvised parodying of each other's styles must have taken place when they met up. It was a good joke by Shakespeare to ventriloquize Marlowe when he had Joan la Pucelle adopt the verbal style of Tamburlaine in *1 Henry VI*. Second, I wish I had invited—and someone should—a good statistician to analyze the graphs and findings published in papers like Gary Taylor, "Shakespeare and Others: The Authorship of *1 Henry VI*." The amount of data is comparatively small (and Taylor's tables contain inaccuracies), and I have a hunch that the neo-disintegrationists are guilty of exaggerating the significance of their deviance curves, ignoring random statistical variation. Sir Brian Vickers, "Incomplete Shakespeare: or, Denying Coauthorship in *1 Henry VI*," uses metrical tests and source material to much better effect and adduces a quantity of evidence that supports the case for Nashe's hand in the play. It is surprising, however, that he does not address the problem of dating or examine in detail the case for Marlowe's contribution. He also fails to consider the implications of Nashe's famous reference to Talbot on the stage in *Pierce Penilesse* (1592)—a puff for Nashe's own work? I have to admit that my interest in performance possibilities outweighs my concerns over authorship problems, yet, having revisited the debate, I would not, at the moment, be tempted to rewrite radically what I had to say about that topic in my introduction to *1 Henry VI*, where I relate the first part of the play to the structure of the whole trilogy. Nor would I want "Shakespeare, Nashe, *et al.*" to appear on the front of the volume.

Which books are especially helpful to you as an editor of Shakespeare?

I was exceedingly fortunate, as an MA student at Victoria University of Wellington, New Zealand, to study Shakespeare with the late Don McKenzie (the bibliographer D. F. McKenzie who was, also, a critic and a charismatic teacher who had absorbed the best of what F. R. Leavis had to offer). The acute logical processes Don brought to bibliographical evidence and his passionate concern for accuracy inspire (or rather haunt) my work—I could never match his standards. But I am always inclined to believe that very few books have the same kind of publishing and printing history. (See D. F. McKenzie, *Making Meaning*). Another fellow New Zealander, Andrew Gurr, has written a number of histories of playhouses, companies, and performance conditions, which are essential. His *The Shakespearean Stage 1574–1642* has been revised several times, showing how it has become a standard reference for a couple of generations of historians and students; *Playgoing in Shakespeare's London* and *The Shakespearian Playing Companies* are also standard works—although they have not replaced E. K. Chambers, *The Elizabethan Stage*. Of course they add a great deal of information, but they present it in a different way. Like everyone, I constantly use Charlton Hinman's facsimile of the Folio, and Michael Allen and Kenneth Muir's volume *Shakespeare's Plays in Quarto* that reprints all of the Quartos, but now, of course we have the riches of the internet. The British Library's Quarto website is a masterpiece of electronic design.

I have just finished writing an e-book on *Richard II*. I enjoyed the task, especially the possibility of inserting hyperlinks. An assiduous student, perhaps in an institution without a good library, could go straight from my e-text to look at some quarto editions of the play, a facsimile of Holinshed, or to a translation of the anonymous *Vindiciae contra tyrannos*. People lambaste the Internet because it encourages plagiarism: properly used it can foster originality. I use "Literature Online" and "Early English Books Online" constantly as an editor and author. Frankly, however, the *Oxford English Dictionary* may be my greatest support. You would think that Shakespearean texts would, by now, have been properly glossed—one of the prime tasks of an editor. They have not. When Le Beau says of Celia that she is "taller" than Rosalind, he does not mean she is bigger, but that she is feistier. I discovered that in *OED*. It destroys the case of earlier critics who thought that the fact that Rosalind says that she is "more than common tall" indicates some large-scale revision for a revival when a different pair of boys was used for these two parts. *OED* and Gordon Williams's dictionaries of the sexual language of the time (*Shakespeare's Sexual Language*) also revealed that Rosalind often speaks more "greasily" than previous generations thought. It's not easy, however, to find an appropriate register when glossing what is called in this context "bawdy"—and sometimes rather tedious.

In your edition of 3 Henry VI, *you compare that play favorably with some other early modern English plays, such as* Locrine *and* Thomas Lord Cromwell *that are not as fine. Are there, however, good chronicle plays that are not by Shakespeare?*

To be truthful, I am not very taken by non–Shakespearean chronicles—with the exception of course of *Edward II*. Marlowe and Shakespeare established the genre, and others bob in their wake. I don't for a moment believe that much of *Edward III* is by Shakespeare—its registers and especially its ideology seem totally "Peelean" to me. Again, the RSC did a good production in 2002 (with one of my ex-students, Caroline Faber, playing the Countess of Salisbury), but I felt I was watching a curiosity that had been extracted from its cabinet. I was, however, very enthusiastic about the production by the RSC in 2005 of an almost-chronicle, the collaborative play *Sir Thomas More*. That along with the other plays in the "Gunpowder Season" was well worth reviving.

And on the subject of other playwrights, your Elizabethan Popular Theatre *looks at stage practices in part by studying* Titus Andronicus, *Marlowe's* Edward II *and* Doctor Faustus, *the anonymous* Mucedorus, *and* The Spanish Tragedy *by Thomas Kyd. I would guess that not all* SNL *readers have read all of these plays, and they are missing a lot. Well, OK, lest I get all self-righteous, I'll admit that I have not read* Mucedorus *yet. Why should the Shakespeare-centric look at these other plays?*

The Spanish Tragedy is a great thing—I like to compare its mixtures of long set speeches, or "passions," as the Elizabethans called them, with the arias in Monteverdi's operas, with which they are roughly contemporaneous. But it also packs a political punch, asking the radical question, where do you go for justice when the fountainhead of justice, the monarchy, is itself polluted? As for *Mucedorus*, we should simply read it because it was one of the most popular plays of its age—judged by the number of times it was reprinted. It is a romance, and that reminds us that the straitjackets of the Aristotelian dramatic categories, tragedy and comedy, don't help us much with this period. We need to remember the chronicles, the romances, the problem plays (in the sense that *The Spanish Tragedy*, like *Measure for Measure*, is a problem play). As in *The Winter's Tale*, a bear makes an entrance in *Mucedorus*.

Oh, fun. I enjoyed your editions of Knight *and* New Inn. *What is the best way to learn about Beaumont and Jonson?*

I think it is better to read more plays than more criticism. *Knight* engages with the citizen comedies that were being written at the time and, like *A Midsummer Night's Dream,* pillories those who assume that theatrical performances should create illusion. It is a revel, offering pastiche versions of various kinds of folk-drama of the period—Rafe comes out and presents himself to his audience as do actors in "mummers" plays. Like *Don Quixote,* it offers affectionate parodies of the romances of the period, although its own structure is like theirs, episodic, and it ignores the Aristotelian imperatives of knotting up and then unknotting a plot or intrigue. Ben Jonson was always one to mock romance conventions, but *The New Inn* may be a slightly awkward tribute to his late rival, Shakespeare. Jonson takes a romance plot and gives it a local habitation in Barnet in Hertfordshire, near London. It remembers Shakespeare's late romances, although it eschews any exotic setting such as Bohemia or Sicily, and does what Jonson had scarcely even done, in plays or poems, includes amused but warm wooing sequences. (One of Jonson's poems in *The Forest* begins, "Why I write not of love.") The hero and heroine exhibit the kind of diffident feelings for one another that we see in Beatrice and Benedick, and need the help of their friends to forge a betrothal one with another.

The Forest *was first printed in Jonson's* Workes. *I recently noticed a possible resonance for the Citizen who leaps upon the stage in the induction to* Knight. *He is free of the grocer's guild. Both he and his apprentice do time on stage in the play, especially the apprentice. Thanks to Dave Kathman, we know that many actors were apprenticed to or freed from the grocer's guild, more than most other guilds. His article is "Grocers, goldsmiths, and drapers: freemen and apprentices in the Elizabethan theater." I wonder if this was a bit of a goof on Beaumont's part, as if he were joking, "Geez, every grocer thinks he's an actor." At the very least, Beaumont took the trouble to make him a grocer, when he could have left his profession out. Are there other playwrights from this era who should not be missed?*

There is still a lot of Middleton and Massinger that scarcely ever gets performed—I'd love to see a production of Fletcher and Massinger's *The Sea Voyage* which, like the plays I have just mentioned, mingles conventions, and again remembers Shakespeare, this time *The Tempest.* I hope that the RSC's Swan Theatre in Stratford, presently closed because of the rebuilding of the complex, will revert to the kind of repertory, based on Jacobean plays, for which it was built.[2]

So do I. Aside from readings at the Globe in London and performances at the Blackfriars in Virginia, you don't see these plays performed. Your "Critics Debate" Hamlet *does a great job of giving voice to the many* Hamlet *argu-*

ments up until shortly before 1987, when the book was published. Who has argued since, and why should we listen to them?

I have become particularly interested in seeing and reading about "foreign" productions, which used Shakespeare as a tool for exploring the forms and pressures of our times. I was lucky enough to be taken by some students, when I was in Krakow during the period of Solidarity and martial law, to see a revival of Andrzej Wajda's production of *Hamlet*. It is not just a question of the frisson of being present when a production becomes a political event, but of experiencing what is necessary for every critic, a way of making strange an over-familiar text. Later in Sofia at the "Shakespeare in the New Europe" conference, with my Bulgarian colleagues Alexander Shurbanov and Boika Sokolova, with Marta Gabinska from Poland, and Jim Siemon from Boston, I learned so much about the way the world changed in 1989—not in the way we thought at the time. Then, three years ago, with gifted Shakespeareans like Madalina Nicolaescu, I was at the magnificent Craiova Shakespeare Festival in Romania. About seven plays in seven days, the majority from Eastern Europe. These were as stimulating times as I have ever had. I am honored to have been co-opted onto the new executive committee of the European Shakespeare Research Association[3] which had one of its biennial conferences in Iasi, Romania, last year. This is a unique non–Anglophone organization, and I think that all native speakers of the language in which Shakespeare wrote have so much to learn from productions in other languages and writings from other cultures. This is partly because so much Anglophone Shakespeare criticism, in the last decades of the twentieth century, was written for a coterie of elite academics. It's highly intelligent, and occasionally fascinating, but I prefer readings that can be tested by the disciplines of performance.

Let me confess that I have great affection for Branagh's Much Ado, *despite your quite valid comments. You have not done much Shakespeare film criticism, but it is on a higher level that most than I have read. Whose work has impressed you?*

I'd recommend books by Kenneth Rothwell and Anthony Davies as well as Jonathan Miller (see above). Rothwell's *A History of Shakespeare on Screen*, is a genial and informed volume that artfully combines critique with chronicle, and Davies' *Filming Shakespeare's Plays: The Adaptations of Laurence Olivier, Orson Welles, Peter Brook and Akira Kurosawa*, establishes the "great tradition" in this field. In France, Sarah Hatchuel and Nathalie Vienne-Guerrin have edited various useful collections of criticism of screen and television Shakespeare. Their *Shakespeare on Screen* series, with volumes devoted to single plays, have grown out of splendid conferences that have attracted established and emerging scholars from around the world. Barbara Hodgdon's essays are unparalleled. See, for example, *The Shakespeare Trade.* Diana E. Henderson, *A Concise Companion to Shakespeare on Screen* complements Russell Jackson's *Cambridge Companion* to the same topic. When I'm writing about film, I usually have a good anthology of theoretical essays to hand: Gerald Mast, Leo Braudy, Marshall Cohen, editors of *Film Theory and Criticism, 4e.* I find it perpetually useful—it is large and includes classic essays from both Europe and the United States. I am often surprised at how "old" essays in that volume, for example Erwin Panofsky 1934 essay, "Style and Medium in the Motion Pictures" and Hugo Münsterberg's "The Means of the Photoplay" of 1916, continue to stimulate me.

Thanks for giving me an excuse to set the record straight about something in Henderson's book. Antony R. Gunerante's essay cites an article of mine, for which I thank him, but he has a fact wrong. I reproduced some on-set photographs of scenes not used in the release print of A Midsummer Night's Dream *(1935). These are not frame-blowups, as Gunerante states on page 42. Frame blow-ups would prove these scenes, in the screenplay but not in the movie, were filmed. I can only prove that the actors were in costume and on those sets, which suggests that those scenes were filmed, but falls short of proving it, so that is not my claim. Enough of that. Here is a purely selfish question. No one has published a book on an important area of Shakespeare film studies. A friend and I have discussed editing one, but one of our challenges is finding contributors. Mick, you have 51 different people in the Blackwell* Companion, *including yourself. How on earth did you find them all?*

Yet again Dame Fortune has played a part. The great Reformation historian Patrick Collinson was at Kent during the last years of my career there, and I was able to run interdisciplinary seminars with him. It happened that we both moved to Sheffield the same summer, and I was able to continue working with him in South Yorkshire. Through him, I got to know about those cultural historians who were making waves. I much admire those critics who write about history as well as literature—not necessarily the New Historicists. Names like that of Michael Neill and Susan Ceresano come to mind. Although I am an atheist, I believe that we must study the religious movements of the early modern period in order to understand it. Obviously Patrick gave me a steer in this direction as well. Sometimes I think we ought to junk the concept of "Renaissance England" and write about "Reformation England" in the way people write about "Reformation Germany." That is why I called my last monograph *Renaissance and Reformations*: I am afraid you have to stick "Renaissance" into a title for marketing purposes. Incredible though it may seem, Blackwell have asked me, and I have accepted the invitation, to revise that Blackwell *Companion* and increase its length by 50%—into two volumes.[4] I have asked all current contributors to recommend the names of brilliant younger colleagues, and have reaped a goodly crop of suggestions. I am also Master Accost at the Folger or the International Shakespeare Conference, and ask people I meet there. It is more important to have first-rate contributors than to have "coverage" of the field—which is impossible anyway.

Which books helped direct your career?

Although the New Critics have gone out of fashion, the conviction that the study of literature is a moral activity came to me through exposure to the writings of F. R. Leavis, some of whose supervisions I attended in Cambridge—although by then he had lost his flair and was endlessly repetitive. L. C. Knights had been a fellow *Scrutiny* editor, and although their visions of the good society and the good life seem quaint fantasies now, I often feel I am still a Leavisite in my bones. Knights' Cambridge lectures on Shakespeare were superb. Then of course Raymond Williams was in Cambridge at that time, and I have used his categories on many occasions. Later I was a colleague of Molly Mahood, whose *Shakespeare's Wordplay* is a book to which I regularly return. It was chastening to be appointed to the Chair at Sheffield which Knights had held—as had Geoffrey Bullough and, later, Sir William Empson. Empson's writings make us learn that language "creates what it conveys" (that formula was in fact deployed by Leavis), and the work I am currently doing uses a rhetorical approach to social analysis. What I mean by that is that what the rhetoricians called "discovery" (the mental retrieval of words and material) leads to "discovery" in the modern sense of exploration of the external world. Quentin Skinner has recently been fascinated by the rhetorical figure of *paradiastole* or redefinition (see *Reason and Rhetoric in the Philosophy of Hobbes*). His discussions have helped give a focus to my next monograph, which I think of as a respectful rewriting of Knights' *Drama and Society in the Age of Jonson*. But Empson will also have left a mark: Knights was a Marxist—I shall be concerned much more with ambiguity and the structure of complex words (see Empson's *Seven Types of Ambiguity* and *The Structure of Complex Words*).

Reflecting on this as I write it makes me realize that it was the books I read forty years ago that have made a mark, along with more recent writings by social and cultural historians. This either says something about me, or indicates that perhaps the New Critics made a greater contribution than the structuralists, historicists, psychoanalytic writers, and postmodernists who have raised so many waves recently.

I hope that others will think about that. Thanks, Mick. I really appreciate your thoughtful answers and the insights into your work.

Notes

1. Lodge's proto-novel *Rosalynde, Euphues Golden Legacie* was published in 1590. It was Shakespeare's primary source for *As You Like It.*
2. The Swan reopened in November 2010.
3. http://www.um.es/shakespeare/esra
4. Published in 2010 as, *A New Companion to English Renaissance Literature and Culture.*

Barbara Hodgdon

Barbara Hodgdon starts her first book, *The End Crowns All: Closure and Contradiction in Shakespeare's History*, with quotes from John Webster, John Berger, A. A. Milne, Yogi Berra, and Karl Marx. That is a widely cast net. Beginning with the observation that Shakespeare's plays "remain open-ended only when waiting to be read or performed: the moment a reader, a group of theatrical practitioners, or a spectator begin to work with a text, each is constructing closure" (xv), the book is a study of endings and closures in Shakespeare's history plays, looking at both printed texts and the choices made by theater professionals.

The Shakespeare Trade: Performances and Appropriations examines the tension inherent in the modern Shakespearean appropriations as diverse as advertisements, films, paintings, later stagings, the Shakespeare properties in and near Stratford, and items in the Birthplace gift shop. Hodgdon also considers the afterlives of Cleopatra and the first Queen Elizabeth.

In between came *Shakespeare in Performance: Henry IV, part two* which looks at notable productions of selected plays on stage, film, and television. The above described books are drenched in feminist and cultural theory, and this one has more of it than is usual in this series, but Hodgdon still includes who made the shows, reveals what happened on stage and screen, and why these things are noteworthy. Also in the performance vein is the thick *Companion to Shakespeare in Performance,* co-edited with W. B. Worthen. It is notable for bringing together different performance sites such as stage, film, and television in a single companion, and reading across time from the early modern to the very modern, including Shakespeare as an exemplar of national pride in different eras. Noteworthy is Douglas Lanier's important chapter on phonographic Shakespeare, and the volume includes always interesting scholars such as Peter Donaldson, Carol Chillington Rutter, Tiffany Stern, and "Talking Books" guests such as Peter Holland, and Anthony B. Dawson.

A sharp break from performance studies is *The First Part of King Henry the Fourth* in Bedford's Texts and Contexts series. The series uses the David Bevington text, which in this case is about one-third of the book, supplemented by well-chosen documents that create contexts for the play both on-stage and in early modern culture. Hodgdon chooses roughly 40 pages from Edward Hall, Raphael Holinshed, and Samuel Daniel, Shakespeare's historical sources, then adds excerpts from others on political power, the education of princes, English militarism, the Oldcastle controversy,[1] and what she calls cultural territories: places such as alehouses, theaters, and Wales. It is a terrific series, and this is a terrific edition of the play. Hodgon is the editor of the Arden 3 *Taming of the Shrew*, which was in preparation during our interview and released in 2010. A comparison of the comments in the following pages with the published book is rewarding.

Barbara Hodgdon

We discussed studying Shakespeare performance using archival material during our interview. Hodgdon published *Shakespeare, Performance and the Archive* in 2016, a book that fleshes out our discussion by modeling the way scholars and students might use use archives in the United Kingdom to understand performances of the past.

Hodgdon asked me to list a number of chapters and articles written prior to our interview. These are in the bibliography.

Hodgdon received her Ph.D. from the University of New Hampshire, taught at Drake University for many years, and retired after many more years from the University of Michigan. I learned that Barbara Hodgdon passed away on the day I began the final edit of the bibliography for this book. This interview was originally published in *Shakespeare Newsletter*, 58:1, #274, Spring/Summer 2008.

• •

MPJ: The End Crowns All *is not just a brilliant title, but a nicely balanced book on endings published at a time when ambiguity is practically a moral principle. You maneuver in the tension between them.*

Barbara Hodgdon: Barbara Herrnstein Smith's study of *Poetic Closure:*

A Study of How Poems End spurred my interest in exploring endings. To my knowledge, there has been little concentrated interest in or work on formal structures of late, given these New Historicist times: that arena of study seems to have dropped off the critical landscape in Shakespeare studies. *End* was my attempt to write about performances, or to privilege the study of performances at a high moment of textuality. The move to adopt the term "performance text" was aimed at thinking about performances as particular kinds of texts; I would make a different argument now. It seems to me that theatrical practitioners are far more intrigued by playing with endings than critics are.

What should grad/post-doctoral students be alert for when reading prompt books and other archival material?

By and large, graduate and post-doc students have not consulted prompt books or other archival materials having to do with theatrical performances. A short answer to your question is that these students need to be carefully taught (yes, I know it's a line from a song),[2] beginning with understanding the various notation systems stage managers use, and then finding out and thinking about what kind of "text," if you will, a prompt book represents. Since much notation is now computerized, the prompt books from the mid–1980s forward tend to be less detailed than those from the 1960s–1980s. Prompt books need to be read in conjunction with stage managers' reports, light and music cues, photos and reviews in order to reconstruct performances past. I now regularly include work with prompt books and other archival materials in grad courses. One day, I hope, one of my students will be interested in theorizing the prompt book.

Who are the performance critics that you read?

Carol Rutter, Peter Holland, Robert Shaughnessy, Ric Knowles, Bill Worthen—for Shakespeare performance studies—are at the top of my list. Also, anything by Peggy Phelan and Joseph Roach. All of these writers provide insights into how to talk about the material theatre; their work offers a series of trampolines, in a sense: I can bounce off them. Just incidentally, it's my sense that the term "performance critic" needs rethinking and relabeling. Unfortunately, "performance critic" is an umbrella term that catches up anything from reviewing to an occasional mention of performance in an essay—often as a footnote.

Carol Rutter's *Shakespeare and Child's Play* undertakes the difficult double project of setting early modern discourses and sources on childhood side by side with how children have been performed on present-day stages; Rutter's richly textured prose gives the reader a sense of "being there" at the performances she describes. Robert Shaughnessy's *The Shakespeare*

Effect offers an elegantly written, historically inflected study of a series of performances. Ric Knowles's *Reading the Material Theatre* is the clearest and most efficient tripartite model I know for approaching the very difficult business of talking about material theatre in ways that acknowledge, up front, the complications and difficulties of doing so. Worthen's *Shakespeare and the Force of Modern Performance*, which capitalizes on his earlier book (*Shakespeare and the Authority of Performance*), makes its arguments even more forceful. What's intriguing to me is that Worthen's arguments, while admired, have not incorporated into the stories we tell ourselves about the distinctions between texts and performances: I hope that day will come. Peggy Phelan's *UnMarked: The Politics of Performance*: I regularly assign sections of Phelan's book in both undergraduate and graduate courses. Her thinking is informed by both theory and practice; she has an infallible eye. Joseph Roach's *Cities of the Dead: Circum-Atlantic Performances* brings together cultural and textual theory and work in performance studies with trenchant case studies of local and global performances that again, offers models for "thinking about Shakespeare performances." I might also suggest Roach's most recent book, *it*—a witty study of the origins and definitions of that term, of how various phenomena of "It-ness" march through cultural histories.

Your 21 page bibliography in The Shakespeare Trade *shows that you assembled information and ideas from an extraordinary number of places. Given how disparate this subject is, how did you go about researching these later uses of Shakespeare?*

I read—and raid. I read indexes (we all do, but we pretend that we don't). When I'm working on something, I read eclectically—nearly everything (performance studies, performance theory, film theory, history, poetry, reviews) I think might make a contribution or just get me thinking—with a difference. And I look at films—not just Shakespeare films but other films as well.

Who was especially formative in your thinking?

That's tough to answer, since *Shakespeare Trade* touches so many bases: it's basically a collection of essays jammed together under an umbrella. Some of the readings I most enjoyed were the various biographies of Elizabeth I—I much admire Susan Frye's *Elizabeth I: The Competition for Representation*, for instance, for her wide learning and incisive prose.

I learned a lot from the studies of museum culture about how to talk about museum artifacts and exhibition practices and from reading film theory. Good places to begin would be with Tony Bennett, *The Birth of the Museum*; Eilean Hooper-Greenhill, *Museums and the Shaping of Knowledge*;

Museum Studies in Material Culture, edited by Susan M. Pearce; and *Museums and Communities: The Politics of Public Culture,* edited by Ivan Karp, Chrtistine Mullen Kreamer and Steven D. Lavine. These are sources I turned to for writing about "Shakespeare objects" in the Stratford properties, but there undoubtedly are more recent books, especially those available from the Smithsonian.

For film language and (some) theory, a good place to begin would be with David Bordwell and Kristin Thompson's introductory text *Film Art: An Introduction, 5e.* Their bibliography provides a useful list of anthologies of theory and criticism. Beyond that, it is difficult to recommend one or two single sources: the theoretical paradigms film historians use draw from an eclectic range of theoretical discourses; journals such as *Cinema Journal, camera obscura* and *Jump Cut,* among others, provide "state of the art" work.

This sort of cultural criticism has really come into its own, and I would argue this is evidenced by some bad work in the field. Who is doing it well?

Bad work? Good work? Hmmmm. I'm not going to go there—in either direction: let's just say that I'm suspicious of binaries? In many ways, state-of-the-art writing about Shakespeare films has become increasingly alert to cultural contexts; perhaps this is a response to New Historicist work? Certainly the idea of "contexts" is more dominant than it used to be: I find work by Courtney Lehmann and Doug Lanier consistently thought-provoking. They see well, use theory with flair and in distinctive ways and are sensitive to and sensible about the relations between performances and cultural critique.

In *Shakespearean Remains: Theater to Film, Early Modern to Postmodern,* Lehmann brings a dazzling command of cultural theory and film theory to bear on a series of films to argue how recent film directors collaborate with Shakespeare; Diana Henderson's *Concise Companion to Shakespeare on Screen* contains a number of essays that situate film texts within their cultural milieux; *World-Wide Shakespeares: Local Appropriations in Film and Performance,* edited by Sonia Massai, is an outstanding collection of essays, all of which explore local Shakespeares; overall, the volume works towards refining notions of adaptation; Douglas Lanier's *Shakespeare and Modern Popular Culture* also covers a wide range of "Shakespeare-Cultures"; I much admire his essay, "Shakescorp *Noir,*" in the 2002 *Shakespeare Quarterly* issue devoted to film.

Everything by Doug is worth the time it takes to read it. The possible connection with New Historicism is fascinating, and I had not thought of it that way before. You have a chapter on Queen Elizabeth I. The study of her afterlife had begun to receive similar treatment, hasn't it?

Yes, of course—occasioned in part by the 2003 celebrations of her life. Michael Dobson has written extensively about Elizabeth I, in a particularly engaging book *England's Elizabeth: An Afterlife in Fame and Fantasy*, written with Nicola J. Watson. And several films about her post-date those I wrote about in *Shakespeare Trade*. Given the current revival of Elizabethan and Shakespearean biofictions, the "Elizabeth phenomenon" probably will continue.

You and Professor Worthen are very inclusive about the meaning of "performance" in your Blackwell Companion. *What sites for performance do most of us tend to overlook, and who has written about them?*

I think that the "sounds" of Shakespeare have been overlooked—you're wise to notice Lanier's essay in the *Companion*. Bruce Smith, of course, has written marvelously about "acoustical Shakespeare"; it would be grand to have further studies beyond two I admire: *The Acoustic World of Early Modern England: Attending the O-Factor* and "Ragging *Twelfth Night*: 1602, 1996, 2002–3" in the Blackwell *Companion to Shakespeare and Performance*.

The Festival Shakespeare phenomenon is, I think, given short shrift—except for spotty reviews: this needs a thorough-going "cultural studies" kind of examination. Manga Shakespeare, digital Shakespeare, comic books such as Neil Gaiman's *Sandman* series, Peter Donaldson's archive of streaming video of Asian Shakespeares, the blogosphere—all these open possibilities for further work.

Pete Donaldson's archive is in the bibliography under MIT Global Shakespeares. Shakespeare films keep cropping up in your books, including one film and some television versions in your book on Henry IV, part two. *You have also written chapters on films in books edited by others that are not mentioned in my introduction. Which Shakespeare films are the most interesting?*

Orson Welles's *Chimes at Midnight* (1966), Julie Taymor's *Titus* (1999), Tim Blake Nelson's *O* (2002), Kenneth Branagh's *Henry V* (1989), Richard Loncraine's *Richard III* (1995), Baz Luhrman's *William Shakespeare's Romeo + Juliet* (1996), Michael Almereyda's *Hamlet* (2000), Akira Kurosawa's *Throne of Blood* (1957), Grigori Kozintsev's *Hamlet* (1964) and *King Lear* (1971), Peter Brook's *King Lear* (1971). These are in no particular order, except for *Chimes*—perhaps my favorite. Both of Kozintsev's films are stunning; so is Brook's *Lear*. My students's favorites are those four plus Almereyda's *Hamlet*.

Why these films and not others?

That's a huge question! Perhaps the simplest answer to that question is that when I return to them, time after time, I see things I'd not seen before: in its own way, each offers a deep, rich viewing and listening experience. In teaching those films with subtitles, I've been especially intrigued by how not having Shakespeare's language on the sound track—or, as with Luhrmann's *Romeo + Juliet* or Loncraine's *Richard III*, not having a whole lot of it—invites students to look more closely. Taymor's film, I think, offers an extraordinary amalgam of performance modes—theatre and film—and so becomes a model for, if you will, the Shakespeare film "with a difference."

Which writers and theater/screen productions have shaped your thinking about the Henry IV *plays? I'll assume Shakespeare.*

Welles's *Chimes at Midnight* and Bogdanov's *Wars of the Roses* on stage in 1987 and televised in 1990. Welles's film is simply stunning: for me, it exhibits what I'll call "Shakespearean energy." The filmed-for-TV performances of Bogdanov's project are somewhat disappointing (as are many films of stage performances), but Bogdanov's work was seminal to an understanding of how the histories were being thought about as a "national" project in the 1980s–early 1990s. Others raided his work, often without acknowledgment—but theatre does that all the time: it's called homage.

As imperfect as those programs are at capturing the theater experience, they come closer to doing that than anything I have read about them, and so I am grateful they exist. You seem to discuss English theater productions, especially the Royal Shakespeare Company, more than others.

I talk about English theatre productions because I've seen them—it's as simple as that. Until recently, my travel was somewhat limited: seeing RSC productions as well as productions in London were tied to archive research trips. Currently, the work that I find most interesting is happening, not at the RSC but at the National Theatre, done by various directors, and in performances by Cheek by Jowl.

I'm interested in your forthcoming edition of the Shrew. *Which resources do you find most helpful?*

Long ago, Lynda Boose's brilliant article, "Scolding Brides, Bridling Scolds: Taming the Woman's Unruly Member," got me started on thinking and writing about *Shrew* and was the genesis of what became a chapter in *Shakespeare Trade*. Fran Dolan's work on the play, her Bedford edition as well as several sections in her recent *Marriage and Violence* has been stimulating and invaluable, of great help in fleshing out some of the historical materials that play into *Shrew*. Feminist colleagues have been extremely generous in sharing work in progress, sending me "the latest" in their thinking about the play. Lately, with a view to understanding how to talk about textual matters, I've been reading theatre historians—William Ingram, Roz Knutson, Andrew Gurr, and David Kathman in particular—and work on textual editing matters—essays by Paul Werstine, Margaret Jane Kidnie; Joseph Grigely's *Textualterity: Art, Theory and Textual Criticism*, Jerome McGann's *Radiant Textuality: Literature after the World Wide Web*.

Will you please give us some titles for each, a place to begin?

William Ingram, *The Business of Playing: The Beginnings of the Adult Professional Theater in Elizabethan England*; Andrew Gurr, *The Shakespeare Company*; Meredith Anne Skura, *Shakespeare the Actor and the Purposes of Playing*; David Kathman's essay, "Reconsidering *The Seven Deadly Sins*" in *Early Theatre*; Margaret Jane Kidnie, "Text, Performance and the Editors: Staging Shakespeare's Drama" and Paul Werstine, "Narratives about Printed Shakespeare Text," both in *Shakespeare Quarterly*. Essentially, in terms of editing *Shrew*, I've taken a kind of crash course in textual editing and theatre history, and the books and essays in this list are among those with which I find myself engaged: good conversations all round.

I like the way you put that. Which books helped direct your career?

My dissertation director, Robert Hapgood, brought John Russell Brown's *Shakespeare's Plays in Performance* to my attention, and I suppose the notion of writing about performances grew from reading that—the very idea that "it could be done." Peter Brook's *The Empty Space*; Jack Jorgens's *Shakespeare on Film*, C. L. Barber's *Shakespeare's Festive Comedy*, Jonathan Dollimore's and Alan Sinfield's *Political Shakespeare*, Kate Belsey's *The Subject of Tragedy*, Stephen Greenblatt's *Renaissance Self-fashioning*. Whether these "directed" my career or not? Certainly all of these have shaped my thinking at particular times. I reread Brook rather often—and urge the book on students, too.

In amassing this list (and I know that I've left many unmentioned), I suppose I'm creating a kind of personal canon: in one way or another, these are all readings that sent me off towards further explorations. As I look back at the list I created, one way to explain why these books and not others is because, like many of these writers, my thinking about politics, culture and texts and the relations among them was shaped by the 60s, by Vietnam and post–Vietnam events. What Brook has to say about theatrical enactment is extremely resonant and pertinent nearly 50 years after its appearance. Jorgens's book reads Shakespeare films in relation to how they rethink the plays for the screen, but also points towards later studies which focus more on film qua film. Barber's book, again, is a classic: he points ahead to work that situates Shakespeare in cultural history, edges toward interdisciplinary studies. *Renaissance Self-fashioning* and *The Subject of Tragedy* are both deep studies of subjects and subjectivity. *Political Shakespeare* offers the first sustained statement of cultural materialism that queries the work of Greenblatt and others.

Who should be rediscovered?

Bullough's studies of sources and A. C. Bradley. Actually, Bullough (*Narrative and Dramatic Sources of Shakespeare*) gets re-thought in the Bedford Texts and Contexts series, doesn't he? A "big" study that expanded the notion of "sources" would be grand to have—yes?

Enthusiastically.

As for Bradley (*Shakespearean Tragedy*), the notion of "character criticism" has had recent treatments, but Bradley still has much to say, and a study of his methodology might be fun to do. Might we re-read E. M. W. Tillyard, too (*The Elizabethan World Picture*)?—if only to discover that his work needs to be restored to the critical canon, for he anticipated, in some ways, the ways we think about texts and histories at present.

I think we've tossed the baby with the bath when it comes to Tillyard. Many seem to take an "all or nothing at all" approach, instead of reading him for what is still worthwhile, or so it seems to me from my reading and conversations. What is the most important book on Shakespeare, his times, or early modern theatre you have read?

This seems to me to be a time-sensitive question: different books serve different functions at particular times. Perhaps Bernard Beckerman's *Shakespeare at the Globe 1599–1609* for me, represents a "seminal read"; at the time I read it, it served to point me to arenas of study that eventually became central to my own work, so this is a very selfish sort of response to your question.

When I first read Beckerman's book, I was struck by how it seemed so sensible: it provided what I'll call a "hopeful read" in that it sketched out a series of paradigms for thinking about how Shakespeare once moved through a theatrical marketplace, and thus opened the possibility that there was more to be said—and to be discovered, not just within the arena of early modern theatre history, but also in terms of exploring present-day performances.

Whose books do you greatly admire that have not yet been mentioned?

Susan Stewart's *On Longing: Narratives of the Miniature, the Gigantic, the Souvenir, the Collection*, comes to mind this morning: lucid, fascinating, generous in its scope. It's a study that extends Gaston Bachelard's phenomenological studies of spaces, and it addresses the various topics mentioned in the subtitle, constructing stories about stories, expanding one small memory, or several, connected to an item such as a souvenir and endowing it with significance. Clearly, I've gone "outside" Shakespeare studies, haven't I?

That's fine.

Again, I'm uncomfortable with drawing up an all-time list of admired critics or historians, but let me settle for saying that I'd rush right out and buy anything Jean Howard writes. She invites readers to think with her. *The Stage and Social Struggle in Early Modern England* is an excellent place to begin: it's become a classic and represents a foundation for much of Howard's more recent work, such as *Engendering a Nation: A Feminist Account of Shakespeare's English Histories*, written with Phyllis Rackin. Howard's more recent *Theater of a City: The Places of London Comedy, 1598–1642* is a book I've only browsed so far, but its "take" on the notion of place as essential to the ways in which we think through texts is especially resonant. She currently is at work on a study of Caryl Churchill's plays, to which I much look forward.[3]

What are you reading now?

Anything to do with *Taming of the Shrew*—and I literally do mean anything. I just finished rereading *The Beard of Avon*, which includes a terrific and witty riff on "what to do with the ending of the *Shrew.*" Answer: ask Queen Elizabeth I.

The Beard of Avon *is a play about whether or not Shakespeare was a writer. My standard joke is to say, "I wonder who really wrote* The Beard of Avon*?" I'm pretty sure playwright Amy Freed would not be happy if someone else is named. What needs are there crying out for a book that perhaps you don't want to write?*

A book that lays out the "next new paradigm" for (re)studying/rereading early modern texts. As I talk with graduate students, what I'm hearing from them—and sensing also from conversations at conferences over the past several years—is that everyone is waiting with (somewhat) bated breath for the next "big" bandwagon, for a model, or several models, for rethinking how we think about Shakespeare. It's not that there aren't indications of movements in that direction: it seems to me that print culture, textual editing, and performance studies are currently hot topics. But what lies beyond New Historicism, cultural materialism, and the new wave feminist studies, all of which generated intense excitement at one time? Is it time to return to talking "in old ways" about structures, about language? Or to find some great new paradigm that will magically restore a balance between text and context? And must it be "new"? The current critical-textual climate is especially troubling, I think, for those proposing and writing dissertations: if they choose to frame their thinking within familiar paradigms, extending those parameters or calling them into question, their work will be instantly recognizable by advisors as well as hiring committees. But if they attempt to fashion a methodology or generate a different way of talking, that may not be the case. If I knew the direction this might take, I could be more precise, but I don't.

These are stimulating thoughts. Thanks, Barbara. You have introduced a number of books and a couple of writers that are new to me, and I appreciate it.

Notes

1. The character named Falstaff was originally called Oldcastle in *Henry IV, part one* until Oldcastle's powerful decedents objected. The name was changed by the time the play was published and the sequels were written.
2. The song is, "You've Got to Be Carefully Taught," from the 1949 show *South Pacific*, music by Richard Rogers and lyrics by Oscar Hammerstien, II.
3. This project is mentioned as still in the works in a somewhat different form on Howard's Columbia University faculty webpage accessed March 2018: http://english.columbia.edu/people/profile/390.

Robert S. Miola

Greek and Latin texts in translation continue to fascinate and entertain me, so I envy Robert S. Miola who mastered the languages in addition to becoming one of our finest current Shakespeareans. It is the Latin classics that inform some of his most vibrant Shakespeare work.

In his introduction to *Shakespeare's Rome*, Miola shows that a lot of value and a lot of tosh have been written about Shakespeare's attitude towards and use of Rome in his plays. He concludes that Rome "is sometimes metaphor, sometimes myth, sometimes both, sometimes neither," that the city "maintains a distinct identity," yet is an "ever-changing presence," and notes that in the arc of Shakespeare's plays, he becomes critical of Rome, yet finally writes "a valediction to the Eternal City" (all quotations are from p. 17). Individual chapters on the Roman works, from *The Rape of Lucrece* through *Cymbeline*, show this process.

Shakespeare and Classical Tragedy: The Influence of Seneca and *Shakespeare and Classical Comedy: The Influence of Plautus and Terrence* tease out from Shakespeare's plays how the works read at his grammar school prepared the future playwright, and in doing so gave Shakespeare plot types used throughout his career. Chapters study big categories such as revenge stories and plots about tyrannous characters in the tragedies, and plots based on errors and intrigue in the comedies. *Hamlet* and *King Lear* receive sections in both books, and *A Midsummer Night's Dream* and *The Winter's Tale* are discussed at length in *Tragedy*. I hope that mentioning this will send readers to Miola's books to learn why.

The books are preoccupied with Shakespeare's reading and the ways he used it, so it is fitting that Miola contribute *Shakespeare's Reading* to the Oxford Shakespeare Topics series. Organized by genre, with a chapter on Elizabethan reading and a concluding chapter titled "Shakespeare as Reader," Miola takes the opportunity to explore the rich mosaic of writers we can deduce he read. Thomas Kyd, Arthur Golding, Edward Hall, Raphael Holinshed, Giovanni Fiorentino, and many others make appearances, giving us a glance into Shakespeare's rich and varied reading life and a better understanding of how he constructed his plays and poems.

Robert S. Miola

Miola edited the anthology *The Comedy of Errors: Critical Essays* with the usual suspects such as Samuel Taylor Coleridge and T. W. Baldwin, but with a nice mix of newer school writers such as Douglas Lanier and Laurie Maguire. There are about 150 pages of performance criticism, from the Gray's Inn account through the Shenandoah Shakespeare Express production of 1992.

Miola edited two Norton Critical editions. *Macbeth* supplements the well-edited text with the usual Norton bells and whistles, which makes this book akin to the *Errors* anthology, but with the play included. Excerpts range from Simon Forman and Samuel Johnson through Harry Levin and Stephen Orgel. In other words, this is a good classroom text. Peter Holland's essay on *Macbeth* films may prove indispensable to film scholars working on that play. A second edition was published in 2014 after our interview.

In the interview, Miola discusses his then forthcoming Norton *Hamlet*, published in 2011. The general description of the *Macbeth* very much applies, and several of the *Hamlet* books discussed in our interview are excerpted as readings for this edition.

Miola's edition of Ben Jonson's *Every Man in His Humor: Quarto Version* is wonderfully clean and readable, the appendix has all substantial variations from the Folio, and the introduction is more than I hoped for. Most importantly, this edition reclaims the play to the genre of Italy-set comedies. The quarto and folio are so different that you simply do not have all of Jonson unless you have the quarto in addition to F. Miola was preparing a new edition of *The Case is Altered* for the *Cambridge Edition of the Works of Ben Jonson* during our interview. It was published in 2012.

The anthology *Early Modern Catholicism: An Anthology of Primary Sources* blew me away. It excerpts, among other genres, biographies, histories, verse, fiction, Catholic instruction, and drama from the likes of Sir Thomas More, Robert Southwell, Jane Owen, Ben Jonson, and translations produced and read in early modern England, such as Toby Matthew's version of Augustine's *Confessions* from 1620. Miola continues his deep background reading here: portions of *Hamlet* influenced by Catholicism are included, for example. The book delivers a unique collection from a school of thought well represented in early modern England, but neglected today.

Published since our interview is Miola's edition of George Chapman's version of Homer's *Iliad*, the translation used by Shakespeare and many of his contemporizes when writing about Troy. It was released by the Modern Humanities Research Association in 2017. Miola previously wrote about Chapman's *Iliad* in an article called, "On Death and Dying in Chapman's 'Iliad': Translation as Forgery" for the *International Journal of the Classical Tradition*.

Robert S. Miola is Gerard Manley Hopkins Professor of English, and Lecturer in Classics at the Loyola University, Maryland, where he teaches Latin and Greek languages and literature, but publishes mostly on Shakespeare. He received his Ph.D. from the University of Rochester. A mutual friend, the late John W. Velz, urged me to interview Miola for "Talking Books," and I'm glad he did. This interview originally appeared in *Shakespeare Newsletter*, 59:1, #277, Spring/Summer 2009.

••••••••••••••••••••••••••••

MPJ: *I'm sorry this is the longest question on record, but the subject is very personal to me, and I also think of interest to many concerned about religious conflicts today.*

Reading Early Modern Catholicism *challenged me to relive some uncomfortable moments, and I'll tell you about one. A close high school friend was Kent Winters-Hazleton, now a Presbyterian minister. We had lunch a few years ago and talked about the Bible. I told Kent about my close reading of Genesis informed by my agnosticism, and what I think the book means. Kent told me about his close reading of Genesis informed by his faith, and what he thinks the book means. We were so far apart that a Hegelian synthesis was not possible. I felt that his presuppositions kept Kent from seeing what is clearly there to be seen, enjoyed, and profited from, and I assumed he felt the same of me, he says wrongly. I was condescending to him, and assumed he felt the same. Don't get me wrong, this was a very friendly conversation that included other topics, but whenever I have a religious conversation with someone whose views are different than mine, I have felt condescension on both sides, and I think that most of the time that it really is there. I have worked with atheists, Jews, Catholics, Protestants, Muslims, Hindus, Taoists, Buddhists, and have in-laws who are members of a cult. We are far more likely to discuss the World Series and the latest James Bond movie than what we believe. We play it safe. Maybe we should and maybe not, but we usually do, and it is a relief not to feel the condescension of others and to not have to hide mine.*

I found a lot of condescension as I read through Early Modern Catholicism, *condescension by early modern Catholics who wrote about Protestants, plus the condescension they feel from the Protestants in power. Circumstances now are somewhat different, though some things are the same. While today you can find Protestants who say that all Catholics are going to hell, and Catholics who say the same of Protestants, and both publish some really ugly materials to stir up the faithful, at least on our continent, people seldom die for their religious beliefs. Not so for some of the writers excerpted in your anthology, people who died for being vocally Catholic, people who in modern critical terms are the* other *in the Tudor and post–Elizabeth power structure. Early modern England was condescending on its best days and went through periods of horrendous persecution, just as it had in diverse ways under Henry VIII and Queen Mary. There is a lot of ugly to go around. Part of me wants to be flippant, and say that early mods needed the World Series and James Bond movies. Part of me finds all this very disturbing, which is probably why I want to hide behind flippancy. Though you state it clearly in your introduction to your section on the histories (387–391), this is a subtext to the entire book: we view so much of England's Catholic past through the histories of the Protestant victors. We ignore the voices of the* other *reproduced in your book.*

Robert S. Miola: Condescension, born from the certainty that one is right, as you note, is the edge of the attitude that all too often leads to intolerance and persecution. And, yes, both sides are guilty. Both sides committed atrocities; both sides have plenty to be ashamed of. We need to get beyond the grizzly arithmetic of persecution ("You killed x; we only killed y"), and the excuses ("You started it; we are only acting in self-defense"). As the years rolled on as I was working on the anthology I came to a clearer understanding of this; I had myself to get past the destructive binary thinking that fueled the conflicts in the first place while trying to maintain a sense of fairness and purpose. Finally, in the published version of the anthology, I included some Protestant voices in footnotes (William Tyndale responding to More, for example) and Catholics disagreeing with Catholics (Alban Langdale and Robert Persons, e.g., on church papistry; Robert Bellarmine and William Barclay on papal authority). Obviously the point was to listen to Catholic voices for a change, but I wanted to give some sense of the period in its complexity, not just fall into the apologetics that have vitiated so many of the earlier collections. But there is something you have identified in religious discourse that is very disturbing. People want to be, need to be, right on the most important questions and sometimes this need turns destructive.

Something else that fascinated me was not the subtext, but the text of your collection: the Catholic context to many works of literature that we assume are nominally Protestant, or at least do not think of as especially Catholic, such as Jonson's The Alchemist.

Yes that is certainly another part of the picture, figures and texts that have a surprising Catholicity to them. Ben Jonson was a Catholic for the most productive years of his life. He has some very interesting and neglected Catholic poetry. John Donne, for another example, was raised a Catholic and Catholic devotions mark some of his best poetry; he even expresses attitudes and beliefs there, regarding the Virgin Mary and her role as intercessor, for example, that he explicitly denies from the pulpit as Dr. Donne. Shakespeare is in every sense a special case: the arguments for his biographical Catholicity seem unpersuasive to me, but Catholic devotion and doctrine certainly constitute a potent dramatic resource for him throughout his career. *Measure for Measure*, it seems to me, is about religious vocation, clerical and non-clerical, in the fallen world. The last plays feature haunting refigurations of Catholic devotional practices and beliefs—penances, pilgrimages, theophanies, miracles.

Never thought of them that way. I have read through disturbingly few of the people in your collection. Their names are familiar from surveys and anthologies that might contain a poem or two. Are there any important writers who should be rediscovered apart from their function as Catholic voices from the past?

I think Richard Crashaw has been distinctly undervalued as a poet because he has been dismissed as an odd example of the excesses of Catholic Baroque art. "Over-ripeness is all," Douglas Bush once quipped.[1] But his hymns and longer poems, his translations into Latin, his devotional poems really cry out for re-evaluation. To a lesser extent the same thing is true for Robert Southwell, whose poem "The Burning Babe" is well-known but not much else. He wrote wonderfully intricate metaphysical poetry in the late

1590s, some of which shows the influence of Continental styles. Robert Persons is one of the most important prose writers of his day, widely learned, skilled in argument, theologically astute. He has barely gotten a mention in standard histories of the period. He also wrote an extremely popular devotional work, *The Christian Exercise* which was read, imitated, and even plagiarized, by Protestants. Many of the best works are in un-translated or partially translated Latin. I think of Philip O'Sullivan Beare, an Irish historian who writes partially out of his and his family's experiences in the war against the English (*Historiae Catholicae Iberniae Compendium* [History of Catholic Ireland]). He is worth reading for his own sake and as an antidote to Edmund Spenser's propaganda in *A View of the Present State of Ireland*. And there is also the glorious music of that Catholic composer, William Byrd.

Let me recommend some Byrd CDs to readers, and I hope listeners. The Cardinall's Musick in England released a uniform edition of Byrd's sacred music on ten disks between 1997 and 2006. The label is AVS. Gorgeous stuff. The budget minded will find some Byrd on Naxos's Early Music label, such as the masses for four and five voices. All are worth seeking out. Were there any contributions that broke your heart to cut for space, and where can we find them?

Yes, I continually had to make cuts and compromises. The Jesuit John Gerard's *Autobiography* (1609), his clash with Richard Topcliffe, the psychopathic priest hunter, and his dramatic escape from prison; Nicholas Roscarrock's writings on the lives of the saints in Cornwall and Devon (recently published by N. Orme,), which gives insight into regional practices and features such figures as Saint Endelient, virgin, and her sister, Saint Menfre. Gregory Martin's *Preface* to the Rheims New Testament is a little known but fascinating chapter in sacred philology, wrong I think in many respects but an articulate voice of opposition to Erasmus. There are lots of other things in manuscript, the letters of Henry Walpole, Jesuit martyr, and those of Anne Dacres Howard. Some poets were hard to lose: the Marian poet Miles Huggard, especially his dream vision *The Pathway to the Tower of Perfection* and his bird poem *The Mirror of Love*; William Forrest's praise of Catherine of Aragon, *Griseld the Second*, along with Laurence Vaux and Kenelm Digby. Earlier versions of the book included early modern statutes against Catholics and some decrees from the Council of Trent. Some of these items are available in Victorian editions, in publications from the Catholic Record Society, and in *Early English Books Online*.

To conclude the Catholic portion of our discussion, you wrote a well-deserved blistering review of a "Shakespeare was a Catholic" book called "The Canon-

ized Bones" that concluded with the wonderful statement, "Dante was a Catholic; Milton was a Protestant; Shakespeare was a *dramatist.*" *The emphasis is yours. The Catholic Shakespeare movement strikes me as less insane, but of a kind with the "Shakespeare was de Vere" and "Shakespeare was Marlowe" movements. Have you seen any sensible books on this?*

Yes, that review got some attention on television, radio, and in print and cyber space. Everyone is eager to claim the big prize, Shakespeare, for his or her own side and that results in lots of silliness. But there are some very good recent things in *Shakespeare Survey 54*, which includes essays from the Stratford Conference on "Shakespeare and Religion." Arthur Marotti (*Religious Ideology and Cultural Fantasy*), Phebe Jensen (*Religion and Revelry in Shakespeare's Festive World*), Alison Shell (*Catholicism, Controversy and the English Literary Imagination*), and Alexandra Walsham (*Church Papists*) have all written very valuable studies of the period. Some sensible works on Shakespeare and Catholicism that wisely avoid the biographical fallacies for an examination of religious traces and Catholic elements in Shakespeare's work are J. C. Mayer, *Shakespeare's Hybrid Faith: History,* and Beatrice Groves, *Texts and Traditions: Religion in Shakespeare 1592–1604.*

I should say that Phebe Jensen and I are not related, as far as I know. Which are the important books that brought discussion of Shakespeare and the Classical tradition to the point where you began work?

It was really the reading of classical authors themselves, Vergil, Homer, Seneca, Plautus, Ovid, the Greek tragedians, and Aristophanes that was decisive. John Velz's *Shakespeare and the Classical Tradition*, remarkably thorough and concise, was a call to work and a guide to what might be done in the field. I admired Reuben Brower's *Hero and Saint: Shakespeare and the Greco-Roman Heroic Tradition*, and Douglas Bush's *Mythology and the Renaissance Tradition in English Poetry.*

Should any of these still be read today, or has scholarship moved beyond them?

Well of course recent scholars have taught us many new things and many new ways to ask old questions. But studies born of real intelligence and hard work, such as these, stay useful.

You discuss a number of books about Rome published in Shakespeare's time that informed and sometimes misinformed early moderns about Rome. These works are important to grasping their understanding of Rome. Which are the most important of these?

Rome was a literary construct, made of thousands of references, myths, and legends, grammar school Latin, and scores of authors in translation:

Plutarch's *Lives*, Vergil's *Aeneid*, Ovid's *Metamorphoses*, Suetonius, Tacitus, and so on. So these are the best place to start, preferably in early modern translations, which give lots of clues to contemporary understanding and reception.

Shakespeare's Rome *was published 25 years ago. Who has written sensibly on the Roman theme and Rome based works? Who has added to your ideas, or argued with you with merit?*

Lots of folks have added to the picture, Coppélia Kahn (*Roman Shakespeare*) has re-examined the role of women in the Roman plays, Margaret Tudeau-Clayton (*Jonson, Shakespeare, and Early Modern Vergil*) has established a context for the reception and appropriation of Vergil, and Heather James, (*Shakespeare's Troy*) has explored the way cultural authority migrated from Troy to Rome to Britain. One book by Holderness, Loughrey, and Murphy came out a few years ago and reprinted part of my book as an example of old-fashioned, naïve criticism, insufficiently attuned to lit crit developments that came out years after its publication. (They never explained how I should have foreseen the future work in theory.) Anyway, they erroneously reprinted my essay under the name of Paul Cantor and that caused quite a flap, including some legal action, some interesting correspondence with my publisher, Cambridge UP, and some choice exchanges in *TLS*, the *Shakespeare Newsletter*, and the *shakspear* listserve.[2] Can't say I learned anything new about Shakespeare's Rome from that book and all that fuss, however.

I have chosen not to plug the Holderness book here. I read Seneca in the Penguin and the Loeb editions, but I have never been able to get into him. I realize the problem may be me, but can you recommend a translation that is perhaps more readable than these while being reasonably fair to the Latin?

Part of the problem is that Seneca is really much better in the original—mouth filling, lively, fun-to-say-out-loud Silver Age Latin. The Elizabethans knew that and enjoyed themselves immensely in oral declamation. I generally use the Loeb translations, partially because they provide the Latin right there to check against.

I've read a bit of Plautus in both Loeb and Penguin translations, but it never occurred to me to look for the roots of Hamlet *or* Lear *there.*

Shakespeare has a retentive, unpredictable memory for his reading. He may remember the pirate episode from Plutarch's *Julius Caesar* and put it in *Hamlet*; the story of Apollonius of Tyre from his early days with *The Comedy of Errors* and reuse it for the frame of *Pericles.* Phrases and plots and incidents from popular, biblical, classical, and contemporary works all go into the mix. And he is never very respectful of dramatic rules, arbitrary classifications, and generic boundaries. This latter quality greatly disturbed Voltaire and the neoclassical critics, but we are more likely to regard it as strength than a weakness. One gets the impression always of a very quick, associative mind, making all sorts of rapid connections without bothering much about literary proprieties. So comic subplots appear in the tragedies and tragic forms in the comedies. *King Lear* has great anti-pastoral scenes, as Maynard Mack explained in *King Lear in Our Time*. The histories are everywhere.

You could have easily written about As You Like It *with the "error" plays in* Shakespeare and Classical Comedy, *and* Love's Labour's Lost *might be a candidate for an intrigue play. Which of Shakespeare's other plays not discussed at length can be studied with profit using the ideas in that book?*

Yes, there are lots of other possibilities. I think I could have done a bit more with Plautine and Shakespearean romance, especially Plautus' *Rudens*, which Shakespeare's Globe staged a few years ago in a new translation. When I wrote the program notes for their season, I was struck by how suggestive and interesting a play it is. And I certainly think that the collaborations with John Fletcher can be reexamined.

Incidentally, the book I wish you'd write next is one where you do the same for Middleton, Lyly, Peele, Heywood, and others, some mentioned briefly in your work. My guess is that you are writing something else instead.

Yes, at the moment I have two projects: an edition of Ben Jonson's *The Case Is Altered* for the new Cambridge Ben Jonson. This Cambridge edition is a huge and complicated undertaking, very ably directed by Ian Donaldson, Martin Butler, and David Bevington, which aims to replace the monumental Herford and Simpson edition. It has taken many scholars and many years, but we can look for it (and its electronic archive) in 2010.[3] I am also editing *Hamlet* for Norton, losing sleep over the text but enjoying the rich critical and theatrical history. I found comments on *Hamlet* by two U.S. presidents, John Quincy Adams and Abraham Lincoln; some interesting handwritten observations in Edwin Booth's promptbook. I watched some silent films (Forbes-Robertson, 1913, and Asta Nielsen, 1920) and read some wild adaptations and parodies, everything from John Poole's nineteenth-century travesty *Hamlet Travestie in Three Acts* to *The Skinhead Hamlet* and *Green Eggs and Hamlet*. I also read some very revealing actor's accounts, including those of Michael Pennington (*Hamlet: A User's Guide*), John Gielgud (Rosamund Gilder's *John Gielgud's Hamlet: A Record of Performance*), and Richard Burton (R. L. Sterne's *John Gielgud Directs Richard Burton in Hamlet*).

The Skinhead Hamlet *was written by Richard Curtis.* Green Eggs and Hamlet *is anonymous. Let's go back to Jonson for a moment. I want to say with mock outrage, "Replace Herford and Simpson?" I have been aware of the forthcoming edition for years, and hope to interview one of the general editors when it becomes available, but I'll keep my beloved Herford and Simpson. It needs updating; too much has been learned and editing theory has changed over the decades, but just as you keep Chambers* The Elizabethan Stage, *you keep Herford and Simpson, edition of Jonson, or I do. This does bring us to something I've wondered about: editions must pay attention to singularities in a text, but generally speaking, do you need a different approach to editing Jonson than you do to editing Shakespeare?*

Interesting question. David Bevington emphasizes similarities first, the need for an editor of either to be sensitive to language change and theatrical practice, and the like, and to be consistent. Then one can go on to the differences. Jonson's early printed texts may reflect more closely his preferred spelling and punctuation practices than do Shakespeare's; he was more of a classicist (so he puns in Latin more), and his masques require special consideration. Jonson had an un-Shakespearean flair for self-dramatization, actually killed a fellow actor, propounded a version of himself in prefaces, and so on.

Shakespeare's Reading *is a fun book. Many people prepared the way for you. In fact, because of alphabetical accident, your book is to the left of Kenneth Muir's two volume* Shakespeare's Sources *on my shelf. I constantly find little pieces in* Notes and Queries *claiming that Shakespeare read this bit of Thomas Nashe or that bit of someone else. What would you add to your book if a new edition were offered, or would have added if space permitted?*

Well, Nashe is everywhere, as you suggest and as John Tobin has well shown, though most of the *NQ* stuff records verbal echo and near echo, the least interesting kind of evidence in my view. (By the way, am looking forward to reading Charles Nicholl on Nashe, *A Cup of News: The Life of Thomas Nash.*) I could have done more with the local dramatic scene, the plays in the company repertory and in rival repertories, which certainly constituted a kind of reading. I also would take a careful turn through Stuart Gillespie's Ashgate dictionary, *Shakespeare's Books: A Dictionary of Shakespeare's Sources*, to look for new leads. I am glad you mentioned Muir's work, which I regard as unsurpassed in its substance and concision. I told Oxford University Press at the outset that I did not think it likely that one could match that volume if one started from the same assumptions. My approach differed in that I included traditions as a viable category.

Let me make a plea for a smart publisher to reprint Nicholl's A Cup of News. *In the unlikely event you find a copy for sale, it is prohibitively expensive and interest in Nashe is very much ascending amongst Shakespeareans. Who has written most illuminatingly about* Macbeth?

Al Braunmuller, whose Cambridge edition is first rate through and through. He thinks about everything seriously and skeptically. I learned from the essays of Stephen Orgel and Peter Holland, which I was able to print in the volume. There is a good essay by David Norbrook on the play and its sources, but it was a bit dense for the readership ("*Macbeth* and the politics of historiography"). I learned a lot from Welcome Msomi's Zulu version, *Umabatha* (1971, revived 1997), a brilliant and poetic adaptation, as well as the films: Trevor Nunn's wonderfully spare version with Ian McKellen and Judi Dench,[4] Kurosawa's *Throne of Blood*, and William Reilly's *Men of Respect* (1991).

If I were doing another edition I would include more information on Ninagawa's adaptation (1980, with a second version in 2001), and the recent Patrick Stewart Chichester *Macbeth* (2007), which played to packed houses on both sides of the Atlantic and broke some new ground in interpretation.[5]

Whose books helped direct your career?

Classical texts and critics, at first. I wrote out a translation of Vergil's *Aeneid* while I was in graduate school, wholly under its spell. Vergil continually called me to a deeper engagement with Classics. Back then a number of classical critics were also formative. I was fortunate enough to hear Bernard Knox deliver an unforgettable lecture on Euripides' *Medea*; after hearing that, I knew I could not live without Greek so I set about learning it. Eventually I got to read the *Oresteia* with Knox in a graduate seminar at Johns Hopkins. Back then Michael Putnam's loving and careful book on Vergil's *Eclogues*, *Vergil's Pastoral Art*, opened up some of the wonders of Latin verse to me and taught me about close reading. Later I discovered Aristophanes, Sophocles, and Homer with Diskin Clay and the Cambridge commentaries on Homer; Euripides with Richard Hamilton, and W. S. Barrett's edition of *Hippolytus*, Ovid with Georg Luck and the Renaissance commentaries. In my first years of teaching I spent some lovely lunch hours reading Horace with a wonderful classicist, appropriately named Howard Marblestone. I remember his reading a gloss from one of the commentaries on *Nunc est bibendum, nunc pede libero/pulsanda tellus* ("Now is the time for drinking, now the time to beat the earth with free foot"), to the effect that "the ancients danced vigorously, having little use for the effete gliding that passes for dancing today." Wonderful fun, and in classics, one is a student, happily, always.

A selection of Latin commentaries on Ovid was edited and translated by Ann Moss. Which books influenced you the most?

Aside from the classical texts and scholars, Dante was primary from my undergraduate days at Fordham, though I did not have enough Italian then to read him in the original. Still, reading the *Vita Nuova* in translation was a formative experience thanks to the ministrations of a learned teacher, Paul Memmo, and Charles Singleton's luminous essay (*An Essay on the "Vita Nuova"*). I began to see that the slim and rarified book of sonnets and prose paragraphs actually celebrated a pure and ennobling love, one that would lead the lover eventually to the love that moves the circling stars. Singleton's commentary on the *Commedia* as well as Allen Mandelbaum's translation and commentary (*The Divine Comedy*) later continued my illumination. Shakespeare, I suppose, goes without saying. As for critics, Northrop Frye's *Anatomy of Criticism*, abstract and perceptive, spoke to me back then, as did Harry Levin, who wrote comparative literature studies with broad learning and effortless elegance (*The Question of Hamlet*; *The Overreacher: A Study of Christopher Marlowe*). Also, the edition of Donne's *Ignatius his Conclave: An Edition of the Latin and English Texts with Introduction and Commentary* by Timothy Healy, S.J., friend and mentor, taught me about real scholarship and started me thinking about the Catholic issues.

Later, I learned the most about editing from David Bevington, who was my general editor for both Jonson plays (*Every Man In* and *Case*). A learned and generous scholar, he set very high standards of precision and consistency, thought through every problem, and delighted in the work.

Name a Shakespeare book that is just plain fun.

I really enjoyed Ralph Cohen's *ShakesFear and How to Cure It!*, born out of years of mounting productions and establishing the creative American Shakespeare Center; the book is challenging, witty, funny, direct. Tiffany Stern's *Making Shakespeare: from Stage to Page*—is lively and learned and in its way comprehensive; *omnia insunt*, "it's all in there." She and Lukas Erne (*Shakespeare as Literary Dramatist*) and Sonia Massai (*Shakespeare and the Rise of the Editor*) belong to a new generation of scholars who are moving the profession past the sterile fixation with theory and back into archives and patient historical and theatrical research. It is an exciting time in Shakespeare and early modern studies. For a different kind of fun there is Charles Nicholl's books, *The Lodger: Shakespeare on Silver Street*, about Shakespeare's role in the Monjoy-Belott suit, and *The Reckoning: The Murder of Christopher Marlowe*, about Marlowe's death. Nicholl writes with real imagination and flair but he is a rock-solid researcher who has made an exhaustive study of primary sources and records, particularly manuscripts. And of course Michael Dobson is always a treat, especially his annual reviews of productions in *Shakespeare Survey 54–61* (2001–8).

Are any non-lit-crit books particularly enriching in your thinking and writing about Shakespeare and early modern theatre?

Histories, mainly, done by Tudor-Stuart historians and archivists—John Hungerford Pollen, who gathered important records in *Unpublished Documents Relating to English Martyrs*, and Eamon Duffy, who really inspired a lot of revisionist history with his *The Stripping of the Altars*, and the journal *Recusant History*, and the publications of the Catholic Record Society.

Are there any books you'd like to mention, but I lacked the wit to ask about?

Hamlet is much on my mind lately and I enjoyed Margreta de Grazia's brilliant "*Hamlet*" *without Hamlet*, which turns our attention to the broader dynastic picture, and away from our own obsessions with the main character; Tony Howard's study, *Women as Hamlet: Performance and Interpretation in Theatre, Film and Fiction* is a searching and revealing performance history. Dennis Kennedy's books (*Looking at Shakespeare* and *Foreign Shakespeare*) provide fascinating leads on global productions of Shakespeare and examples of cultural appropriation.

What needs are there crying out for a book that perhaps you don't want to write?

I can think of two things, not books but series, that need doing and that would inflect the profession for the better. And these would be well beyond the capacities, if not the wishes, of any single writer. The first is a collection of crucial Catholic texts in modern spelling editions. The facsimiles of the Catholic Record Society are wonderful but sometimes hard to get and even harder for students to understand. The second is a series on the early modern texts, commentaries, and translations of classical writers. The sort of thing that Julia Haig Gaisser has done for Catullus (*Catullus and his Renaissance Readers*) and for Apuleius (*The Fortunes of Apuleius and the Golden Ass*) could be enormously useful for understanding the period.

News of that do I long to hear. Bob, thanks for always translating the Greek and Latin for dummies like me, and for talking to me about these books. I also want to thank the Rev. Kent Winters-Hazelton for giving me permission to tell our story in that endless first question.

Notes

1. Bush, Douglas, *English Literature in the Earlier Seventeenth Century 1600–1660*, 2e (Oxford University Press, 1962), p. 147.
2. http://shaksper.net/
3. The seven-volume set was eventually published by Cambridge University Press in 2012.
4. This was produced for television.
5. This production was filmed for television in 2010.

Appendix: Films Referenced in the Interviews

Films with the same title are listed chronologically. Director's names follow the title. Because films are often financed by multiple production companies, only the lead production company is listed.

As You Like It, Christine Edzard, Sands Films, 1992.
Being Shakespeare, John Wyver, Illuminations, 2012.
The Children's Midsummer Night's Dream, Christine Edzard, Sands Films, 2001.
Chimes at Midnight (alternate title, *Falstaff*), Orson Welles, International Films, 1965.
Dead Again, Kenneth Branagh, Paramount, 1991.
Dr. Zhivago, David Lean, MGM, 1965.
Full Metal Jacket, Stanley Kubrick, Natant, 1987.
Gone with the Wind, Victor Fleming, Selznick International Pictures, 1939.
Hamburger Hill, John Irvin, RKO Pictures, 1987.
Hamlet, Cecil Hepworth, Gaumont, 1913.
Hamlet, Svend Gade, Art-Film, 1920.
Hamlet, Laurence Olivier, Two Cities, 1948.
Hamlet (original title: Гамлет), Grigori Kozintsev, Lenfilm, 1964.
Hamlet, Franco Zeffirelli, Nelson Entertainment, 1990.
Hamlet, Kenneth Branagh, Castle Rock Entertainment, 1996.
Hamlet, Michael Almereyda, Miramax Films, 2000.
Henry V, Kenneth Branagh, BBC Films, 1989.
Henry V, Laurence Olivier, Two Cities, 1944.
In the Bleak Midwinter (U.S. title: *A Midwinter's Tale*), Kenneth Branagh, Castle Rock Entertainment, 1995.
Julius Caesar, Joseph L. Mankiewicz, MGM, 1953.
King and the Playwright: A Jacobean History, The, three parts, Steven Clarke, BBC, 2012.
King Lear (original title: Король Лир), Grigori Kozintsev, Lenfilm, 1971.
King Lear, Peter Brook, Athéna Films, 1971.
King Lear, Richard Eyre, BBC, 1998.
Love's Labour's Lost, Kenneth Branagh, Miramax Films, 2000.
Macbeth, Roman Polanski, Playboy Productions, 1971.

Macbeth, Trevor Nunn and Philip Casson, Thames Television, 1979.
Macbeth, Gregory Doran, BBC, 2001.
Macbeth, Rupert Goold, BBC Four, 2010.
The Magnificent Seven, John Sturges, Mirisch Company, 1960.
Mary Shelley's Frankenstein, Kenneth Branagh, American Zoetrope, 1994.
Men of Respect, William Reilly, Columbia Pictures, 1991.
A Midsummer Night's Dream, Max Reinhardt and William Dieterle, Warner Bros., 1935.
A Midsummer Night's Dream, Adrian Noble, Capitol Films, 1996.
Much Ado About Nothing, Kenneth Branagh, BBC Films, 1993.
My Own Private Idaho, Gus Van Sant, Fine Line Features, 1991.
O, Tim Blake Nelson, Daniel Fried Productions, 2002.
Othello, Orson Welles, United Artists, 1952.
Platoon, Oliver Stone, Hemdale Film Corporation, 1986.
Richard III, Laurence Olivier, London Films, 1955.
Richard III, Richard Loncraine, Bayly / Paré Productions, 1995.
Romeo and Juliet, Franco Zeffirelli, BHE Films, 1968.
Scotland, PA, Billy Morrissette, Lot 47 Films, 2001.
Shakespeare in Love, John Madden, Universal Pictures, 1997.
10 Things I Hate About You, Gil Junger, Touchstone Pictures, 1999.
Throne of Blood (original title, 蜘蛛巣城), Akira Kurosawa, Toho, 1957.
Titus, Julie Taymor, Clear Blue Sky Productions, 2000.
Titus Andronicus, Lorn Richey, Lorn Richey Productions, 1997.
Titus Andronicus, Christopher Dunne, Joe Redner Film and Productions, 1999.
Titus Andronicus, Richard Griffin, South Main Street Productions, 2000.
The Wars of the Roses, a seven part television series, Michael Bogdanov, Portman Productions, 1990.
William Shakespeare's Romeo + Juliet, Baz Luhrman, Bazmark Productions, 1996.

Bibliography

Several "Talking Books" guests mentioned authors without the titles of their books or a series of books without giving specific titles. These titles have been supplied in this bibliography. The films mentioned in the interviews are listed in the Appendix.

The books that Robert S. Miola call the "Cambridge commentaries on Homer" are found under the names of the authors of this series: G. S. Kirk, Mark W. Edwards, Brian Hainsworth, Richard Janko, and Nicholas Richardson. According to Miola there is debate amongst classical scholars as to whether the Roman poet's name should be spelled Vergil or Virgil. Miola prefers Vergil and uses that spelling in our interview. Everybody has been given their preference—sometimes Vergil and sometimes Virgil.

Abbott, E. A., *Shakespearian Grammar: An Attempt to Illustrate Some of the Differences Between Elizabethan and Modern English* (London: Macmillan and Company, 1870).

Abrams, M. H., General Ed., *Norton Anthology of English Literature*, first edition (New York: W. W. Norton & Company, 1962).

Adamson, Sylvia, Lynette Hunter, Lynne Magnusson, et. al, *Reading Shakespeare's Dramatic Language: A Guide* (London: Arden, 2000).

Adelman, Janet, *Suffocating Mothers: Fantasies of Maternal Origin in Shakespeare's Plays, Hamlet to the Tempest* (London: Routledge, 1992).

Agate, James, *Brief Chronicles: A Survey of the Plays of Shakespeare and the Elizabethans in Actual Performance* (London: Jonathan Cape, 1943).

Alighieri, Dante, *The Divine Comedy*, Allen Mandelbaum, translator (New York: Alfred A. Knopf, 1980).

_____, *The Divine Comedy: Translated with a Commentary by Charles S. Singleton*, six volumes (Princeton: Princeton University Press, 1970–5).

_____, *La Vita Nuova*, Barbara Reynolds translator (Harmondsworth, U. K.: Penguin, 1969).

Altman, Joel B., "'Preposterous Conclusions': Eros, *Energeia*, and the Composition of *Othello*," *Representations* 18, Spring 1987, pp. 129–57.

_____, *Tudor Play of Mind: Rhetorical Inquiry and the Development of Elizabethan Drama* (Berkeley: University of California Press, 1978).

_____, 'Vile Participation': The Amplification of Violence in the Theatre of Henry V," *Shakespeare Quarterly*, 42:1, Spring 1991, pp. 1–32.

American Heritage Dictionary of the English Language, 4e (Boston: Houghton Mifflin, 2000).

Anderegg, Michael, "Branagh and the Sons of Ken," *Cinematic Shakespeare* (Lanham, MD: Rowman & Littlefield, 2004), pp. 123–6.

Anonymous, *Green Eggs and Hamlet*: http://physics.weber.edu/carroll/honors/GreenEggs.htm

_____, *The Lamentable Tragedy of Locrine* (London: 1595).

_____, *Look About You* (London, 1600).

_____, *A Most Pleasant Comedie of Mucedorus the King's sonne of Valentia* (London: 1610).
_____, *No-Body and Some-Body* (London: 1606).
_____, *The Trail of Treasure* (London: 1567).
_____, *The True Chronicle Historie of the whole life and death of Thomas Lord Cromwell* (London: 1602).
_____, *Vindiciae contra tyrannos* (Basil: 1579).
Apollonius Rhodius, *Argonautica* translated by William H. Race (Cambridge, MA: Loeb, 2009).
Arden, John, *Books of Bale* (London: Methuen, 1988).
Aristophanes, *Clouds, Wasps, Peace*, Jeffrey Henderson, translator (Cambridge MA: Loeb, 1998).
Armstrong, Edward A., *Shakespeare's Imagination: A Study in the Psychology of Association and Inspiration* (London: Lindsay Drummond, 1946).
Atwood, Margaret, *Cat's Eye* (New York: Knopf Doubleday, 1998).
Auden, W. H., *The Dyer's Hand: Essays* (New York: Random House, 1962).
_____, "The Sea and the Mirror," *The Collected Poetry of W. H. Auden* (New York: Random House, 1945), pp. 349–404.
Auerbach, Erich, *Mimesis: Dargestellte Wirklichkeit in der abendländischen Literatur* (Bern: A. Francke Verlag, 1946, English translation: *Mimesis: The Representation of Reality in Western Literature*, Princeton: Princeton University Press, 1953).
Bachelard, Gaston, *La Poétique de l'Espace* (Paris: Presses Universitaires de France, 1958, English translation: *The Poetics of Space* (Boston: Beacon Press, 1969).
Bacon, Delia, *The Philosophy of the Plays of Shakespeare Unfolded* (London: Groonbridge and Sons, 1857).
Bacon, Francis, "*The Advancement of Learning*," *Francis Bacon*, Brian Vickers, ed. (Oxford: Oxford University Press, 1996), pp. 120–229.
_____, *The Essays or Counsels Civil and Moral*, Brian Vickers, ed. (Oxford: Oxford University Press, 1999).
_____, *Francis Bacon*, Brian Vickers, ed. (Oxford: Oxford University Press, 2008).
_____, *The History of the Reign of King Henry VII: And Selected Works*, Brian Vickers, ed. (Cambridge: Cambridge University Press, 1998).
_____, "Of Tribute; Or, Giving That Which is Due," *Francis Bacon*, Brian Vickers, ed. (Oxford: Oxford University Press, 1996), pp. 22–51.
Bakeless, John, *The Tragicall History of Christopher Marlowe* (Hamden, Connecticut: Archon Books, 1964).
Baker, William, *Shakespeare: The Critical Tradition: The Merchant of Venice* (London: Continuum, 2005).
Baldwin, T. W., *Shakespeare's Small Latine & Lesse Greeke*, two volumes (Champaign, Illinois: University of Illinois Press, 1944).
Baldwin, William, and George Ferrers, eds., *The Mirror for Magistrates* (London, multiple editions 1559–1610).
Barber, C. L., *Shakespeare's Festive Comedy: A Study of Dramatic Form and its Relation to Social Custom* (Princeton: Princeton University Press, 1953).
Barber, C. L., and Richard P. Wheeler, *The Whole Journey: Shakespeare's Power of Development* (Berkeley: University of California Press, 1986).
Barish, Jonas A., *Ben Jonson and the Language of Prose Comedy* (New York: W. W. Norton and Company, Inc., 1960).
Barkan, Leonard, *The Antitheatrical Prejudice* (Berkeley: University of California Press, 1981).
_____, *The Gods Made Flesh: Metamorphous and the Pursuit of Paganism* (New Haven: Yale University Press, 1986).
Barker, Francis, and Peter Hulme, "'Nymphs and Reapers Heavily Vanish': The Discursive Con-texts of the *The Tempest*," *Alternative Shakespeares*, John Drakakis, ed. (London: Methuen, 1985), pp. 191–205.
Barker, Harley Granville, *Prefaces to Shakespeare*, two volumes (Princeton: Princeton University Press, 1946–7).
Barker, Richard Hindry, *Thomas Middleton* (New York: Columbia University Press, 1958).
Barton, Anne, *Ben Jonson, dramatist* (Cambridge: Cambridge University Press, 1984).
_____, "Byron and Shakespeare," *The Cambridge Companion to Lord Byron*, Drum-

mond Bone, ed. (Cambridge: Cambridge University Press, 2004), pp. 224–35.
_____, *Don Juan* (Cambridge: Cambridge University Press, 1992).
_____, *Essays, Mainly Shakespearean* (Cambridge: Cambridge University Press, 1994).
_____, "Introduction," *Hamlet* by William Shakespeare (New York: Penguin Books, 2002).
_____, *The Names of Comedy* (Toronto: University of Toronto Press, 1990).
_____, "Parks and Ardens," *Proceedings of the British Academy 80* (London: The British Adacemy, 1993), pp. 49–71.
_____, *Shakespeare and the Idea of the Play* (London: Chatto & Windus, 1962, written under the name Anne Righter).
_____, *The Shakespearean Forest* (Cambridge: Cambridge University Press, 2017).
Barton, Anne, and Eugene Giddens, eds., *The Sad Shepherd, The Cambridge Edition of the Works of Ben Jonson, Volume 7*, David Bevington, Martin Butler, Ian Donaldson, eds. (Cambridge: Cambridge University Press, 2012), pp. 417–80.
Bate, Jonathan, *Arden Shakespeare: Texts and Sources for Shakespeare Studies*, CD-ROM (London: Arden, 1996).
_____, *The Cure for Love* (New York: Picador, 1998).
_____, *The Genius of Shakespeare* (Oxford: Oxford University Press, 1998, tenth anniversary edition, 2008).
_____, *How the Classics Made Shakespeare* (Princeton: Princeton University Press, 2019).
_____, "Introduction," *Titus: The Illustrated Screenplay* by Julie Taymor (New York: Newmarket Press, 2000), pp. 6–16.
_____, *John Clare: A Biography* (New York: Farrar Straus & Giroux, 2003).
_____, *Romantic Ecology: Wordsworth and the Environmental Tradition* (London: Routledge, 1991).
_____, *Shakespeare and Ovid* (Oxford: Oxford University Press, 1994).
_____, *Shakespeare and the English Romantic Imagination* (Oxford: Oxford University Press, 1986).
_____, "A Shakespeare Tale Whose Time has Come," *New York Times*, 2 January 2000: http://www.nytimes.com/2000/01/02/movies/film-a-shakespeare-tale-whose-time-has-come.html
_____, *Shakespearean Constitutions: Politics, Theatre, Criticism 1730–1830* (Oxford: Oxford University Press, 1989).
_____, *The Song of the Earth* (Cambridge, MA: Harvard University Press, 2000).
_____, *Soul of the Age: A Biography of the Mind of William Shakespeare* (New York: Random House, 2009).
_____, *Ted Hughes: An Unauthorized Life* (New York: Harper, 2015).
Bate, Jonathan, ed., *John Clare: Selected Poems* (London: Faber & Faber, 2003).
_____, *Ovid's Metamorphosis*, Arthur Golding, translator (Philadelphia: Paul Dry Books, 2000).
_____, *Oxford English Literary History*, thirteen volumes (Oxford: Oxford University Press, 2002–14).
Bate, Jonathan, and Eric Rasmussen, eds., *The RSC Shakespeare: The Complete Works* (London: Palgrave, 2007).
_____, *William Shakespeare and Others: Collaborative Plays* (London: Palgrave, 2013).
Bate, Jonathan, Jill L. Levenson, and Dieter Mehl, eds., *Shakespeare in the Twentieth Century: The Selected Proceedings of the International Shakespeare Association World Congress, Los Angeles, 1996* (Newark: University of Delaware Press, 1998).
Bate, Jonathan, and Russell Jackson, eds., *Shakespeare: An Illustrated Stage History* (Oxford: Oxford University Press, 1996).
Beal, Peter, ed., *Index of English Literary Manuscripts*, two volumes (New Providence, NJ: R. R. Bowker, 1980 and 1993).
Beare, Philip O'Sullivan, *Historæ Catholicæ Ibernæ Compendium* (English title: *History of Catholic Ireland*, Vlyssippone: 1621).
Beaumont, Francis, *The Knight of the Burning Pestle*, Andrew Gurr, ed. (Edinburgh: Oliver & Boyd, 1968).
_____, *The Knight of the Burning Pestle*, Michael Hattaway, ed. (London: Unwin, 1968 and Bloomsbury, 2003).
Beaumont, Francis and John Fletcher, *The Maid's Tragedy*, Andrew Gurr, ed. (Edinburgh: Oliver & Boyd, 1969).
_____, *Philaster: or Love Lies A-Bleeding*, Andrew Gurr, ed. (Manchester: Manchester University Press, 2003).

Beckerman, Bernard, *Shakespeare at the Globe, 1599–1609* (New York: Collier Macmillan, Ltd., 1962).

_____, *Theatrical Presentation: Performer, Audience and Act* (London: Routledge, 1990).

Bednarz, James P., *Shakespeare and the Poets' War* (New York: Columbia University Press, 2001).

Beerbohm, Max, *Around Theatres* (New York: Taplinger Publishing Company, 1969).

Behn, Aphra, *Oroonoko, or the Royal Slave* (London: 1688).

Belsey, Cathernie, *The Subject of Tragedy: Identity and Difference in Renaissance Drama* (London: Routledge, 1985).

Bennett, Tony, *The Birth of the Museum* (London: Routledge, 1995).

Bentley, G. E., *The Jacobean and Caroline Stage*, seven volumes (Oxford: Oxford University Press, 1968).

Berger, Harry, *Imaginary Audition: Shakespeare on Stage and Page* (Berkeley: University of California Press, 1989).

Bevington, David, *Action Is Eloquence: Shakespeare's Language of Gesture* (Cambridge, MA: Harvard University Press, 1984).

_____, *From Mankind to Marlowe: Growth of Structure in the Popular Drama of Tudor England* (Cambridge, MA: Harvard University Press, 1962).

Bishop's Bible, The (London: 1568).

Blake, N. F., *A Grammar of Shakespeare's Language* (London: Palgrave, 2002).

Blayney, Peter W. M., "The Publication of Playbooks," *New History of Early English Drama*, John D. Cox and David Scott Kastan, eds. (New York: Columbia University Press, 1970), pp. 383–422.

_____, *The Stationers' Company and the Printers of London, 1501–1557*, two volumes (Cambridge: Cambridge University Press, 2013).

Bloom, Harold, *Anxiety of Influence: A Theory of Poetry* (Oxford: Oxford University Press, 1973).

Bohannan, Laura, "Shakespeare in the Bush," *Critical Essays on Shakespeare's Hamlet*, David Scott Kastan, ed. (Boston: G. K. Hall, 1995).

Boose, Lynda, "Scolding Brides, Bridling Scolds: Taming the Woman's Unruly Member," *Shakespeare Quarterly*, 42:2, Summer 1991, pp. 179–213.

Boose, Lynda E., and Richard Burt, eds., *Shakespeare the Movie: Popularizing the Plays on Film, TV, and Video* (London: Routledge, 1997).

Booth, Stephen, *King Lear, Macbeth, Indefinition and Tragedy* (New Haven: Yale University Press, 1983).

Booth, Wayne, *The Rhetoric of Fiction* (Chicago: University of Chicago Press, 1961).

Bordwell, David, and Kristin Thompson, *Film Art: An Introduction, 5e* (New York: McGraw-Hill, 1996).

Bowers, Fredson, *Textual and Literary Criticism* (Cambridge: Cambridge University Press, 1959).

Bowsher, Julian, *The Rose Theatre: An Archaeological Discovery* (London: Museum of London, 1998).

Boyd, Brian, *Nabokov's "Pale Fire": The Magic of Artistic Discovery* (Princeton: Princeton University Press, 1999).

Boyd, Brian, ed., *Words That Count: Essays on Early Modern Authorship in Honor of MacDonald P. Jackson* (Newark: University of Delaware Press, 2004).

Bradbrook, M. C., *Elizabethan Stage Conditions: A Study of Their Place in the Interpretation of Shakespeare's Plays* (Cambridge: Cambridge University Press, 1931).

_____, *The Rise of the Common Player: A Study of Actor and Society in Shakespeare's England* (Cambridge: Cambridge University Press, 1962).

_____, *Themes and Conventions of Elizabethan Tragedy* (Cambridge: Cambridge University Press, 1935).

Bradley, A. C., *Shakespearean Tragedy: Lectures on Hamlet, Othello, King Lear, Macbeth* (London: Macmillan and Co. Limited, 1904).

Bradshaw, Graham, *Misrepresentations: Shakespeare and the Materialists* (Ithaca, NY: Cornell University Press, 1993).

_____, *Shakespeare's Skepticism* (New York: St. Martin's Press, 1987).

Brahms, Caryl, and S. J. Simon, *No Bed for Bacon* (London: Michael Joseph, 1941).

Bräker, Ulrich, *A Few Words about William Shakespeare's Plays*, Derek Bowman, translator (New York: Continuum, 1979).

Braunmuller, A. R., and Michael Hattaway, eds. *The Cambridge Companion to English renaissance Drama, 2e* (Cambridge: Cambridge University Press, 2003).

Bristol, Michael, *Shakespeare's America; America's Shakespeare* (London: Routledge & Kegan Paul, 1990).

British Library Shakespeare Quarto Archive: http://www.bl.uk/treasures/shakespeare/homepage.html

Brockbank, Philip (unnumbered volume), Russell Jackson and Robert Smallwood (volumes 2 and 3), and Robert Smallwood (volumes 4–6), *Players of Shakespeare*, 6 volumes (Cambridge: Cambridge University Press, 1985–2004).

Brogan, T. V. F., *English Versification, 1570–1980: A Reference Guide with a Global Appendix* (Baltimore: Johns Hopkins University Press, 1981).

Brook, Peter, *The Empty Space: A Book About the Theatre: Deadly, Holy, Rough, Immediate* (New York: Atheneum, 1968).

Brooke, C. F. Tucker, *The Shakespeare Apocrypha: Being a Collection of Fourteen Plays Which Have Been Ascribed to Shakespeare* (Oxford: Oxford University Press, 1908, reprinted 1967).

Brooke, Nicholas, "Romeo and Juliet," *Shakespeare's Early Tragedies* (London: Methuen, 1968, reprinted 1973), pp. 80–106.

Brooks, Cleanth, and Robert Penn Warren, *Understanding Poetry: An Anthology*, four editions (Henry Holt and Company, 1938–76).

Brower, Reuben A., *Hero and Saint: Shakespeare and the Greco Roman Heroic Tradition* (Oxford: Oxford University Press, 1971).

Brown, John Russell, *Shakespeare in Performance: An Introduction Through Six Major Plays* (New York: Harcourt Brace Jovanovich, 1967).

Bruster, Douglas, review may be accessed here: http://www.academia.edu/22529387/Review_of_Steven_May_and_William_Ringler_A_Bibliography_and_First-line_Index_of_English_Verse_1559-1603_

Brydon, Diana, and Irena R. Makaryk, *Shakespeare in Canada: A World Elsewhere* (Toronto: University of Toronto Press, 2002).

Buchanan, Judith, *Shakespeare on Film* (London: Routledge, 2005).

Bullough, Geoffrey, *Narrative and Dramatic Sources of Shakespeare*, eight volumes (New York: Columbia University Press, 1957–1975).

Bulman, James C., ed., *Shakespeare in Performance: The Merchant of Venice* (Manchester: Manchester University Press, 1991).

_____, *Shakespeare, Theory and Performance* (London: Routledge, 1996).

Burke, Kenneth, *Counter-Statement* (Berkeley: University of California Press, 1931).

Burnett, Mark Thornton, and Ramona Wray, eds., *Shakespeare on Screen in the Twenty-First Century* (Edinburgh: Edinburgh University Press, 2006).

Burt, Richard, *Unspeakable ShaXXXspeares: Queer Theory & American Kiddie Culture* (New York: St. Martin's Press, 1998).

Burton, Robert, *Some Anatomies of Melancholy, What it is with All the Kinds, Causes, Symptoms, Prognistickes, and Several Cures of it* (Oxford: 1621).

Bush, Douglas, *Mythology and the Renaissance Tradition in English Poetry*, revised edition (New York: W. W. Norton & Company, 1963).

Callow, Simon, *Charles Laughton: A Difficult Actor* (London: Methuen, 1987).

Candido, Joseph, ed., *Shakespeare: The Critical Tradition: King John* (London: Continuum, 1996).

Capell, Edward, *Notes and Various Reading to Shakespeare*, three volumes (London: 1779–1783).

Carr, Virginia Mason, *Drama as Propaganda: A Study of the Troublesome Raigne of King John*, two editions (Salzburg: Universität Salzburg, 1974, reprinted by Lewiston, NY: Edwin Mellen Press, 2002).

Carroll, William C., *Fat King, Lean Beggar: Representations of Poverty in the Age of Shakespeare* (Ithaca, NY: Cornell University Press, 1996).

Cervantes, Miguel de, *El Ingenioso Hidalgo Don Quijote de la Mancha*, two parts (English title: *The Aventures of Don Quixote*, Madrid: 1605 and 1615).

Chambers, E. K., *The Disintegration of Shakespeare* (Oxford: Oxford University Press, 1924).

_____, *The Elizabethan Stage*, four volumes (Oxford: Oxford University Press, 1923).

_____, *The Medieval Stage*, two volumes (Oxford: Oxford University Press, 1903).

_____, *William Shakespeare: A Study of Facts and Problems*, two volumes (Oxford: Oxford University Press, 1930).

Champion, Larry S., *The Noise of Threatening Drum: Dramatic Strategy and Political Ideology in Shakespeare and the English Chronicle Plays* (Newark: University of Delaware Pres, 1990).

Chapman, George, *Homer's Iliad*, Robert S. Miola, ed. (Cambridge: Modern Humanities Research Association, 2017).

Charlton, H. B., *Romeo and Juliet as an Experimental Tragedy* (Folcroft, PA: Folcroft Library Editions, 1933).

Cheney, Patrick, *Shakespeare, National Poet-Playwright* (Cambridge: Cambridge University Press, 2004).

_____, *Shakespeare's Literary Authorship* (Cambridge: Cambridge University Press, 2008).

Cheney, Patrick, ed., *The Cambridge Companion to Shakespeare's Poetry* (Cambridge: Cambridge University Press, 2007).

Chernaik, Warren, *The Cambridge Introduction to Shakespeare's History Plays* (Cambridge: Cambridge University Press, 2007).

Clare, John, *John Clare: Selected Poems*, Jonathan Bate, ed. (London: Faber & Faber, 2003).

Clarke, Mary Cowden, *The Girlhood of Shakespeare's Heroines: A Series of Tales* (New York: A. C. Armstrong & Son, 1879).

Clemen, Wolfgang, *The Development of Shakespeare's Imagery*, two editions (London: Methuen, 1951 and 1977).

_____, *English Tragedy Before Shakespeare: The Development of Dramatic Speech* (London: Methuen, 1961).

Cocklin, James N., ed., *Shakespeare in Production: Romeo and Juliet* (Cambridge: Cambridge University Press, 2002).

Cohen, Ralph Alan, *ShakesFear and How to Cure It!*, two editions (Smyrna, DE: Pestwick House, 2007 and London: Bloomsbury, 2018).

Coleridge, Samuel Taylor, *Coleridge on Shakespeare: The Text of the Lectures 1811–12*, R. A. Foakes, ed. (Detroit: Wayne State University Press, 1989, reprint London: Routledge, 2004).

_____, *Coleridge's Criticism of Shakespeare*, R. A. Foakes, ed. (London: Athlone Press, 1989).

_____, *Lectures, 1809–1819, On Literature*, two volumes, R. A. Folkes, ed. (Princeton: Princeton University Press, 1987).

Colie, Rosalie L., "*Othello* and the Problematics of Love," *Shakespeare's "Living Art"* (Princeton: Princeton University Press, 1974), pp. 135–67.

Cordner, Michael, and Peter Holland, eds., *Redefining British Theatre History: Players, Playwrights, Playhouses: Investigating Performance, 1660–1800* (London: Palgrave, 2007).

Coursen, H. R., "Searching for *Hamlet*: Branagh's Film," *Shakespeare: The Two Traditions* (Madison, NJ: Fairleigh Dickson University Press, 1999), pp. 216–37.

Cox, John D., and David Scott Kastan, *New History of Early English Drama* (New York: Columbia University Press, 1997).

Craig, Hugh, "George Chapman, John Davies of Hereford, William Shakespeare, and 'A Lover's Complaint,'" *Shakespeare Quarterly*, 63:2, January 2012, pp. 147–174.

_____, "The 1602 Additions to *The Spanish Tragedy*," *Shakespeare, Computers and the Mystery of Authorship*, Hugh Craig and Arthur Kinney, eds. (Cambridge: Cambridge University Press, 2009), pp. 162–80.

Crashaw, Richard, *Steps to the Temple. Sacred Poems, with Other Delights of the Muses* (London: 1646).

Creaser, John W., ed., *Volpone: or, the Fox* by Ben Jonson (New York: New York University Press, 1978).

Crosby, Joseph, and Joseph Parker Norris, *One Touch of Shakespeare: Letters of Joseph Crosby and Joseph Parker Norris*, John W. Velz and Francis N. Teague, eds. (Washington D.C.: Folger Shakespeare Library, 1986).

Crowl, Samuel, "Chain Reaction: A Study of Roman Polanski's *Macbeth*," *Soundings: A Journal of Interdisciplinary Studies*, 59:2, Summer 1976. pp. 226–33.

_____, *The Films of Kenneth Branagh* (Santa Barbara, CA: Praeger, 2006).

_____, "Flamboyant realist: Kenneth Branagh," *The Cambridge Companion to Shakespeare on Film, 2e,* Russell Jackson, ed. (Cambridge: Cambridge University Press, 2007).

_____, "The Marriage of Shakespeare and Hollywood: Kenneth Branagh's *Much Ado About Nothing,*" *Spectacular Shakespeare: Critical Theory and Popular Cinema,* Courtney Lehmann and Lisa S. Starks, eds. (Madison, NJ: Fairleigh Dickinson University Press, 2002), pp. 110–24.

_____, *Shakespeare at the Cineplex: The Kenneth Branagh Era* (Athens: Ohio University Press, 2006).

_____, *Shakespeare Observed: Studies in Performance on Stage and Screen* (Athens: Ohio University Press, 1992).

_____, *Shakespeare on Film: A Norton Guide* (New York: W. W. Norton and Company, 2007).

_____, *Shakespeare's Hamlet: The Relationship Between the Text and the Film* (London: Arden, 2014).

_____, "A world elsewhere: The Roman plays on film and television," *Shakespeare and the Moving Image: The plays on film and television,* Anthony Davies and Stanley Wells, eds. (Cambridge: Cambridge University Press, 1994), pp. 146–62.

Crystal, David, and Ben Crystal, *Shakespeare's Words: A Glossary and Language Companion* (London: Penguin, 2002).

Cummings, Peter, "Hamlet to Ophelia," *In a Fine Frenzy: Poets Respond to Shakespeare,* David Starkey and Paul J. Willis, eds. (Iowa City: University of Iowa Press, 2005), p. 129.

_____, "Sonnets on Shakespeare's Sonnets," *Shakespeare Newsletter,* 51:3, Fall 2001, p. 61.

Cunningham, Andrew, and Ole Peter Grell, *The Four Horsemen of the Apocalypse: Religion, War, Famine and Death in Reformation Europe* (Cambridge: Cambridge University Press, 2000).

Curtis, Richard, *Skinhead Hamlet*: http://web.mit.edu/johanna/Public/skinhead.hamlet

Danby, John F., *Shakespeare's Doctrine of Nature: A Study of King Lear* (London: Faber & Faber, 1961).

Dane, Clement, *Will Shakespeare: An Invention in Four Acts* (London: Heinemann, 1921).

Dash, Irene G., *Wooing, Wedding, and Power: Women in Shakespeare's Plays* (New York: Columbia University Press, 1981).

David, Richard, *Shakespeare in the Theatre* (Cambridge: Cambridge University Press, 1978).

Davidson, Donald, "What Metaphors Mean," *Philosophical Perspectives on Metaphor,* Mark Johnson, ed. (Minneapolis: University of Minnesota Press, 1978), pp. 200–20.

Davies, Anthony, *Filming Shakespeare's Plays: The Adaptations of Laurence Olivier, Orson Welles, Peter Brook and Akira Kurosawa* (Cambridge: Cambridge University Press, 1990).

Davies, Anthony, and Stanley Wells, eds., *Shakespeare and the Moving Image* (Cambridge: Cambridge University Press, 1994).

Davies, Helen D., and Michael P. Jensen, *Alzheimer's: The Answers You Need* (Forest Knolls, CA: Elder Books, 1998).

Davies, Matthew, and Ann Saunders, *The History of the Merchant Taylors' Company* (Leeds, UK: Maney Publishing, 2004).

Davis, Natalie Zemon, *Trickster Travels: A Sixteenth-Century Muslim Between Worlds* (New York: Hill and Wang, 2006).

Davis, Tracy C., and Peter Holland, *Redefining British Theatre History: The Performing Century: Nineteenth-Century Theatre's History* (London: Palgrave, 2007).

Dawson, Anthony B., *Indirections: Shakespeare and the Art of Illusion* (Toronto: University of Toronto Press, 1978).

_____, *Shakespeare in Performance: Hamlet* (Manchester: Manchester University Press, 1995).

_____, *Watching Shakespeare: A Playgoers Guide* (New York: St. Martin's Press, 1988).

Dawson, Anthony B., and Philip Yachnin, *The Culture of Playgoing in Shakespeare's England: A Collaborative Debate* (Cambridge: Cambridge University Press, 2001).

Day, Gilian, *Shakespeare at Stratford: King Richard III* (London: Arden Shakespeare, 2002).

Delius, Nicholas, *Die Tieck'sche Shake-*

spearekritik (Cologne, Germany: König, 1846).

Dent, R. W., *John Webster's Borrowing* (Berkeley: University of California Press, 1960).

_____, *Shakespeare's Proverbial Language: An Index* (Berkeley: University of California Press, 1981).

Dessen, Alan C., *Elizabethan Drama and the Viewer's Eye* (Chapel Hill: University of North Carolina Press, 1977).

_____, *Elizabethan Stage Conventions and Modern Interpreters* (Cambridge: Cambridge University Press, 1984).

_____, *Jonson's Moral Comedy* (Evanston, IL: Northewstern University Press, 1971).

_____, *Recovering Shakespeare's Theatrical Vocabulary* (Cambridge: Cambridge University Press, 1995).

_____, *Rescripting Shakespeare: The Text, the Director, and Modern Productions* (Cambridge: Cambridge University Press, 2002).

_____, *Shakespeare and the Late Moral Plays* (Lincoln: University of Nebraska Press, 1986).

_____, *Shakespeare in Performance: Titus Andronicus* (Manchester: Manchester University Press, 1989).

Dessen, Alan C., and Leslie Thomson, *A Dictionary of Stage Directions in English Drama 1580–1642* (Cambridge: Cambridge University Press, 1999).

Diehl, Huston, *Staging Reform, Reforming the Stage: Protestantism and Popular Theater in Early Modern England* (Ithaca, NY: Cornell University Press, 1997).

Digby, Kenelm, *Discours sur la vegetation des plantes* (Paris: 1667).

Dobson, Michael, and Nicola J. Watson, *England's Elizabeth: An Afterlife in Fame and Fantasy* (Oxford: Oxford University Press, 2002).

Dobson, Michael, and Stanley Wells, eds., *Oxford Companion to Shakespeare* (Oxford: Oxford University Press, 2001).

Dolan, Frances E., *Marriage and Violence: The Early Modern Legacy* (Philadelphia: University of Pennsylvania Press, 2008).

Dollimore, Jonathan, *Radical Tragedy: Religion, Ideology and Power in the Drama of Shakespeare and His Contemporaries* (Chicago: University of Chicago Press, 1984).

Dollimore, Jonathan, and Alan Sinfield, *Political Shakespeare: New Essays in Cultural Materialism* (Manchester: University of Manchester Press, 1985).

Donaldson, Peter S., *Shakespearean Films/ Shakespearean Directors* (London: Unwin and Hyman, 1990).

Donne, John, *Ignatius his Conclave*, Timothy Healy, S.J., ed. (Oxford: Oxford University Press, 1969).

Doran, Madeleine, *Endeavors of Art: A Study of Form in Elizabethan Drama* (Ann Arbor, MI: Bell & Howell Information & Learning, 1954).

Dostoevsky, Fyodor, Преступлéние и наказáние (English title: *Crime and Punishment*) (serialized 1866, first English translation by Frederick Whishaw, London: 1885).

Drakakis, John, *Alternative Shakespeares* (London: Routledge, 2002).

Dryden, John, *All for Love: Or The World well Lost* (London: 1678).

Duffin, Ross W., *Shakespeare's Songbook* (New York: W. W. Norton and Company, 2004).

Duffy, Eamon, *The Stripping of the Altars: Traditional Religion in England, c. 1400–c. 1580* (New Haven: Yale University Press, 1992).

Duncan-Jones, Katherine, "Leader of the Media Pack," *Times Literary Supplement*, 14 October 2005, p. 20.

_____, *Portraits of Shakespeare* (Oxford: Bodleian Library, 2015).

_____, *Shakespeare: from Upstart Crow to Sweet Sawn: 1592–1623* (London: Arden, 2011).

_____, *Shakespeare's Life and World* (London: The Folio Society, 2004).

_____, *Sir Philip Sidney: Courtier Poet* (New Haven: Yale University Press, 1991).

_____, *Ungentle Shakespeare: Scenes from His Life* (London: Arden, 2001).

_____, "Who Wrote *A Funerall Elegye*?" *Shakespeare Studies 25*, 1997, pp. 192–210.

Dunn, Esther Cloudman, *Shakespeare in America* (New York: Macmillan, 1939).

Dusinberre, Juliet, ed., *Shakespeare and the Nature of Women*, two editions (Basingstoke, UK: Macmillan, 1975 and 1996).

Dutton, Richard, "The Birth of the Author," *Texts and Cultural Change in Early*

Modern England, Cedric Brown and Arthur Marotti, eds. (Houndmills, UK: Palgrave, 1997), pp. 153–78.

Ebisch, Walther, and Levien Ludwig Schücking, *A Shakespeare Bibliography* (Oxford: Oxford University Press, 1931), with a *Supplement*, two editions (Oxford: Oxford University Press, 1936 and 1964).

Edmondson, Paul, and Stanley Wells, *Shakespeare's Sonnets* (Oxford: Oxford University Press, 2004).

Edmondson, Paul, and Stanley Wells, eds., *The Shakespeare Circle: An Alternate Biography* (Cambridge: Cambridge University Press, 2015).

Elam, Keir, *The Semiotics of Theatre and Drama, 2e* (London: Routledge, 2002).

Eliot, T. S., *On Poetry and Poets* (New York: Farrar, Straus, Cudahy, 1957).

_____, *Selected Essays* (New York: Harcourt, Brace & Company, 1950).

Elliott, Ward, and Robert J. Valenza, "Did Shakespeare Write 'A Lover's Complaint'? The Jackson Ascription Revisited," *Words That Count*, Brian Boyd, ed. (Newark: University of Delaware Press, 2004), pp. 117–140.

Ellmann, Richard, *The Identity of Yeats, 2e* (New York: Oxford University Press, 1964).

_____, *James Joyce* (New York: Oxford University Press, 1959).

_____, *Yeats: The Man and the Masks* (New York: Dutton, 1948).

Empson, William, *Seven Types of Ambiguity*, three editions (London: Chatto and Windus, 1930–1953).

_____, *Some Versions of Pastoral* (London: Chatto & Windus, 1935).

_____, *The Structure of Complex Words* (Norfolk, CT: New Dimensions, 1951).

Erne, Lukas, *Beyond* The Spanish Tragedy*: A Study of the Works of Thomas Kyd* (Manchester: Manchester University Press, 2001).

_____, "Biography, Mythography and Criticism: The Life and Works of Christopher Marlowe," *Modern Philology*, 103:1, August, 2005, pp. 28–50.

_____, *Shakespeare and the Book Trade* (Cambridge: Cambridge University Press, 2013).

_____, *Shakespeare as Literary Dramatist*, two editions (Cambridge: Cambridge University Press, 2003 and 2013).

_____, *Shakespeare's Modern Collaborators* (New York: Continuum, 2007).

Erne, Lukas, and Devani Singh, eds., *Belvedere, or the Garden of the Muses: An Early Modern Commonplace Book* (Cambridge: Cambridge University Press, forthcoming).

Erne, Lukas, Florence Hazrat, and Maria Shmygol, eds., *Early Modern German Shakespeare, Volume Two* (to be determined).

Erne, Lukas, and Guillemette Bolens, eds., *The Limits of Textuality* (Tübingen, Germany: G. Narr, 2000).

_____, *Medieval and Early Modern Authorship* (Tübingen, Germany: G. Narr, 2011).

Erne, Lukas, and Kareen Seidler, eds., *Early Modern German Shakespeare, Volume One* (to be determined).

Erne, Lukas, and Margaret Jane Kidnie, eds. *Textual Performances: The Modern Reproduction of Shakespeare's Drama* (Cambridge: Cambridge University Press, 2004).

Euripides, *Hippolytus*, W. S. Barrett, ed. (Oxford: Oxford University Press, 1964).

Eyre, Richard, *National Service: A Diary of a Decade* (London: Bloomsbury, 2003).

Farabee, Darlene, Mark Netzloff, and Bradley D. Reyner, ed., *Early Modern Drama in Performance* (Newark: University of Delaware Press, 2014).

Farnham, Willard, *The Medieval Heritage of Elizabethan Tragedy* (Berkeley: University of California Press, 1936).

Faulkner, William, *The Sound and the Fury* (New York: Jonathan Cape and Harrison Smith, 1929).

Fineman, Joel, *Shakespeare's Perjured Eye: The Invention of Poetic Subjectivity in the Sonnets* (Berkeley: University of California Press, 1986).

Fiorentino, Giovanni, *Il Pecorne* (Milan: 1558).

Flatter, Richard, *Shakespeare's Producing Hand: A study of his marks of expression to be found in the First folio* (London: Heineman, 1948).

Fleay, F. G., *Shakespeare Manual* (London: Macmillan, 1876).

Fletcher, John, *The Woman's Prize*, Lucy Munro, ed. (Manchester: Bloomsbury Publishing, 2014).

Fletcher, John, and Philip Massinger, *The Sea Voyage* (London: 1622).

Foakes, R. A., *Hamlet verses Lear: Cultural Politics and Shakespeare's Art* (Cambridge: Cambridge University Press, 1993).

_____, *Illustrations of the English Stage, 1580–1642* (Stanford, CA: Stanford University Press, 1985).

_____, *Marston and Tourneur* (Harlow, UK: Longman, 1978).

_____, "The Player's Passion: Some Notes on Elizabethan Psychology and Acting," *Essays and Studies 7*, 1954, pp. 62–77.

_____, *Shakespeare and Violence* (Cambridge: Cambridge University Press, 2003).

_____, *Shakespeare: from the Dark Comedies to the Last Plays: from Satire to Celebration* (Charlottesville: University of Virginia Press, 1971, reprint London: Routledge, 2004).

Foakes, R. A., and Mary Foakes, *The Columbia Dictionary of Quotations from Shakespeare* (New York: Columbia University Press, 1998).

Folger Shakespeare Library Digital Editions: http://www.folgerdigitaltexts.org

Ford, John, *The Chronicle History of Perkin Warbeck. A Strange Truth* (London: 1634).

_____, *The Collected Works of John Ford, Vol. 1*, G. D. Monsarrrat, Brian Vickers, and R. J. C. Watt, eds. (Oxford: Oxford University Press, 2012).

_____, *The Collected Works of John Ford, Volumes 2 and 3*, Brian Vickers, ed. (Oxford: Oxford University Press, 2017).

Forker, Charles R., *Skull Beneath the Skin: The Achievement of John Webster* (Champaign: University of Illinois Press, 1986).

Forker, Charles R., ed., *Shakespeare: The Critical Tradition: Richard II* (London: Continuum, 1998).

Forrest, William, *The History of Griseld the Second*, Rev. W. D. McCray, ed. (London: 1875).

Forsyth, Neil, *The Satanic Epic* (Princeton: Princeton University Press, 2002).

Foster, Donald W., *Elegy by W. S.: A Study in Attribution* (Newark: University of Delaware Press, 1989).

Fraser, Russell, *Shakespeare, the Later Years* (New York: Columbia University Press, 1992).

_____, *Young Shakespeare* (New York: Columbia University Press, 1988).

Freed, Amy, *The Beard of Avon* (New York: Samuel French, 2004).

Frye, Northrop, *Anatomy of Criticism* (Princeton: Princeton University Press, 1957).

_____, "The Argument of Comedy," *The English Institute Essays: 1948*, D. A. Robertson, ed. (New York: Columbia University Press, 1949), pp. 58–73.

_____, *Fables of Identity: Studies in Poetic Mythology* (New York: Harcourt, Brace, and World, 1963).

_____, *Fools of Time: Studies in Shakespearean Tragedy* (Toronto: University of Toronto Press, 1967).

_____, *A Natural Perspective: The Development of Shakespearean Comedy and Romance* (New York: Columbia University Press, 1988).

Frye, Susan, *Elizabeth I: The Competition for Representation* (Oxford: Oxford University Press, 1996).

Gabrieli, Vittorio, and Giorgio Melchiori, eds., *Sir Thomas More* by Anthony Munday and others (Manchester: Manchester University Press, 1990).

Gaiman, Neil and various artists, *Sandman*, seventy-five issues (New York: Vertigo Comics, 1989–1996).

Gaisser, Julia Haig, *Catullus and His Renaissance Readers* (Oxford: Oxford University Press, 1993).

_____, *The Fortunes of Apuleius and the Golden Ass* (Princeton: Princeton University Press, 2008).

Geckle, Georg L., *Shakespeare: The Critical Tradition: Measure for Measure* (London: Continuum, 2001).

The Geneva Bible (Geneva, Switzerland, 1560).

Geneva Bible: The Bible of the Protestant Reformation, 1560 Edition, Berry, Lloyd E., ed. (Peabody, MA: Henderickson Publishers, 2007).

George, David, *Shakespeare: The Critical Tradition: Coriolanus* (Bristol, England: Continuum, 2004).

Gerard, John, *The Autobiography of a Hunted Priest* (San Francisco: Igantius Press, 2012).

_____, *Autobiography of an Elizabethan*, Philip Caraman, S. J., translator (London: Longmans, 1951).

Gervinus, Georg Gottfried, *Shakespeare*, four volumes (Leipzig: Wilhelm Engelmann, 1849–52).

Gibbons, Brian, *Jacobean City Comedy: A Study of Satiric Plays by Jonson, Marston and Middleton*, two editions (London: Methuen, 1968 and 1980).

Gibbs, Wolcott, "Ring Out, Wild Bells," *The New Yorker*, 4 April 1936, p. 21.

Gilbert, Miriam, *Shakespeare in Performance: Love's Labour's Lost* (Manchester: Manchester University Press, 1993).

Gilder, Rosamund, *John Gielgud's Hamlet: A Record of Performance* (London: Methuen, 1937).

Gillespie, Stuart, *Shakespeare's Books: A Dictionary of Shakespeare's Sources* (Burlington, VT: Ashgate, 2001).

Godschalk, William, "The Texts of *Troilus and Cressida*," *Early Modern Literary Studies* 1.2, August 1995, http://extra.shu.ac.uk/emls/01-2/godsshak.html.

Goldman, Michael, "Marlowe and the Histrionics of Ravishment," *Two Renaissance Mythmakers, Christopher Marlowe and Ben Jonson (Selected Papers from the English Institute: 1973–76)*, Alvin Kernan, ed. (Baltimore: Johns Hopkins University Press, 1977), pp. 22–40.

Graves, R. B., *Lighting the Shakespearean Stage, 1567–1642* (Carbondale, Southern Illinois University Press, 1999).

Grazia, Margreta de, *"Hamlet" without Hamlet* (Cambridge: Cambridge University Press, 2007).

Greenblatt, Stephen, *Learning to Curse: Essays in Early Modern Culture* (London: Routledge, 1992).

_____, "Marlowe and Renaissance Self-fashioning," *Two Renaissance Mythmakers, Christopher Marlowe and Ben Jonson (Selected Papers from the English Institute: 1973–76)*, Alvin Kernan, ed. (Baltimore: Johns Hopkins University Press, 1977), pp. 41–69.

_____, *Renaissance Self-fashioning: From More to Shakespeare* (Chicago: University of Chicago Press, 1980).

_____, *Shakespearean Negotiations: The Circulation of Social Energy in Renaissance England* (Berkeley: University of California Press, 1988).

_____, *Will in the World: How Shakespeare Became Shakespeare* (New York: W. W. Norton & Company, 2004).

Greenblatt, Stephen, General Ed., *Norton Anthology of English Literature, 9e* (New York: W. W. Norton & Company, 2006).

Greenblatt, Stephen, Walter Cohen, Jean E. Howard, et. al, eds., *The Norton Shakespeare, 2e* (New York: W. W. Norton & Company, 2008).

Greenblatt, Stephen, Walter Cohen, Suzanne Gossett, et. al, eds., *The Norton Shakespeare, 3e* (New York: W. W. Norton & Company, 2015).

Greene, Gayle, and Coppélia Kahn, eds., *Making a Difference: Feminist Literary Criticism* (London: Routledge, 1990).

Greene, Thomas, *The Light in Troy: Imitation and Discovery in Renaissance Poetry* (New Haven: Yale University Press, 1982).

Greg, W. W., *A Bibliography of the English Printed Drama to the Restoration*, four volumes (London: Bibliographical Society, 1939–59).

_____, *The Shakespeare First Folio, Its Bibliographical and Textual History* (Oxford: Oxford University Press, 1955).

_____, "The Works of Thomas Kyd" *Modern Language Quarterly*, 1901, pp. 185–90.

Grigely, Joseph, *Textualterity: Art, Theory and Textual Criticism* (Ann Arbor: University of Michigan Press, 1995).

Griswold, Wendy, *Renaissance Revivals: City Comedy and Revenge Tragedy in the London Theatre, 1576–1980* (Chicago: University of Chicago Press, 1986).

Gross, John, *After Shakespeare: An Anthology* (Oxford: Oxford University Press, 2003).

Groves, Beatrice, *Texts and Traditions: Religion in Shakespeare 1592–1604* (Oxford: Oxford University Press, 2007).

Gunerante, Antony R., "'Thou Dost Usurp Authority': Beerbohm Tree, Reinhardt, Olivier, Welles, and the Politics of Adapting Shakespeare," *A Concise Companion to Shakespeare on Screen*," Diana E. Henderson, ed. (Malden, MA: Blackwell Publishing, 2006), pp. 31–53.

Gurr, Andrew, "Maximal and Minimal Texts: Shakespeare v. the Globe," *Shakespeare Survey 52* (Cambridge: Cambridge University Press, 1999), pp. 68–87.

_____, *Playgoing in Shakespeare's London*, three editions (Cambridge: Cambridge University Press, 1987–2004).

_____, *Rebuilding Shakespeare's Globe* (London: Orion Publishing, 1989).

_____, *The Shakespeare Company, 1592–1642* (Cambridge: Cambridge University Press, 2004).

_____, *The Shakespearean Playing Companies* (Oxford: Oxford University Press, 1996).

_____, *The Shakespearean Stage, 1574–1642, 4e* (Cambridge: Cambridge University Press, 2009).

_____, *Shakespeare's Hats* (Rome: Piccoli Libri, 1993).

_____, *Shakespeare's Opposites: The Admiral's Company 1594–1625* (Cambridge: Cambridge University Press, 2012).

_____, *William Shakespeare: His Life and Times* (Glasgow: Collins, 1995).

_____, *Writers in Exile: The Identity of Home in Modern Literature* (Brighton: Harvester Press, 1981).

Gurr, Andrew, and Angus Calder, eds., *Writers in East Africa* (Nairobi: East African Literature Bureau, 1973).

Gurr, Andrew, and Farah Karim-Cooper, eds., *Moving Shakespeare Indoors: Performing and Repertoire in the Jacobean Playhouse* (Cambridge: Cambridge University Press, 2014).

Gurr, Andrew, and Mariko Ichikawa, *Staging in Shakespeare's Theatres* (Oxford: Oxford University Press, 1996).

Gurr, Andrew, and Pio Zimiru, eds., *Black Aesthetics* (Nairobi: East African Literature Bureau, 1973).

Gurr, Andrew, J. R. Mulryne, and Margaret Shewring, *The Design of the Globe: Conclusions from the Archaeological Evidence for Shakespeare's Globe Theatre* (Warwick, UK: International Shakespeare Globe Center, 1993).

Halio, Jay L., *Shakespeare in Performance: A Midsummer Night's Dream* two editions (Manchester: Manchester University Press, 1995 and 2003).

Hall, Edward, *The Union of the Two Noble and Illustre Families of Lancaster and York* (London: 1584).

Hanson, Clare, and Andrew Gurr, *Katherine Mansfield* (Houndmills, UK: Palgrave, 1981).

Hapgood, Robert, *Shakespeare the Theatre-Poet* (Oxford: Oxford University Press, 1988).

Harbage, Alfred, *As They Liked It: A Study of Shakespeare's Moral Artistry* (New York: Harper Torchbooks, 1947, reprinted 1961).

_____, *Shakespeare and the Rival Traditions* (London: Macmillan, 1952).

Harbage, Alfred, and S. Schoenbaum, *Annals of English Drama, 975–1700, an Analytical Record of All Plays, Extant or Lost, Chronologically Arranged and Indexed by Authors, Titles and Dramatic Companies* (London: Methuen, 1964, and with supplement, 1970).

Harp, Richard, "Jonson's late plays," *The Cambridge Companion to Ben Jonson*, Richard Harp and Stanely Steward, eds. (Cambridge: Cambridge University Press, 2000), pp. 90–102.

Harris, Jonathan Gil, and Natasha Korda, *Staged Properties in Early Modern English Drama* (Cambridge: Cambridge University Press, 2002).

Harrison, Robert Pogue, *The Body of Beatrice* (Baltimore: Johns Hopkins University Press, 1988).

_____, *The Dominion of the Dead* (Chicago: University of Chicago Press, 2003).

_____, *Forests: The Shadow of Civilization* (Chicago: University of Chicago Press, 1992).

Hart, Alfred, *Stolne and Surreptitious Copies: A Comparative Study of Shakespeare's Bad Quartos* (Melbourne: Melbourne University Press, 1942).

Hatchuel, Sarah, and Nathalie Vienne-Guerrin, *Shakespeare on Screen: A Midsummer Night's Dream* (Rouen, France: Publications de l'Université de Rouen, 2004).

Hattaway, Michael, "'By Indirections Find Directions Out': Shakespeare, His Restoration Adapters, and Early Modern Myths of Nature," *Cahiers élisabéthains*, 2016, pp. 1–16.

_____, "The comedies on film," *The Cambridge Companion to Shakespeare on Film, 2e*, Russell Jackson, ed. (Cambridge:

Cambridge University Press, 2007), pp. 87–101.

_____, *The Critics Debate: Hamlet* (Atlantic Highlands, NJ: Macmillian, 1987).

_____, *Elizabethan Popular Theatre: Plays in Performance* (London: Routledge & Keegan Paul, 1983).

_____, "'Enter Celia, the Fairy Queen, in her Night Attire': Shakespeare and the Fairies," *Shakespeare Survey 65* (Cambridge: Cambridge University Press, 2013), pp. 26–41.

_____, "'I've processed my guilt': Shakespeare, Branagh, and the Movies," *Shakespeare and the Twentieth Century: The Selected Proceedings of the International Shakespeare Association World Congress Los Angeles, 1996*, Jonathan Bate, Jill L. Levenson, and Dieter Mehl, eds. (Newark: University of Delaware Press, 1998), pp. 194–214.

_____, "Lands, Realms, Women, and Texts: Possession, Entitlement, and Occupation," *Cahiers élisabéthains*, 94:2, March 2018, pp. 2–21.

_____, "Reading Early Modern Theatrical Performance and a Skimmington at Horn Fair: Evidence from Sibiu," *East-West Cultural Passage16*, 2016, pp. 36–65.

_____, *Renaissance and Reformation: An Introduction to Early Modern English Literature* (Oxford: Basil Blackwell, 2005).

_____, "Re-Shaping *King Lear*: Space, Place, Costume and Genre," *Linguaculture*, 8.1, 2017, pp. 9–22.

Hattaway, Michael, ed., *The Cambridge Companion to Shakespeare's History Plays* (Cambridge: Cambridge University Press, 2003).

_____, *A Companion to English Renaissance Literature and Culture*, two editions (Oxford: Basil Blackwell, 2000 and 2010).

Hattaway, Michael, Boika Sokolova, and Derek Roper, eds., *Shakespeare in the New Europe* (Sheffield, UK: Sheffield Academic Press, 1995).

Hawkes, Terence, *That Shakespeherian Rag: essays on a critical process* (London: Methuen, 1986).

Hawkins, Harriett, *The Devil's Party: Critical Counter-interpretations of Shakespearian Drama* (Oxford: Oxford University Press, 1985).

Hazlitt, William, *Table-Talk: or, Original Essays*, two volumes (London: John Warren, 1821–2).

Hedrick, Donald, "War is Mud: Branagh's Dirty Harry V and the Types of Political Ambiguity," *Shakespeare, The Movie, 2e*, Lynda Boose and Richard Burt, eds. (London: Routledge, 2003), pp. 213–30.

Heilman, Robert B., *Magic in the Web: Action and Language in Othello* (Lexington: University of Kentucky Press, 1956).

Helgerson, Richard, *Self-Crowned Laureates: Spenser, Jonson, Milton and the Literary System* (Berkeley: University of California Press, 1983).

Henderson, Diana E., *A Concise Companion to Shakespeare on Screen* (Oxford: Blackwell, 2006).

Henslow, Philip, *The Henslowe Papers*, R. A. Foakes, ed. (London: Scholar Press, 1977).

_____, *Henslowe's Diary*, R. A. Foakes and R. T. Rickert, eds. (Cambridge: Cambridge University Press, 1961).

_____, *Henlsowe's Diary, 2e*, R. A. Foakes, ed. (Cambridge: Cambridge University Press, 2002).

Heywood, Thomas, *The English Traveller* (London: 1633).

Highfall, Philip J., Jr., Kalman A. Burnim, and Edward A. Langhans, *Biographical Dictionary of Actors, 1600–1800*, sixteen volumes (Carbondale: Southern Illinois University Press, 1973–1993).

Hinman, Charlton, *The Printing and Proof-Reading of the First Folio of Shakespeare*, two volumes (Oxford: Oxford University Press, 1963).

_____, ed., *The Norton Facsimile: The First Folio of Shakespeare* (New York: W. W. Norton & Company, 1968).

Hobday, Charles, "Why the Sweets Melted: A Study in Shakespeare's Imagery," *Shakespeare Quarterly* 16.1, Winter 1965, pp. 3–17.

Hodgdon, Barbara, "Bride-ing the Shrew: Costumes that Matter," *Shakespeare Survey 60* (Cambridge: Cambridge University Press, 2007), pp. 72–83.

_____, *The End Crowns All: Closure and Contradiction in Shakespeare's History* (Princeton: Princeton University Press, 1991).

_____, "'Here Apparent': Photography, History, and The Theatrical Unconscious"

Textual and Theatrical Shakespeare: Questions of Evidence, Edward Pechter, ed. (Iowa City: University of Iowa Press, 1996), pp. 181–209.

_____, "Inoculating the Old Stock: Shakespearean Chorographies," *Renaissance Drama 34*, 2005, pp. 3–30.

_____, "New Collaborations with Old Plays: The (Textual) Politics of Performance Commentary," *Textual Performances: The Modern Reproduction of Shakespeare's Drama*, Lukas Erne and Margaret Jane Kidnie, eds. (Cambridge: Cambridge University Press, 2004), pp. 210–23.

_____, "Photography, Theatre, Mnemonics; or Thirteen Ways of Looking at a Still," *Theorizing Pratice: Redefining Theatre History*, W. B. Worthen with Peter Holland, eds. (London: Palgrave, 2003), pp. 88–119.

_____, "Reincarnations," *Remaking Shakespeare: Performance Across Media, Genres and Cultures*, Pascale Aebischer, Edward J. Esche, and Nigel Wheale, eds. (London: Palgrave, 2003), pp. 190–209.

_____, "Sexual Disguise and the Theatre of Gender," *The Cambridge Companion to Shakespearean Comedy*, Alexander Leggatt, ed. (Cambridge: Cambridge University Press, 2002), pp. 179–197.

_____, *Shakespeare in Performance: Henry IV, Part Two* (Manchester: Manchester University Press, 1993).

_____, *Shakespeare, Performance and the Archive* (Abingdon, UK: Routledge, 2016).

_____, *The Shakespeare Trade: Performances and Appropriations* (Philadelphia: University of Pennsylvania Press, 1998).

_____, "Shopping in the Archives: Material Mnemonics," *Remembering Shakespeare, Memory, Performance*, Peter Holland, ed. (Cambridge: Cambridge University Press, 2006), pp. 135–67.

Hodgdon, Barbara, and W. B. Worthen, eds., *A Companion to Shakespeare in Performance* (Oxford: Basil Blackwell, 1993).

Hodges, Walter, *The Globe Restored: A Study of the Elizabethan Theatre* (London: Ernest Benn Ltd., 1953).

Hoenselaars, Ton, ed., *Shakespeare and the Language of Translation*, two editions (London: Arden, 2004 and 2012).

Holdsworth, Roger V., "Middleton and Shakespeare: The Case for Middleton's Hand in *Timon of Athens*" (Ph.D. thesis, University of Manchester, 1982).

Holinshed, Raphael, *The Chronicles of England, Scotland, and Ireland*, two volumes (London: 1577).

Holland, Peter, "Beginning in the Middle," (London: The British Academy, 2000), https://www.britac.ac.uk/pubs/proc/files/111p127.pdf

_____, *English Shakespeares: Shakespeare on the English Stage in the 1990s* (Cambridge: Cambridge University Press, 1997).

_____, "Film Editing," *Shakespeare Performed: Essays in Honor of R. A. Foakes*, Grace Ioppolo, ed. (Newark: University of Delaware Press, 2000), pp. 273–98.

_____, "Forgetting Performance," *The Oxford Handbook of Shakespeare and Performance*, James C. Bulman, ed. (Oxford: Oxford University Press, 2017), pp. 170–83.

_____, *The Ornament of Action: Text and Performance in Restoration Comedy* (Cambridge: Cambridge University Press, 1979, reissued 2010).

_____, "'Stands Scotland Where It Did?': The Location of *Macbeth* on Film," William Shakespeare, *Macbeth, 2e*, Robert S. Miola, ed. (New York: W. W. Norton & Company, 2014), pp. 270–94.

_____, *William Shakespeare* (Oxford: Oxford University Press, 2007).

Holland, Peter, ed., *Great Shakespeareans, Volume II, Garrick, Kemble, Siddons, Kean* (London: Bloomsbury, 2010).

_____, *Great Shakespeareans, Volume XVIII, Brook, Hall, Ninagawa, Lepage* (London: Bloomsbury, 2013).

Holland, Peter, and Stephen Orgel, eds., *Redefining British Theatre History: From Performance to Print in Shakespeare's England, Volume 1* (London: Palgrave, 2006).

_____, *Redefining British Theatre History: From Script to Stage in Early Modern England, Volume 2* (London: Palgrave, 2004).

Holland, Peter, and W. B. Worthen, eds., *Redefining British Theatre History: Theorizing Practice, Volume 3* (London: Palgrave, 2003).

Holm, Ian, *Acting My Life* (New York: Bantam, 2004).

Holmes, Martin, *Shakespeare and His Players* (London: John Murray, 1972).

Holste, Gayle, " Branagh's *Love's Labour's Lost*: Too Much, Too Little, Too Late, *Literature/Film Quarterly*, 30:3, 2002, pp. 228–30.

Honan, Park, *Shakespeare: A Life* (Oxford: Oxford University Press, 2000).

Honigmann, Ernst, *Shakespeare: The Lost Years* (Manchester: Manchester University Press, 1985).

_____, *The Stability of Shakespeare's Texts* (Lincoln: University of Nebraska Press, 1965).

Hooper-Greenhill, Eilean, *Museums and the Shaping of Knowledge* (London: Routledge, 1992).

Hope, Jonathan, *The Authorship of Shakespeare's Plays: A Socio-Linguistic Study* (Cambridge: Cambridge University Press, 1994).

_____, *Shakespeare's Grammar* (London: Arden, 2003).

Hopkirk, Peter, *The Great Game: On Secret Service in High Asia* (London: John Murray, 1990).

Hornblower, Simon, and Antony Spawforth, eds., *The Oxford Classical Dictionary, 3e* (Oxford: Oxford University Press, 2003).

Hosley, Richard, *La reconstruction du Théâtre du Swan* (Éditions du Centre national de la recherche scientifique, 1963).

Houseman, A. E., "The Application of Thought to Textual Criticism," *Proceedings of the Classical Association*, August 1921, vol. XVIII.

Houston, John Porter, *Shakespearean Sentences: A Study in Style and Syntax* (Baton Rouge: Louisiana State University Press, 1988).

Howard, Jean, "The New Historicism in Renaissance Studies," *English Literary Renaissance* 16:1, December 1986, pp. 13–43.

_____, *The Stage and Social Struggle in Early Modern England* (London: Routledge, 1993).

_____, *Theater of a City: The Places of London Comedy, 1598–1542* (Philadelphia: University of Pennsylvania Press, 2006).

Howard, Jean E., and Phyllis Rackin, *Engendering a Nation: A Feminist Account of Shakespeare's English Histories* (London: Routledge, 1997).

Howard, Tony, *Women as Hamlet: Performance and Interpretation in Theatre, Film and Fiction* (Cambridge: Cambridge University Press, 2007).

Hoy, Cyrus, "The Shares of Fletcher and His Collaborators in the Beaumont and Fletcher Canon," seven parts in *Studies in Bibliography* volumes 8 and 9 and 11–15, 1956–62.

Huffman, Clifford Chalmers, and John W. Velz, *The Rape of Lucrece, Titus Andronicus, Julius Caesar, Antony and Cleopatra, and Coriolanus: An Annotated Bibliography of Shakespeare Studies 1910–2000* (Fairview, NC: Pegasus Press, 2002).

Huggard, Miles, *The Mirrour of Love* (London: 1555).

_____, *The Pathway to the Tower of Perfection* (London: 1556).

Hulme, Peter, "Hurricane in the Caribbees: The Constitution of the Discourse of English Colonialism," *1642: Literature and Power in the Seventeenth Century*, Francis Barker, Jay Bernstein, John Coombes, et al., eds. (Wivenhoe Park, Clocheste, UK: University of Essex, 1981), pp. 55–83.

_____, "Stormy Weather: Misreading the Postcolonialist Tempest" *Early Modern Culture 3*, 2003, pp. 1–22.

Hulme, Peter, and William H. Sherman, eds., *"The Tempest" and its Travels* (Islington, UK: Reakton Books, 2000).

Hunter, G. K., *John Lyly: The Humanist as Courtier* (Cambridge, MA: Harvard University Press, 1962).

_____, *Oxford History of English Literature, English Drama 1586–1642: The Age of Shakespeare* (Oxford: Oxford University Press, 1997).

Hunter, Lynette, Lynne Magnusson, Sylvia Adamson, eds., *Reading Shakespeare's Dramatic Language, a Guide* (London: Arden, 2000).

Hyman, Stanley Edgar, *Iago: Some Approaches to the Illusion of His Motivation* (New York: Anthemeum, 1970).

Ichikawa, Mariko, *Shakespearean Entrances* (London: Palgrave, 2002).

Ingram, W. G., and Theodore Redpath, eds. *Shakespeare's Sonnets*, two editions (London: University of London Press, 1964, and London: Hodder and Stoughton, 1978).

Ingram, William, *The Business of Playing: The Beginning of the Adult Professional Theatre in Elizabethan London* (Ithaca, NY: Cornell University Press, 1992).

Ioppolo, Grace, ed., *Shakespeare Performed: Essays in Honor of R. A. Foakes* (Plainsboro Township, NJ: Associated University Press, 2000).

Jackson, MacDonald P., *Defining Shakespeare:* Pericles *as Test Case* (Oxford: Oxford University Press, 2003).

_____, *Determining the Shakespeare Canon:* Arden of Facersham *& "A Lover's Complaint"* (Cambridge: Cambridge University Press, 2014).

_____, "Shakespeare and the Quarrel Scene in Arden of Faversham," *Shakespeare Quarterly*, 57:3, Fall 2006, pp. 249–93.

_____, *Shakespeare's A Lover's Complaint: its date and authenticity, University of Auckland Bulletin* 72, English Series 13, 1965.

_____, *Studies in Attribution: Middleton and Shakespeare* (Salzburg: Institut für Anglistik und Amerikanistik, Universität Salzburg, 1979).

_____, *Who Wrote "The Night Before Christmas"?: Analyzing the Clement Clarke Moore vs. Henry Livingston Question* (Jefferson, NC: McFarland, 2016).

Jackson, Russell, *Cambridge Companion to Shakespeare on Film*, two editions (Cambridge: Cambridge University Press, 2000 and 2007).

James, Heather, *Shakespeare's Troy: Drama, Politics and the Translation of Empire* (Cambridge: Cambridge University Press, 2007).

James, Henry, *What Maisie Knew* (London: Heinemann, 1897).

Jensen, Michael P., "Finding Shakespeare: Brian Vickers vs. the Attributers," *Shakespeare Newsletter*, 53:3, Fall 2003, pp. 67–8, 70, 72, 74, 83–4, 86, 92.

_____, "Fragments of a *Dream*: Photos of Three Scenes Missing from the Reinhardt-Dieterle *Dream*," *Shakespeare Bulletin*, 16:4, Fall 2000, pp. 37–8.

_____, "Mel Gibson on Hamlet," *Shakespeare on Film Newsletter*, 15:2, April 1991, pp. 1–2, and 12.

Jensen, Mike, "Essays, Mainly Shakespearean," *Small Press*, 12:4, Fall 1994, p. 74.

Jensen, Phebe, *Religion and Revelry in Shakespeare's Festive World* (Cambridge: Cambridge University Press, 2009).

Johnson, Samuel, ed., *The Dramatic Works of William Shakespeare: from the Corrected Edition of Isaac Reed, Esq. with Copious Annotations, Volume 1* (London: J. Walker, G. Offor, Sharpe and Sons, 1820), pp. 85–6.

Jones, Emrys, *Origins of Shakespeare* (Oxford: Oxford University Press, 1977).

_____, *Scenic Form in Shakespeare* (Oxford: Oxford University Press, 1971).

Jones, John, *Shakespeare at Work* (Oxford: Oxford University Press, 1995).

Jonson, Ben, *The Alchemist* (London, 1612).

_____, *Ben Jonson*, eleven volumes, C. H. Herford, Percy Simpson, and Evelyn Simpson, eds. (Oxford: Oxford University Press, 1925–52).

_____, *Every Man in his Humor: Quarto Version*, Robert S. Miola, ed. (Manchester: Manchester University Press, 2000).

_____, *The New Inn*, Michael Hattaway, ed. (Manchester: Revels, 1984).

_____, *Volpone: or, the Fox*, John W. Creaser, ed. (New York: New York University Press, 1978).

_____, *The Workes of Beniamin Jonson* (London: 1616).

Jorgens, Jack, *Shakespeare on Film* (Bloomington: Indiana University Press, 1977).

Joseph, Sister Miriam, *Shakespeare's Use of the Arts of Language* (New York: Columbia University Press, 1947).

Kahan, Jeffrey, *Bettymania and the Birth of Celebrity Culture* (Bethlehem, PA: Lehigh University Press, 2010).

_____, *The Cult of Kean* (Burlington, VT: Ashgate, 2006).

_____, *Getting Published in the Humanities: What to Know, Where to Aim, How to Succeed* (Jefferson, NC, McFarland, 2011).

_____, *Reforging Shakespeare* (Plainsboro, NJ: Associated University Presses, 1998).

_____, *Shakespiritualism: Shakespeare and the Occult, 1850–1950* (London: Macmillan, 2013).

Kahan, Jeffrey, ed., *Imitations, Parodies and Forgeries, 1710–1820*, 3 volumes (New York: Routledge, 2004)

Kahn, Coppélia, *Man's Estate: Masculine*

Identity in Shakespeare (Berkeley: University of California Press, 1981).

_____, *Roman Shakespeare: Warriors, Wounds and Women* (London: Routledge, 1997).

Kantorowicz, Ernst H., *The King's Two Bodies: A Study in Medieval Political Theology* (Princeton: Princeton University Press, 1957).

Karp, Ivan, Christine Mullen Kreamer, and Steven D. Lavine, eds., *Museums and Communities: The Politics of Public Culture* (Washington D.C.: Smithsonian Institution Press, 1992).

Kastan, David Scott, "'The Duke of Milan/ And His Brave Son': Dynastic Politics in *The Tempest*," *Critical Essays on* Shakespeare's The Tempest, Virginia Mason Vaughan and Alden T. Vaughan, eds. (Boston: G. K. Hall and Co., 1998), pp. 91–103.

_____, *A Companion to Shakespeare* (Oxford: Basil Blackwell, 1999).

Kathman, David, "Grocers, Goldsmiths, and Drapers: Freemen and Apprentices in the Elizabethan Theater" *Shakespeare Quarterly*, 55:1, Spring 2004, pp. 1–49.

_____, "Reconsidering *The Seven Deadly Sins*," *Early Theatre* 7:1, 2004, pp. 13–44.

Katz, David S., *Philo-Semitism and the Readmission of the Jews to England, 1603–1655* (Oxford: Oxford University Press, 1982).

_____, *Sabbath and Sectarianism in Seventeenth-Century England* (Leiden, Netherlands: E. J. Brill, 1988).

Kaul, Mythili, ed., *Othello: New Essays by Black Writers* (Washington D.C.: Howard University Press, 1997).

Keats, John, *Letters of John Keats*, Robert Gittings, ed. (Oxford: Oxford University Press, 1970).

Kennedy, Dennis, *Foreign Shakespeare: Contemporary Performance* (Cambridge: Cambridge University Press, 1995).

_____, *Looking at Shakespeare: A Visual History of Twentieth-Century Performance*, two editions (Cambridge: Cambridge University Press, 1993 and 2001).

Kennedy, Judith M., and Richard F. Kennedy, *Shakespeare: The Critical Tradition: A Midsummer Night's Dream* (London: Continuum, 1999).

Kenner, Hugh, *The Pound Era* (Berkeley: University of California Press, 1971).

Kermode, Frank, *The Classic: Literary Images of Permanence and Change* (Cambridge, MA: Harvard University Press, 1983).

_____, *The Sense of an Ending: Studies in the Theory of Fiction* (Oxford: Oxford University Press, 1967).

_____, *Shakespeare's Language* (New York: Farrar, Straus, Giroux, 2000).

Kernan, Alvin, ed., *Two Renaissance Mythmakers, Christopher Marlowe and Ben Jonson (Selected papers from the English Institute; 1975–76)* (Baltimore: Johns Hopkins University Press, 1977).

Kerrigan, John, *Revenge Tragedy from Aeschylus to Armageddon* (Oxford: Oxford University Press, 1996).

Kidnie, Margaret Jane, "Text, Performance and the Editors' Staging Shakespeare's Drama," *Shakespeare Quarterly* 51:4, Winter 2000, pp. 456–73.

Kingsolver, Barbara, *The Poisonwood Bible* (New York: HaprerCollins, 1998).

Kirk, G. S., General ed., *The Iliad: A Commentary*, six volumes (Cambridge: Cambridge University Press, 1985–1993).

Kittay, Eva F., and Adrienne Lehrer, "Semantic Fields and the Structure of Metaphor," *Studies in Language 5* (1981) pp. 31–63.

Kliman, Bernice W., *Shakespeare in Performance: Macbeth*, two editions (Manchester: Manchester University Press, 1992 and 2004).

Knight, G. Wilson, *The Crown of Life: Essays in Interpretation of Shakespeare's Final Plays* (Oxford: Oxford University Press, 1947).

_____, *The Shakespearian Tempest* (Oxford: Oxford University Press, 1932).

_____, *The Wheel of Fire: Interpretations of Shakespearian Tragedy*, two editions (Oxford: Oxford University Press, 1930 and 1949).

Knights, L.C., *Drama and Society in the Age of Jonson* (London: Chato and Windus, 1937).

_____, *Some Shakespearean Themes* (Stanford, CA: Stanford University Press, 1959).

Knowles, Ric, *Reading the Material Theatre* (Cambridge: Cambridge University Press, 2004).

Knutson, Roslyn Lander, *The Repertory of Shakespeare's Company* (Fayetteville: University of Arkansas Press, 1991).

Kökeritz, Helge, *Shakespeare's Pronunciation* (New Haven: Yale University Press, 1953).

Koon, Helene Wickham, *How Shakespeare Won the West: Players and Performances in America's Gold Rush, 1849–1865* (Jefferson, NC: McFarland, 1989).

Kott, Jan, *Shakespeare our Contemporary* (New York: Doubleday, 1964).

Kuhn, Thomas, *The Structure of Scientific Revolutions*, two editions (Chicago: University of Chicago Press, 1962 and 1970).

Kyd, Thomas, *The First Part of Hieronimo* (London, 1605).

_____, *The Spanish Tragedy*, David Bevington, ed. (Manchester: Revels, 1996).

_____, *The Spanish Tragedy,* Philip Edwards, ed. (Manchester: Revels, 1959).

_____, *The Spanish Tragedy*, J. R. Mulryne, ed. (New Mermaids, revised edition, 1989).

_____, *The Works of Thomas Kyd*, Frederick S. Boas, ed. (Oxford: Oxford University Press, 1901).

Kyd, Thomas (attributed), *Soliman and Perseda*, Lukas Erne, ed. (Manchester: Malone Society, 2014).

Lake, David J., *The Canon of Thomas Middleton's Plays* (Cambridge: Cambridge University Press, 1975).

Lakoff, George, and Mark Johnson, *Metaphors We Live By* (Chicago: University of Chicago Press, 1980).

Langbaum, Robert, *The Poetry of Experience: The Dramatic Monologue in Modern Literary Tradition* (New York: Random House, 1957).

Langer, Susanne, *Feeling and Form: A Theory of Art* (New York: Charles Scribner's Sons, 1953).

_____, *Philosophy in a New Key: A Study in the Symbolism of Reason, Rite, and Art* (Cambridge, MA: Harvard University Press, 1942).

Langley, Russell, *Practical Statistics for Non-Mathematical People* (London: Pan Books, 1968).

Lanier, Douglas M., "Shakescorp *Noir*," *Shakespeare Quarterly*, 53:2, Summer 2002, pp. 157–80.

_____, "Shakespeare on the Record," *A Companion to Shakespeare and Performance*, Barbara Hodgdon and W. B. Worthen, eds. (Oxford: Blackwell Publishing, 2005), pp. 415–36.

_____, *Shakespeare and Modern Popular Culture* (Oxford: Oxford University Press, 2002).

la Primaudaye, Pierre de, *L'Academie Française* (Paris: 1577). English translation, *French Academy*, Thomas Bowes, translator (London: 1586).

Leavis, F. R., *Revaluation, Tradition & Development in English Poetry* (New York: W. W. Norton and Company, 1947).

Leggatt, Alexander, *Citizen Comedy in the Age of Shakespeare* (Toronto: University of Toronto Press, 1973).

_____, *Shakespeare in Performance: King Lear* (Manchester: Manchester University Press, 1991).

Lehmann, Courtney, *Shakespeare Remains: Theatre to Film, Early Modern to Postmodern* (Ithaca, NY: Cornell University Press, 2002).

Lehmann, Courtney and Lisa S. Starks: eds., *Spectacular Shakespeare: Critical Theory and Popular Cinema* (Madison, NJ: Farleigh Dickinson University Press, 2002).

Lenz, Carolyn Ruth Swift, Gayle Greene, and Carol Thomas Neely, *The Woman's Part: Feminist Criticism of Shakespeare* (Champaign, University of Illinois Press, 1980).

Levenson, Jill L., "'Alla stoccado carries it away': Codes of Violence in *Romeo and Juliet*," *Romeo and Juliet: Texts, Contexts, and Interpretation*, Jay L. Halio, ed. (Newark: University of Delaware Press, 1996), pp. 83–96.

_____, "Romeo and Juliet on the stage: 'It is a kind of history,'" *Teaching Shakespeare Through Performance*, Milla Cozart Riggio, ed. (New York: Modern Language Association, 1999).

_____, *Shakespeare in Performance: Romeo and Juliet* (Manchester: Manchester University Press, 1987).

_____, "Teaching the Books of the Play," *Approaches to Teaching Shakespeare's Romeo and Juliet*, Maurice Hunt, ed. (New York: Modern Language Association, 2000), pp 153–62.

Levenson, Jill L., and Robert Ormsby,

eds., *The Shakespearean World* (London: Routledge, 2017).

Levin, Harry, "Form and Formality in *Romeo and Juliet*," *Shakespeare Quarterly*, 11:1, Winter 1960, pp. 3–11.

_____, *The Overreacher: A Study of Christopher Marlowe* (Boston: Beacon Press, 1965).

_____, *The Question of Hamlet* (Oxford: Oxford University Press, 1959).

Lewis, C. S., *English Literature in the Sixteenth Century (excluding drama)* (Oxford: Oxford University Press, 1954).

Lindley, David, *Shakespeare at Stratford: The Tempest* (London: Arden, 2003).

Literature Online: http://literature.proquest.com/marketing/index.jsp

Lodge, Thomas, *Rosalynde, Euphues Golden Legacie* (London, 1590).

Long, William B., "'Precious Few': English Manuscript Playbooks," *A Companion to Shakespeare*, David Scott Kastan, ed. (Oxford: Basil Blackwell, 1999), pp. 414–33.

Looney, J. Thomas, *"Shakespeare" Identified in Edward de Vere the Seventeenth Earl of Oxford* (New York: Frederick A. Stokes Company, 1920).

Lott, Eric, *Love and Theft: Blackface Minstrelsy and the American Working Class* (Oxford: Oxford University Preess, 1993).

Love, Harold, *Attributing Authorship: An Introduction* (Cambridge: Cambridge University Press, 2002).

Lucas, F. L., *The CompleteWorks of John Webster*, four volumes (London: Chatto and Windus, 1927).

Lyly, John, *Gallathea* (London: 1585).

MacDonald, Joyce Green, *Women and Race in Early Modern Texts* (Cambridge: Cambridge University Press, 2002).

McClure, Norman Egbert, *The Letters of John Chamberlain*, two volumes (Philadelphia: American Philosophical Society, 1939).

McDonald, Russ, *Shakespeare and the Arts of Language* (Oxford: Oxford University Press, 2001).

McGann, Jerome, *Radiant Textuality: Literature after the World Wide Web* (London: Palgrave, 2001).

McGrail, Mary Ann, ed., *Poetica 48*, special issue: "Shakespeare's Plutarch," 1997.

McJannet, Linda, *The Sultan Speaks: Dialogue in English Plays and Histories About the Ottoman Turks* (New York: Palgrage, 2006).

McKenzie, D. F., *Making Meaning: "Printers of the mind" and other essays*, Peter D. McDonald and Michael Felix Suarez, eds. (Amherst: University of Massachusetts Press, 2002).

McKerrow, Ronald B., *Prolegomena for the Oxford Shakespeare: A Study in Editorial Method* (Oxford: Oxford University Press, 1939).

McManaway, James G., *Studies in Shakespeare, Bibliography, and Theater*, Richard Hosley, Arthur C. Kirsch, and John W. Velz, eds. (New York: Shakespeare Association of America, 1969).

McMillin, Scott, *The Elizabethan Theatre and the Book of Sir Thomas More* (Ithaca, NY: Cornell University Press, 1987).

_____, *Shakespeare in Performance: Henry IV, Part One* (Manchester: Manchester University Press, 1991).

McMillin, Scott and Sally-Beth MacLean, *The Queen's Men and Their Plays*, two editions (Cambridge: Cambridge University Press, 1998 and 2006).

McMullan, Gordon, Lena Cowen Orlin, and Virginia Mason Vaughan, *Women Making Shakespeare: Text, Reception and Performance* (London: Arden, 2014).

Mack, Maynard, *Everybody's Shakespeare: Reflections Chiefly on Tragedies* (Lincoln: University of Nebraska Press, 1993).

_____, *King Lear in Our Time* (Berkeley: University of California Press, 1965).

Magnusson, Lynne, *Shakespeare and Social Dialogue, Dramatic Language and Elizabethan Letters* (Cambridge: Cambridge University Press, 1999).

Maguire, Laurie, *Shakespearean Suspect Texts: The 'Bad' Quartos and Their Contexts* (Cambridge: Cambridge University Press, 1996).

Mahood, M. M., *Bit Parts in Shakespeare's Plays* (Cambridge: Cambridge University Press, 1992).

_____, *Shakespeare's Wordplay* (London: Methuen, 1957).

Marienstras, Richard, *New Perspectives on the Shakespearean World* (Cambridge: Cambridge University Press, 1981), pp. 40–7.

Marlowe, Christopher, *Edward II* (London: 1594).

_____, *The Jew of Malta* (London: 1633).

_____, *Tamburlaine, Parts One and Two*, Anthony B. Dawson, ed. (New York: W. W. Norton & Co., 1997).

_____, *Tamburlaine, the Great*, J. S. Cunningham, ed. (Manchester: Revels, 1999).

_____, *Tamburlaine, the Great in Two Parts*, Una Ellis-Fermor, ed. (London: Methuen, 1930).

_____, *Tamburlaine, the Great, parts one and two*, J. W. Harper, ed. (London: New Mermaid, 1971).

_____, *The Tragicall History of the Life and Death of Doctor Faustus*, two editions (London: 1604 and 1616).

Marotti, Arthur, *Manuscript, Print, and the English Renaissance Lyric* (Ithaca, NY: Cornell University Press, 1995).

Marotti, Arthur F., *Religious Ideology and Cultural Fantasy: Catholic and Anti-Catholic Discourses in Early Modern England* (Notre Dame, IN: University of Notre Dame Press, 2005).

Marston, John, *The Selected Plays of John Marston*, MacDonald P. Jackson and Michael Neill, eds. (Cambridge: Cambridge University Press, 1986).

_____, *What You Will* (London, 1607).

Martin, Gregory, ed., *The New Testament of Jesus Christ Translated Faithfully into English* (Rheims: 1582).

Marx, Leo, *The Machine in the Garden: Technology and the Pastoral Ideal in America* (Oxford: Oxford University Press, 1967).

Massai, Sonia, *Shakespeare and the Rise of the Editor* (Cambridge: Cambridge University Press, 2007).

Massai, Sonia, ed., *World-Wide Shakespeares: Local Appropriations in Film and Performance* (London: Routledge, 2006).

Mast, Gerald, Leo Braudy, Marshall Cohen, eds., *Film Theory and Criticism: Introductory Readings, 4e* (Oxford: Oxford University Press, 1992).

Matthew, H. C. G., and Brian Harrison, eds., *The Dictionary of National Biography*, sixty volumes (Oxford: Oxford University Press, 2004).

Matus, Irvin Leigh, *Shakespeare, In Fact* (New York: Continuum, 1994).

Maus, Katharine Eisaman, *Inwardness and Theatre in the English Renaissance* (Chicago: University of Chicago Press, 1995).

May, Steven W., *Bibliography and First-line Index of English Verse, 1559–1603* (New York: Continuum, 2004).

May, Steven W., and William Ringler, *English Poetry: A Bibliography and First-Line Index of English Verse, 1559–1603*, three volumes (New York: Continuum, 2004).

Mayer, Jean-Christophe, *Shakespeare's Hybrid Faith: History, Religion and the State* (London: Palgrave, 2006).

Mehl, Dieter, *Shakespeare's Tragedies: An Introduction* (Cambridge: Cambridge University Press, 1986).

Mehl, Dieter, Angela Stock, and Anna-Julia Zwierlein, eds., *Plotting Early Modern London: New Essays on Jacobean City Comedy* (Farnham, UK: Ashgate, 2005).

Melchiori, Giorgio, "*Hamlet*: The Acting Version and the Wiser Sort," *The "Hamlet" First Published (Q1, 1603) Origins, Forms, Intertextualities*, Thomas Clayton, ed. (London: London Associated University Presses, 1992), pp. 195–210.

Menzer, Paul, *Shakespeare in the Theatre: The American Shakespeare Center* (London: Arden, 2017).

Merchant, W. Moelwyn, *Shakespeare and the Artist* (Oxford: Oxford University Press, 1959).

Merleau-Ponty, Maurice, *Phenomenology of Perception* (Evanston, IL: Northwestern University Press, 1945).

_____, *Signs* (Evanston, IL: Northwestern University Press, 1964).

Middleton, Thomas, *The Puritane, or the Widow of Watling-streete* (London: 1606).

_____, *The Revenger's Tragedy*, R. A. Foakes, ed., two editions (London: Methuen, 1966 and 1996).

_____, *The Revengers Tragedy Attributed to Middleton: A Facsimile of the 1607/8 Quarto*, Jackson, MacDonald P., ed. (Rutherford, NJ: Fairleigh Dickinson University Presses, 1983).

_____, *Thomas Middleton: The Collected Works*, Gary Taylor and John Lavagnino, General eds. (Oxford: Oxford University Press, 2007).

_____, *The Yorkshire Tragedy: Not so New and Lamentable and true* (London: 1608).

Middleton, Thomas, and Thomas Dekker, *The Roaring Girl* (London, 1611).

Miles, Josephine, *Eras and Modes in English Poetry* (Berkeley: University of California Press, 1957).

_____, *Style and Proportion: The Language of Prose and Poetry* (Boston: Little, Brown, and Co., 1967).

Miller, Jonathan, *Subsequent Performances* (London: Faber, 1986).

Miola, Robert S., "The Canonized Bones," *First Things: The Journal of Religion, Culture, and Public Life*, August/September 2008. http://www.firstthings.com/article.php3?id_article=6264.

_____, "On Death and Dying in Chapman's 'Iliad': Translation as Forgery," *International Journal of the Classical Tradition*, 3:1, Summer, 1996, pp. 48–64.

_____, *Shakespeare and Classical Comedy: The Influence of Plautus and Terence* (Oxford: Oxford University Press, 1994).

_____, *Shakespeare and Classical Tragedy: The Influence of Seneca* (Oxford: Oxford University Press, 1992).

_____, *Shakespeare's Reading* (Oxford: Oxford University Press, 2000).

_____, *Shakespeare's Rome* (Cambridge: Cambridge University Press, 1983).

Miola, Robert S., ed., *The Comedy of Errors: Critical Essays* (New York: Routledge, 1997).

_____, *Early Modern Catholicism: An Anthology of Primary Sources* (Oxford: Oxford University Press, 2007).

MIT Global Shakespeares: http://globalshakespeares.mit.edu/#

Monaco, James, *How to Read a Film: The Art, Technology, Language, History, and Theory of Film and Media*, four editions (Oxford: Oxford University Press, 1977–2009).

Monsarrrat, G. D., "*A Funeral Elegy*: Ford, W. S., and Shakespeare," *Review of English Studies*, 53:210, May 2002, pp. 186–203.

Montaigne, Machell de, *The Essais or Morall, Politike, and Militarie Discourses*, John Florio, translator (London, 1603).

Montrose, Louis A., "A Kingdom of Shadows," *A Midsummer Night's Dream: Critical Essays*, Dorothea Kehler, ed. (New York: Garland Publishing, 1998), 217–40.

_____, "The Work of Gender in the Discourse of Discovery," *Representations* 33, Winter 1991, pp. 1–41.

Moss, Ann, ed., *Latin Commentaries on Ovid from the Renaissance* (Signal Mountain, TN: Library of Renaissance Humanism, 1998).

Mowat, Barbara A., *The Dramaturgy of Shakespeare's Romances* (Athens: University of Georgia Press, 1976).

_____, "The Form of Hamlet's Fortunes," *Renaissance Drama XIX*, 1988, pp. 97–126.

_____, "Nicholas Rowe and the Twentieth-Century Shakespeare Text," *Shakespeare and Cultural Traditions: The Selected Proceedings of the International Shakespeare Association World Congress, Tokyo, 1991*, Tetsuo Kishi, Roger Pringle, and Stanley Wells, eds. (Newark: University of Delaware Press, 1994), pp. 314–22.

_____, "Prospero's Book," *Shakespeare Quarterly*, 52:1, Spring 2001, pp. 1–33.

Mu, Groupe, *Rhétorique de la poésie* (Paris: Seuil, 1977).

Muir, Kenneth, *Shakespeare as Collaborator* (London: Methuen, 1960).

_____, *Shakespeare's Sources*, reprinted with new appendices, two volumes (London: Methuen, 1961).

Munday, Anthony and others, *Sir Thomas More*, Vittorio Gabrieli and Giorgio Melchiori, eds. (Manchester: Manchester University Press, 1990).

Münsterberg, Hugo, "The Means of the Photoplay," *Film Theory and Criticism, 4e*, Gerald Mast, Marshall Cohen and Leo Braudy, eds. (Oxford: Oxford University Press, 1992), pp. 355–61.

Murphy, Andrew, ed., *The Renaissance Text: Theory, Editing, Textuality* (Manchester: Manchester University Press, 2000).

Nabokov, Vladimir, *Lolita* (Paris: Olympia Press, 1955).

_____, *Pale Fire* (New York: Putnam, 1962).

Nashe, Thomas, *Thomas Nashe: Selected Works*, Stanley Wells, ed. (London: Edward Arnold, 1964).

Nason, Arthur Huntington, *James Shirley, Dramatist: A Biographical and Critical Study* (privately published, 1915, reprint New York: Benjamin Blom, 1967).

Neely, Carol Thomas, *Broken Nuptials in Shakespeare's Plays* (New Haven: Yale University Press, 1985).

Neill, Michael, *Issues of Death: Mortality and*

Identity in English Renaissance Tragedy (Oxford: Oxford University Press, 1997).

Nelson, Alan H., *Monstrous Adversary: The Life of Edward de Vere, 17th Earl of Oxford* (Liverpool: Liverpool University Press, 2003).

_____, "The Universities: Early Staging in Cambridge," *New History of Early English Drama*, John D. Cox and David Scott Kastan, eds. (New York, Columbia University Press, 1997), pp. 59–67.

Nelson, Alan H., ed., *The Records of Early English Drama: Cambridge* (Toronto: University of Toronto Press, 1989).

Nicholl, Charles, *A Cup of News: The Life of Thomas Nashe* (London: Routledge & Keegan Paul, 1984).

_____, *The Lodger: Shakespeare on Silver Street* (London: Penguin, 2007).

_____, *The Reckoning: The Murder of Christopher Marlowe* (London: Jonathan Cape, 1992).

Norbrook, David, "*Macbeth* and the Politics of Historiography," *Politics of Discourse*, Kevin Sharpe and Steven N. Zwicker, eds. (Berkeley: University of California Press, 1987), pp. 78–116.

Nuttall, A. D., *A New Mimesis: Shakespeare and the Representation of Reality* (London: Methuen, 1983).

_____, *Why Does Tragedy Give Pleasure?* (Oxford: Oxford University Press, 1996).

Nye, Robert, *The Late Mr. Shakespeare* (London: Penguin, 1998).

O'Brien, Geoffrey, *The New York Review of Books*, http://www.nybooks.com/articles/2004/03/25/lear-for-real/

Odell, George C. D., *Shakespeare: From Betterton to Irving*, two volumes (New York: Charles Scribner's Sons, 1920).

Oliphant, E. H. C., *The Plays of Beaumont and Fletcher: An Attempt to Determine their Respective Shares and the Shares of Others* (New Haven: Yale University Press, 1927).

Oras, Ants, *Pause Patterns in Elizabethan and Jacobean Drama: An Experiment in Prosody* (Gainesville: University of Florida Press, 1960).

Orgel, Stephen, *The Authentic Shakespeare, and Other Problems of the Early Modern Stage* (London: Routledge, 2002).

_____, *Impersonations: The Performance of Gender in Shakespeare's England* (Cambridge: Cambridge University Press, 1996).

_____, *The Jonsonian Masque* (New York: Columbia University Press, 1967).

_____, "*Macbeth* and the Antic Round," *Shakespeare Survey 52* (Cambridge: Cambridge University Press, 1999), pp. 143–53.

Orgel, Stephen, and Roy C. Strong, *Inigo Jones: The Theatre of the Stuart Court, Including the Complete Designs for Productions at Court for the Most Part in the Collection of the Duke of Devonshire Together with Their Texts and Historical Documentation* (Berkeley: University of California Press, 1973).

Orrell, John, *The Quest for Shakespeare's Globe* (Cambridge: Cambridge University Press, 1983).

Osborn, James S., *Young Philip Sidney, 1572–1577* (New Haven: Yale University Press, 1972).

Ovid, *Metamorphoses*, two volumes, Frank Justus Miller, translator, two editions (Cambridge MA: Loeb, 1977, revised by G. P. Goold 1985).

Oxford English Dictionary online: http://public.oed.com/how-to-subscribe/

Oxford English Dictionary, 2e, twenty volumes (Oxford: Oxford University Press, 1989).

Oxford English Dictionary: Compact Edition, two volumes (Oxford: Oxford University Press, 1971).

Panofsky, Erwin, "Style and Medium in the Motion Pictures," *Film Theory and Criticism, 4e*, Gerald Mast, Marshall Cohen and Leo Braudy, eds. (Oxford: Oxford University Press, 1992), pp. 233–48.

Partridge, Edward, "Jonson's Epigrammes: The Named and the Nameless," *Studies in the Literary Imagination*, 61.1, April 1973, pp. 153–98.

Paster, Gail, *The Body Embarrassed: Drama and the Disciplines of Shame in Early Modern England* (Ithaca, NY: Cornell University Press, 1993).

Pearce, Susan M., ed., *Museum Studies in Material Culture* (Washington D.C.: Smithsonian Institution Press, 1991).

Pearlman, E., "Shakespeare at Work: *Romeo and Juliet*," *English Literary Renaissance*, 22:2, March 1994, pp. 315–342.

Pechter, Edward, *What Was Shakespeare?:*

Renaissance Plays and Changing Critical Practice (Ithaca, NY: Cornell University Press, 1995).

Peele, George, *The Old Wives Tale* (London: 1595).

Pendleton, Thomas A., "Shakespeare, In Fact," *Shakespeare Newsletter*, 44:2, Summer 1994, pp. 21, 26, 28–30. [The author is given as T. A. P. As *Shakespeare Newsletter* co-editor, Thomas A. Pendleton signed his articles with those initials].

Pennington, Michael, *Hamlet: A User's Guide* (London: Nick Hern Books, 1996).

Perseus Digital Library: http://www.perseus.tufts.edu/

Persons, Robert, *The first booke of the Christian exercise, appertayning to Resolution* (Rouen: 1582).

Phelan, Peggy, *UnMarked: The Politics of Performance* (London: Routledge, 1993).

Plautus, *Plautus*, Paul Nixon, translator, five volumes (Cambridge, MA: Loeb, 1916–38).

_____, *The Pot of Gold and Other Plays*, E. F. Watling, translator (Harmondsworth, UK: Penguin, 1965).

Plutarch, *Shakespeare's Plutarch*, T. J. B. Spencer, ed. (Harmondworth, UK: Penguin, 1964).

Pollard, A. W., and G. R. Redgrave, eds., *A Short-Title Catalogue of Books Printed in England, Scotland and Ireland, and of English Books Printed Abroad 1475–1640, 2e* (London: The Bibliographical Society, 1928).

Pollen, John Hungerford, *Unpublished Documents Relating to English Martyrs* (London: Catholic Record Society, 1908).

Poole, John, *Hamlet, Travestie: In Three Acts* (London: J. M. Richardson, 1810).

Porter, Roy, *Enlightenment: Britain and the Creation of the Modern World* (London: Alan Lane, 2000).

_____, *Flesh in the Age of Reason: The Modern Foundation of Body and Soul* (London: Alan Lane, 2004).

Potter, Lois, *A Life of William Shakespeare: A Critical Biography* (Oxford: Basil Blackwell, 2012).

_____, *A Preface to Milton*, two editions (Harlow, UK: Longman, 1971, revised 1986).

_____, *Shakespeare in Performance: Othello* (Manchester: Manchester University Press, 2002).

_____, *Text and Performance: Twelfth Night* (London: Macmillan, 1986).

Potter, Lois, ed., *Playing Robin Hood: The Legend as Performance in Five Centuries* (Newark: University of Delaware Press, 2003).

_____, *Secret Rites and Secret Writing: Royalist Literature 1641–1660, Volume 1* (Cambridge: Cambridge University Press, 1989).

Potter, Lois, General ed., *The Revels History of Drama in English: Medieval Drama, Volume One* (London: Routledge Kegan & Paul, 1976).

Potter, Lois, and Arthur F. Kinney, eds., *Shakespeare: Text and Theatre, Essays for Jay L. Halio* (Newark: University of Delaware Press, 1999).

Potter, Lois and John Broadbent, eds., *Paradise Lost: Books III and IV* (Cambridge: Cambridge University Press, 1976).

Preminger, Alex, and T.V.F. Brogan, eds., *The New Princeton Encyclopedia of Poetry and Poetics* (Princeton: Princeton University Press, 1993).

Prockter, Adrian, Robert Taylor, and John Fisher, et al., *The A to Z of Elizabethan London* (Martlesham, UK: Harry Margary, 1979).

Putnam, Michael C. J., *Vergil's Pastoral Art: Studies in the Eclogues* (Princeton: Princeton University Press, 1970).

Quarshie, Hugh, "Second Thoughts About 'Othello'" (Stratford-upon-Avon: International Shakespeare Association Occasional Paper No. 7, 1999).

Rabkin, Norman, *Shakespeare and the Common Understanding* (New York: Free Press, 1967).

Rackin, Phyllis, "Androgyny, Mimesis, and the Marriage of the Boy Heroine," *Proceedings of the Modern Language Association*, 102:1, June 1987, pp. 29–41.

_____, *Stages of History: Shakespeare's English Chronicles* (London: Routledge, 1990).

Ravenscroft, Edward, *Titus Andronicus, or the Rape of Lavinia* (London, 1687).

Ricks, Christopher, *Allusion to the Poets* (Oxford: Oxford University Press, 2002).

Ricouer, Paul, *Time and Narrative*, three

volumes (Chicago: University of Chicago Press, 1984–1988).

Riehle, Wolfgang, *Shakespeare, Plautus, and the Humanist Tradition* (Cambridge: D. S. Brewer, 1990).

Riggio, M. C., "*Othello:* A Contextual History," *Choice*, 33:3, November 1995. Pages are not numbered.

Righter, Anne, *Shakespeare and the Idea of the Play* (London: Chatto & Windus, 1962).

Ringler, William A., *Bibliography and Index of English Verse Printed 1476–1558* (London: Mansell Publishing, 1988).

Roach, Joseph, *Cities of the Dead: Circum-Atlantic Performances* (New York: Columbia University Press, 1999).

_____, *it* (Ann Arbor: University of Michigan Press, 2007).

Robertson, J. M., *The Shakespeare Canon*, two volumes (London: Routledge, 1922 and 1923).

Roscarrock, Nicholas, *Nicholas Roscarrock's Lives of the Saints: Cornwall and Devon*, Nicholas Orme, ed. (Exeter, UK: Devon and Cornwall Record Society, 1992).

Rose, Mark, *Shakespearean Design* (Cambridge, MA: Harvard University Press, 1972).

Rosenberg, Marvin, *The Masks of Othello: The Search for the Identity of Othello, Iago, and Desdemona by Three Centuries of Actors and Critics* (Newark: University of Delaware Press, 1992).

Ross, J. F., *Portraying Analogy* (Cambridge: Cambridge University Press, 1981).

Rossiter, A.P., *English Drama from Early Times to the Elizabethans* (London: Hutchinson, 1950).

Rothwell, Kenneth S., *A History of Shakespeare on Screen: A Century of Film and Television*, two editions (Cambridge: Cambridge University Press, 1999 and 2004).

_____, *Shakespeare on Screen: An International Filmography and Videography* (Chicago: Neal Schuman, 1990).

Rutter, Carol, *Clamorous Voices: Shakespeare's Women Today* (London: Routledge, 1989).

_____, *Enter the Body: Women and Representation on Shakespeare's Stage* (London: Routledge, 2001).

_____, *Shakespeare and Child's Play: Performing Lost Boys on Stage and Screen* (London: Routledge, 2007).

Sajdak, Bruce T., *Shakespeare Index: An Annotated Bibliography of Critical Articles on the Plays 1959–1983* (Millwood, NY: Kraus International Publications, 1992).

Salingar, Leo, *Shakespeare and the Traditions of Comedy* (Cambridge: Cambridge University Press, 1974).

Sarrazin, Gregor, *Aus Shakespeares Meisterwerkstatt: Stilgeschichtliche Studien* (Weimar, Germany: G. Reimar, 1906).

_____, *Thomas Kyd und sein Kreis* (Berlin: Verlag Von Emil Felber, 1892).

Schabert, Ina, ed., *Shakespeare-Handbuch, 4e* (Stuttgart, Germany: Kröner, 2000).

Schafer, Elizabeth, ed., *Shakespeare in Production: The Taming of the Shrew* (Cambridge: Cambridge University Press, 2002).

Schäfer, Jürgen, *Shakespreares Stil. Germanisches und romanisches Vokabuler* (Frankfurt, Germany: Anthenäum, 1973).

Schlegal, August Wilhelm von, "Ueber Shakespeare's Romeo und Julia," *Die Horen*, 10:6, 1797, pp. 18–48.

Schoenbaum, Marilyn, *A Shakespeare Merriment: An Anthology of Shakespearean Humor* (New York: Garland, 1988).

Schoenbaum, Samuel, *Internal Evidence and Elizabethan Dramatic Authorship: An Essay in Literary History and Method* (Evanston, IL: Northwestern University Press, 1966).

_____, *Shakespeare's Lives*, two editions (Oxford: Oxford University Press, 1970 and 1991).

_____, *William Shakespeare: A Documentary Life* (Oxford: Oxford University Press, 1975).

_____, *William Shakespeare: Records and Images*, two editions (Oxford: Oxford University Press, 1975 and 1981).

Seneca, *Four Tragedies and Octavia*, E. F. Watling, translator (Harmondsworth, UK: Penguin Books, 1966).

_____, *Seneca IX: Tragedies II*, Frank Justus Miller, translator (Cambridge, MA: Loeb, 1927).

_____, *Tragedies: Oedipus, Agamemnon, Thyestes, Hercules on Oeta, Octavia, Volume II*, John G. Fitch, translator (Cambridge, MA: Harvard University Press, 2004).

Shadwell, Thomas, *The History of Timon of Athens the Man Hater* (London: 1678).

Shaheen, Naseeb, *Biblical References in Shakespeare's Plays* (Newark: University of Delaware Press, 1999).

Shakespeare, William, *The Arden Shakespeare Complete Works*, Ann Thompson, David Scott Kastan, and Richard Proudfoot, eds., two editions (London: Arden, 1998 and 2011).

_____, *The Art of Shakespeare's Sonnets*, Helen Vendler, ed. (Cambridge, MA: Harvard University Press, 1997).

_____, *As You Like It*, Juliet Dusinberre, ed. (London: Arden, 2006).

_____, *As You Like It*, Michael Hattaway, ed., two editions (Cambridge: Cambridge University Press, 2000 and 2009).

_____, *The Comedy of Errors*, R. A. Foakes, ed. (London: Arden, 1968).

_____, *The Complete Sonnets and Poems*, Colin Burrow, ed. (Oxford: Oxford University Press, 2002).

_____, *The Complete Works*, Stanley Wells and Gary Taylor, eds., two editions (Oxford: Oxford University Press, 1986 and 2005).

_____, *The Complete Works of William Shakespeare* (New York: Doubleday, 1936).

_____, *Coriolanus*, Jeffrey Kahan, ed. (Newburyport, MA: Focus Publishing, 2011).

_____, *Cymbeline*, Peter Holland, ed. (London: Pelican Books, 2000).

_____, *The Dramatic Works of William Shakespeare: From the Corrected Edition of Isaac Reed, Esq. with Copious Annotations*, Samuel Johnson, ed. (London: J. Walker, G. Offor, Sharpe and Sons, 1820).

_____, *The First Part of King Henry the Fourth: Texts and Contexts*, Barbara Hodgdon, ed. (Boston: Bedford Books, 1997).

_____, *The First Part of King Henry VI*, Michael Hattaway, ed. (Cambridge: Cambridge University Press, 1990).

_____, *The First Quarto of Henry V*, Andrew Gurr, ed. (Cambridge: Cambridge University Press, 2006).

_____, *The First Quarto of Romeo and Juliet*, Lukas Erne, ed. (Cambridge: Cambridge University Press, 2007).

_____, *Hamlet*, Ann Thompson and Neil Taylor, eds., two editions (London: Arden, 2006 and 2016).

_____, *Hamlet*, Anne Barton, introduction (New York: Penguin Books, 2002).

_____, *Hamlet*, Anthony B. Dawson, ed., *Norton Shakespeare, 3e*, Stephen Greenblatt, Walter Cohen, Jean E. Howard, et. al, eds. (New York: W. W. Norton & Co., 2015), pp. 1751–1905.

_____, *Hamlet*, Harold Jenkins, ed. (London: Arden, 1982).

_____, *Hamlet*, Jesus Tronch-Perez, ed. (Valencia, Spain: University of Valencia, 2002).

_____, *Hamlet*, Robert S. Miola, ed. (New York: W. W. Norton & Company, 2011).

_____, *Hamlet and As You Like It*, Thomas Caldecott, ed. (London, 1819).

_____, *Hamlet, Prince of Denmark. A Tragedy*, Charles Jennens, ed. (London: 1773).

_____, *Hamlet: The Texts of 1603 and 1623*, Ann Thompson and Neil Taylor, eds. (London: Arden, 2006).

_____, *Henry V*, Andrew Gurr, ed., updated edition (Cambridge: Cambridge University Press, 2005).

_____, *Henry VI, Part 3*, John D. Cox and Eric Rasmussen, eds. (London: Arden, 2001).

_____, *Henry VIII*, R. A. Fokes, ed. (London: Arden, 1957).

_____, *King Lear*, G. I. Duthie, ed., two editions (Oxford: Blackwell, 1949, Cambridge: Cambridge University Press, 1960).

_____, *King Lear*, R. A. Foakes, ed. (London: Arden, 1977).

_____, *King Lear*, Stanley Wells, ed. (Oxford: Oxford University Press, 2000).

_____, *King Richard II*, Andrew Gurr, ed., updated edition (Cambridge: Cambridge University Press, 2005).

_____, *Love's Labour's Lost*, Peter Holland, ed. (London: Pelican Books, 2000).

_____, *Macbeth*, A. R. Braunmuller, ed., two editions (Cambridge: Cambridge University Press, 1997 and 2008).

_____, *Macbeth*, Robert S. Miola, ed., two editions (New York: W. W. Norton & Company, 2004 and 2014).

_____, *A Midsummer Night's Dream*, R. A. Foakes, ed. (Cambridge: Cambridge University Press, 1984).

_____, *A Midsummer Night's Dream*, Peter Holland, ed. (Oxford: Oxford University Press, 1994).

_____, *Mr. William Shakespeares Histories, Comedies, & Tragedies: Published according to the True Original Copies*, four editions (London: 1623–1685).

_____, *Much Ado About Nothing*, Peter Holland, ed. (London: Pelican Books, 1999).

_____, *Much Ado About Nothing*, R. A. Foakes, ed. (New York: Penguin, 1981).

_____, *A New Variorum Edition of Shakespeare: Troilus and Cressida*, Harold N. Hillebrand, ed. (Philadelphia: Lippincott, 1953).

_____, *The Norton Facsimile: The First Folio of Shakespeare*, Charlton Hinman, ed. (New York: W. W. Norton & Company, 1968).

_____, *The Norton Shakespeare*, Stephen Greenblatt, Walter Cohen, Jean E. Howard, et. al, eds., three editions (New York: W. W. Norton & Company, 1997–2015).

_____, *Le origini di Amleto, La traduzione di Amleto nella cultura europea*, Serpieri, Alessandro, ed. (Padua, Italy: Marsilio Editori, 1997).

_____, *Pericles, Prince of Tyre*, Jeffrey Kahan, ed. (Newburyport, MA: Focus Publishing, 2010).

_____, *The Rape of Lucrece* (London: 1594).

_____, *Richard II*, Anthony B. Dawson and Philip Yuchnin, eds. (Oxford: Oxford University Press, 2011).

_____, *Richard III*, Peter Holland, ed. (London: Pelican Books, 2000).

_____, *Richard III*, John Jowett, ed. (Oxford: Oxford University Press, 2000).

_____, *The Riverside Shakespeare*, G. Blakemore Evans, General ed., two editions (Boston: Houghton Mifflin Company, 1974 and 1996).

_____, *Romeo and Juliet*, G. Blakemore Evans, ed. (Cambridge: Cambridge University Press, 1984).

_____, *Romeo and Juliet*, Jill L. Levenson, ed. (Oxford: Oxford University Press, 2000).

_____. *Romeo and Juliet*, Peter Holland, ed. (London: Pelican Books, 2000).

_____, *Romeo and Juliet, 2e*, Brian Gibbons, ed. (London: Arden, 1980).

_____, *Romeo and Juliet, 1597*, Jill L. Levenson and Barry Gaines, eds. (Manchester: Malone Society, 2001).

_____, *The Second Part of King Henry VI*, Michael Hattaway, ed. (Cambridge: Cambridge University Press, 1991).

_____, *Shakespeare in Production: As You Like It*, Cynthia Marshall, ed. (Cambridge: Cambridge University Press, 2004).

_____, *Shakespeare in Production: Othello*, Julie Hankey, ed. (Cambridge: Cambridge University Press, 2005).

_____, *Shakespeare in Production: Romeo and Juliet*, James N. Cocklin, ed. (Cambridge: Cambridge University Press, 2002).

_____, *Shakespeare in Production: The Taming of the Shrew*, Elizabeth Schafer, ed. (Cambridge: Cambridge University Press, 2002).

_____, *Shakespeare in Production: The Tempest*, Christine Dymkowski, ed. (Cambridge: Cambridge University Press, 2000).

_____, *Shakespeare Tragédies*, two volumes (Paris: Gallimard, 2002).

_____, *Shakespeare's Plays in Quarto: A Facsimile Edition of Copies Primarily from the Henry E. Huntington Library*, Michael J. B. Allen and Kenneth Muir, eds. (Berkeley: University of California Press, 1996).

_____, *Shakespeare's Poems*, Katherine Duncan-Jones and H. R. Woudhuysen, eds. (London: Arden, 2007).

_____, *Shakespeare's Sonnets*, Stephen Booth, ed. (New Haven: Yale University Press, 1977).

_____, *Shakespeare's Sonnets*, Katherine Duncan-Jones, ed. (London: Arden, 1997).

_____, *Shakespeare's Sonnets*, W. G. Ingram and Theodore Redpath, eds., two editions (London: University of London Press, 1964, and London: Hodder and Stoughton, 1978).

_____, *Sixteen Plays of Shakespeare*, G. L. Kittredge, ed. (Boston: Ginn and Company, 1946).

_____, *The Taming of the Shrew: Texts and Contexts*, Frances E. Dolan, ed. (Boston: Bedford Books, 1996).

_____, *The Taming of the Shrew*, Barbara Hodgdon, ed. (London: Arden, 2010).
_____, *The Taming of the Shrew*, Ann Thompson, ed., three editions (Cambridge: Cambridge University Press, 1984–2017).
_____, *The Tempest*, Anne Barton, ed. (New York: Penguin Books, 1968).
_____, *The Tempest*, David Lindley, ed., two editions (Cambridge: Cambridge University Press, 2002 and 2013).
_____, *The Tempest*, Frank Kermode, ed. (London: Arden, 1954).
_____, *The Tempest*, Peter Holland, ed. (London: Pelican Books, 1999).
_____, *The Tempest*, Peter Hulme and William H. Sherman, eds. (New York: W. W. Norton & Company, 2004).
_____, *The Tempest*, Stephen Orgel, ed. (Oxford: Oxford University Press, 1987).
_____, *The Tempest*, Virginia Mason Vaughan and Alden T. Vaughan, eds., two editions (London: Arden, 1999 and 2011).
_____, *The Third Part of King Henry VI*, Michael Hattaway, ed. (Cambridge: Cambridge University Press, 1993).
_____, *Timon of Athens*, Anthony B. Dawson and Gretchen Minton, eds., two editions (London: Arden, 2008 and 2011).
_____, *Titus Andronicus* (London: 1594).
_____, *Titus Andronicus*, Jonathan Bate, ed., two editions (London: Arden, 1995 and 2018).
_____, *Titus Andronicus, 1594*, Thomas L. Berger and Barbara A. Mowat, eds. (London: Malone Society, 2003).
_____, *The Tragedie of Hamlet, Prince of Denmark: A Study with the Text of the Folio of 1623*, George MacDonald, ed. (London: Longmans, Green & Co., 1885).
_____, *Troilus and Cressida*, Alice Walker, ed. (Cambridge: Cambridge University Press, 1957).
_____, *Troilus and Cressida*, Anthony B. Dawson, ed. (Cambridge: Cambridge University Press, 2003).
_____, *Troilus and Cressida*, David Bevington, ed. (London: Arden, 1998).
_____, *Troilus and Cressida*, G. Blakemore Evans, ed., *The Riverside Shakespeare* (Boston: Houghton Mifflin Company, 1974), pp. 443–98.
_____, *Troilus and Cressida*, Kenneth Palmer, ed. (London: Arden, 1982).
_____, *Troilus and Cressida*, R. A. Foakes, ed. (New York: Penguin, 1987).
_____, *Two Noble Kinsmen*, Lois Potter, ed., two editions (London: Arden, 1997 and 2013).
_____, *The Winter's Tale*, Stephen Orgel, ed. (Oxford: Oxford University Press, 1996).
_____, *The Works of Mr. William Shakespear; In Six Volumes*, Nicholas Rowe, ed. (London: 1709).
_____, *The Works of Shakespeare in Seven Volumes*, Lewis Theobald, ed. (London: 1733).
Shakespeare, William, and an unknown collaborator, *The Raigne of King Edward the third*, published without attribution (London: 1596).
_____, *The Tragedy of Master Arden of Faversham*, Martin L. Wine, ed. (London: Methuen, 1973).
Shapiro, James, *Contested Will: The Shakespeare Authorship Controversy* (New York: Simon & Schuster, 2010).
_____, *1599: A Year in the Life of William Shakespeare* (New York: HarperCollins, 2005).
_____, *1599: A Year in the Life of William Shakespeare* (New York: Harper Audio, 2005).
_____, *Oberammergau: The Troubling Story of the World's Most Famous Passion Play* (New York: Pantheon, 2000).
_____, *Rival Playwrights: Marlowe, Jonson, Shakespeare* (New York: Columbia University Press, 1991).
_____, *Shakespeare and the Jews* (New York: Columbia University Press, 1995).
_____, *1606: The Year of Lear* (New York: Simon & Schuster, 2015).
Shapiro, James, ed., *Shakespeare in America: An Anthology from the Revolution to Now* (New York: Library of America, 2014).
Shattuck, Charles, *The London Stage, 1660–1800: A Calendar of Plays, Entertainments & Afterpieces, Together with Casts, Box-Receipts and Contemporary Comment*, five volumes (Carbondale, IL: Southern Illinois University Press, 1960–8).
_____, *Shakespeare on the American Stage,*

two volumes (Washington D.C.: Folger Books, 1976 and 1987).

_____, *The Shakespeare Promptbooks: A Descriptive Catalog* (Champaign, IL: University of Illinois Press, 1965).

Shaughnessy, Robert, *The Shakespeare Effect: A History of Twentieth-Century Performance* (London: Palgrave, 2002).

Shaw, George Bernard, "Bernard Shaw on Johnston Forbes-Robertson as Hamlet," *Shakespeare in the Theatre: An Anthology of Criticism*," Stanley Wells, ed. (Oxford: Oxford University Press, 1997), pp. 144–52.

_____, *Shaw on Theatre*, E. J. West, editor (New York: Hill and Wang, 1958).

Shell, Alison, *Catholicism, Controversy and the English Literary Imagination, 1558–1660* (Cambridge: Cambridge University Press, 1999).

Sidney, Philip, *The Countess of Pembroke's Arcadia: The Old Arcadia*, Katherine Duncan-Jones, ed. (Oxford: Oxford University Press, 1999).

_____, *The Defence of Posey* (London: 1595).

_____, *Sir Philip Sidney*, Katherine Duncan-Jones, ed. (Oxford: Oxford University Press, 1989).

_____, *Sir Philip Sidney: The Major Works*, Katherine Duncan-Jones, ed. (Oxford: Oxford University Press, 2002).

Siemon, James R., *Shakespearean Iconoclasm* (Berkeley: University of California Press, 1985).

_____, *Word Against Word: Shakespearean Utterance* (Amherst: University of Massachusetts Press, 2002).

Singh, Devani, and Lukas Erne, *Shakespeare in Geneva: Early Modern English Books (1475–1700) at the Martin Bodmer Foundation: An Introduction and Catalogue* (Paris: Ithaque, 2017).

Singleton, Charles, *An Essay on the "Vita Nuova*," (Cambridge, MA: Harvard University Press, 1949, reprint Baltimore: Johns Hopkins University Press, 1977).

Sisson, C. J., *Lost Plays of Shakespeare's Age* (Cambridge: Cambridge University Press, 1936).

Skinner, Quentin, *Foundations of Modern Political Thought*, two volumes (Cambridge: Cambridge University Press, 1978).

_____, *Reason and Rhetoric in the Philosophy of Hobbes* (Cambridge: Cambridge University Press, 1996).

Skura, Meredith Anne, *Shakespeare the Actor and the Purposes of Playing* (Chicago: University of Chicago Press, 1993).

Smallwood, Robert, *Shakespeare at Stratford: As You Like It* (London: Arden, 2003).

Smith, Barbara Herrnstein, *Poetic Closure: A Study of How Poems End* (Chicago: University of Chicago, 1968).

Smith, Bruce R., *The Acoustic World of Early Modern England: Attending to the O-Factor* (Chicago: University of Chicago Press, 1999).

_____, "Ragging *Twelfth Night*: 1602, 1996, 2002–3," *A Companion to Shakespeare and Performance*, Barbara Hodgdon and W. B. Worthen, eds. (Oxford: Blackwell Publishing, 2005), pp. 57–78.

Smith, Gordon Ross, *A Classified Shakespeare Bibliography 1936–1958* (University Park: Pennsylvania State University Press, 1963).

Smith, Logan Pearsall, *On Reading Shakespeare* (London: Constable & Co., 1933).

Snow, Edward, "Language and Sexual Difference in *Romeo and Juliet*," *Shakespeare's "Rough Magic": Renaissance Essays in Honor of C. L. Barber*, Peter Erickson and Coppélia Kahn, eds. (Newark: University of Delaware Pres, 1985), pp. 168–192.

Snyder, Susan, "Beyond Comedy: *Romeo and Juliet* and *Othello*," *The Comic Matrix of Shakespeare's Tragedies: Romeo and Juliet, Hamlet Othello, and King Lear* (Chicago: University of Chicago Press, 1979), pp. 56–90.

Sophocles, *Ajax, Electra, Oedipus Tyrannus*, Hugh Lloyd-Jones, translator (Cambridge, MA: Loeb, 1994).

Southwell, Robert, *Mœoniæ, Or Certaine excellent poems and spirituall hymnes: omitted in the last impresson of Peters complaint being needful thereunto to be annexed, as being both divine and witte. All composed by R. S.* (London: 1595).

Spain, Delbert, *Shakespeare Sounded Soundly: The Verse Structure and the Language: A Handbook for Students, Actors, and Directors* (Santa Barbara, CA: Capra Press, 1988).

Spenser, Edmund, *A View of the Present State of Ireland as it was In the Reign of Queen Elizabeth* (Dublin: 1621).

Spevack, Marvin, *The Harvard Concordance to Shakespeare* (Cambridge, MA: Harvard University Press, 1973).

Spivack, Bernard, *Shakespeare and the Allegory of Evil: The History of a Metaphor in Relation to his Major Villains* (New York: Columbia University Press, 1958).

Sprague, Arthur Colby, *Shakespeare and the Actors: The Stage Business in His Plays, 1660–1905* (Cambridge, MA: Harvard University Press, 1944).

_____, *Shakespeare's Histories, Plays for the Stage* (London: Society for Theatre Research, 1964).

Spurgeon, Caroline, *Shakespeare's Imagery and what it tells us* (Cambridge: Cambridge University Press, 1935).

Stallybrass, Peter, "Patriarchal Territories: The Body Enclosed," *Rewriting the Renaissance: The Discourses of Sexual Difference in Early Modern Europe*, Margaret W. Ferguson, Maureen Quilligan, and Nancy Vickers, eds. (Chicago: University of Chicago Press, 1986), pp. 123–42.

Stanford, Rhonda Lemke, *Maps and Memory in Early Modern England: A Sense of Place* (New York: Palgrave, 2002).

States, Bert O., *The Pleasure of the Play* (Ithaca: NY: Cornell University Press, 1994).

Stern, Tiffany, *Making Shakespeare: From Stage to Page* (London: Routledge, 2004).

_____, *Rehearsal from Shakespeare to Sheridan* (Oxford: Oxford University Press, 2000).

_____, "Was *Totus mundus agit histrionem* Ever the Motto of the Globe Theatre?," *Theatre Notebook*, 51:3, 1997, pp. 122–7.

Sterne, Richard L., *John Gielgud Directs Richard Burton in Hamlet: A Journal of Rehearsals* (New York: Random House, 1967).

Stewart, Alan, *Shakespeare's Letters* (Oxford: Oxford University Press, 2008).

Stewart, Susan, *On Longing: Narratives of the Miniature, the Gigantic, the Souvenir, the Collection* (Durham, NC: Duke University Press, 1993).

Stoppard, Tom, *Rosencranz and Guildenstern Are Dead* (London: Samuel French, Inc. 1967).

Stowe, John, *A Survey of London: Contayning the Original, Antiquity, Increase, Moderne estate, and description of that Citie, written in the yeare 1598* (London: 1598).

Strazinky, Marta, "A Stage for the World: Shakespeare on CBC Radio, 1947–1955," *Shakespeare in Canada: A World Elsewhere?*, Diana Brydon and Irena R. Makaryk, eds. (Toronto: University of Toronto Press, 2002), pp. 92–107.

Sturgess, Kim C., *Shakespeare and the American Nation* (Cambridge: Cambridge University Press, 2004).

Styan, J. L., *The Shakespeare Revolution: Criticism and Performance in the Twentieth Century* (Cambridge: Cambridge University Press, 1977).

Suetonius, *The Historie of Twelve Caesars, Emperors of Rome: Written in Latine by C. Suetonius Tranquillus, and newly translated into English by Philemon Holland* (London: 1606).

Tacitus, *The Annales of Cornelius Tacitus. The Description of Germaine*, Henry Savile, translator (London: 1591).

Tanselle, G. Thomas, *A Rationale of Textual Criticism* (Philadelphia: University of Pennsylvania Press, 1987).

Tarlinskaja, Marina, "Looking for Shakespeare in Edward III," *Shakespeare Yearbook 16*, 2007, pp 321–50.

_____, "Shakespeare and Sir Thomas More," *Shakespeare and the Versification of English Drama, 1561–1642* (London: Ashgate, 2014), pp. 176–80.

_____, *Shakespeare's Verse: Iambic Pentameter and the Poet's Idiosyncrasies* (Oxford: Peter Lang, 1987).

_____, "The Verse of *A Lover's Complaint*: Not Shakespeare," *Words that Count: Early Modern Authorship: Essays in Honor of MacDonald P. Jackson*, Brian Boyd, ed. (Newark: University of Delaware Press, 2004).

Taylor, A. P., ed., *Shakespeare's Ovid: The Metamorphoses in the Plays and Poems* (Cambridge: Cambridge University Press, 2000).

Taylor, Gary, "The Canon and Chronology of Shakespeare's Plays," *William Shakespeare: A Textual Companion*, Stanley Wells and Gary Taylor, eds. (Oxford:

Oxford University Press, 1987), pp. 69–144.

_____, "Middleton and Rowley—and Heywood: *The Old Law* and New Attribution Technologies," *Papers of the Bibliographical Society of America* 96:2, June 2002, pp. 165–217.

_____, *Moment by Moment in Shakespeare* (Houndmills, UK: Palgrave, 1985), U.S. title, *To Analyze Delight: A Hedonist Criticism of Shakespeare* (Newark: University of Delaware Press, 1985).

_____, *Reinventing Shakespeare: A Cultural History from the Restoration to the Present* (Oxford: Oxford University Press, 1991).

_____, "Shakespeare and Others: The Authorship of *1 Henry VI*" *Medieval and Renaissance Drama in England 7*, 1995, pp. 145–205.

_____, "Thomas Middleton, Thomas Dekker, and *The Bloody Banquet*," *Papers of the Bibliographical Society of America*, 94:2, June 2000, pp. 197–233.

_____, "*Troilus and Cressida*: Bibliography, Performance, and Interpretation," *Shakespeare Studies 15*, 1982, pp. 99–136.

Taylor, Gary, and Gabriel Egan, eds., *The New Oxford Shakespeare Authorship Companion* (Oxford, Oxford University Press, 2017).

Taylor, Gary, and John Lavagnino, General eds., *Thomas Middleton and Early Modern Textual Culture: A Companion to the Collected Works* (Oxford: Oxford University Press, 2007).

Taylor, Gary, and Michael Warren, eds., *The Division of the Kingdoms: Shakespeare's Two Versions of King Lear* (Oxford: Oxford University Press, 1983).

Taymor, Julie, *Titus* (New York: Newmarket Press, 2000).

Terence, *Terence in English*, Richard Bernard, translator (London: 1614).

Theobald, Lewis, *The Works of Shakespeare in Seven Volumes* (London: 1733).

Thompson, Ann, *Shakespeare's Chaucer: A Study in Literary Origins* (Liverpool: Liverpool University Press, 1978).

_____, *Which Shakespeare?: A User's Guide to Editions* (Maidenhead, UK: Open University Press, 1992).

Thompson, Ann, and Gordon McMullan, *In Arden: Editing Shakespeare, Essays in Honour of Richard Proudfoot* (London: Arden, 2003).

Thompson, Ann, and John O. Thompson, *Shakespeare: Meaning and Metaphor* (Iowa City: University of Iowa Press, 1987).

Thompson, Ann, and Neil Taylor, eds., *Hamlet: A Critical Reader* (London: Arden, 2016).

Thompson, Ann, and Sasha Roberts, eds., *Women Reading Shakespeare 1660–1900: An Anthology of Criticism* (Manchester: Manchester University Press, 1997).

Thurber, James, "The Macbeth Murder Mystery," *The Thurber Carnival* (New York: Harper and Brothers, 1945), pp. 60–3.

Tiffany, Grace, *My Father Had a Daughter: Judith Shakespeare's Tale* (New York: Penguin, 2004).

_____, *Will* (New York: Berkley, 2004).

Tillyard, E. M. W., *The Elizabethan World Picture: A Study of the Idea of Order in the Age of Shakespeare, Donne & Milton* (London: Chatto and Windus, 1943).

Timberlake, P. W., *The Feminine Ending in English Blank Verse. A Study of Its Use by Early Writers in the Measure and it Development in the Drama up to the Year 1595* (Menasha, WI: George Banta Publishing Co., 1931).

Tobin, John J. M., "Antony, Brutus, and Christ's Tears Over Jerusalem," *Notes & Queries* 45, September 1998, pp. 324–31.

_____, "Nashe and Shakespeare: Some Further Borrowings," *Notes & Queries* 39, September 1992, pp. 309–20.

Traversi, Derek, *An Approach to Shakespeare* (New York: Doubleday, 1956).

Tudeau-Clayton. Margaret, *Jonson, Shakespeare, and Early Modern Vergil* (Cambridge: Cambridge University Press, 2006).

Tynan, Kenneth, *A View of the English Stage, 1944–1965* (London: Davis-Poynter, 1975).

Ulrici, Hermann, *On Shakespeare's Dramatic Art: History and Character of Shakespeare's Plays*, four editions, the third translated into English by L. Dora Schmitz (London: George Bell, 1976).

Vaughan, Alden T., *Roots of American Racism: Essays on the Colonial Experience* (Oxford: Oxford University Press, 1995).

Vaughan, Alden T., and Virginia Mason

Vaughan, "Before Othello: Elizabethan Representations of Sub-Saharan Africans," *William and Mary Quarterly*, third series, 54:1, January 1997, pp. 19–44.

_____, *Shakespeare in America* (Oxford: Oxford University Press, 2012).

_____, *Shakespeare's Caliban: A Cultural History* (Cambridge: Cambridge University Press, 1991).

Vaughan, Alden T., and Virginia Mason Vaughan, eds., *The Tempest: A Critical Reader* (London: Arden, 2014).

Vaughan, Virginia Mason, *Antony and Cleopatra, Language and Writing* (London: Arden, 2016).

_____, *Othello: A Contextual History* (Cambridge: Cambridge University Press, 1994).

_____, *Performing Blackness on the English Stages, 1500–1800* (Cambridge: Cambridge University Press, 2005).

_____, *Shakespeare and the Gods* (London: Arden, 2019).

_____, *Shakespeare in Performance: The Tempest* (Manchester: Manchester University Press, 2011).

Vaughan, Virginia Mason, and Alden T. Vaughan, eds., *Critical Essays on Shakespeare's The Tempest* (Woodbridge, CT: Twayne, 1998).

_____, *Shakespeare in American Life* (Washington D.C.: The Folger Shakespeare Library, 2007).

Vaughan, Virginia Mason, and John Gillies, eds., *Playing the Globe: Genre and Geography in English Renaissance Drama* (Rutherford, NJ: Fairleigh Dickinson University Press, 1998).

Vaughan, Virginia Mason, and Kent Cartwright, eds., *Othello: New Perspectives* (Rutherford, NJ: Fairleigh Dickinson University Press, 1991).

Vaughan, Virginia Mason, and Margaret Lael Mikesell, eds., *Othello: An Annotated Bibliography* (New York: Garland, 1990).

Vaux, Laurence, *A Catechisme: or Christian Doctrine* (Manchester: 1583).

Velz, John W., *Exit Pursued by a Bear: Encounters with Shakespeare and Shakespeareans* (Austin, TX: LawProse, 2008).

_____, "The Parliament of Heaven in Two Fifteenth-Century Dramatic Accounts of the Fate of Humankind," *New Approaches to European Theatre of the Middle Ages: An Anthology*, Barbara Gusick and Edelgard E. DuBruck, eds. (Bern: Peter Lang, 2004).

_____, "Shakespeare and Ovid in the Twentieth Century: A critical survey," *Shakespeare's Ovid: The Metamorphoses in the Plays and Poems*, A. B. Taylor, ed. (Cambridge: Cambridge University Press, 2000), pp. 181–94.

_____, *Shakespeare and the Classical Tradition: A Critical Guide to Commentary, 1660–1960* (Minneapolis: University of Minnesota Press, 1968).

_____, "Shakespeare and the Geneva Bible," *Shakespeare, Marlowe, Jonson: New Directions in Bibliography*, Takashi Kozuko and J. R. Molryne, eds. (London: Ashgate, 2006).

_____, *Shakespeare's English Histories: A Quest for Form and Genre* (Tempe, AZ: Medieval & Renaissance Texts and Studies, 1997).

_____, *The Tragedy of Julius Caesar: A Bibliography to Supplement the New Variorum Edition of 1913* (New York: Modern Language Association, 1977).

Velz, John W., and Francis N. Teague, eds., *One Touch of Shakespeare: Letters of Joseph Crosby and Joseph Parker Norris* (Washington D.C.: Folger Shakespeare Library, 1986).

Vendler, Helen, *The Art of Shakespeare's Sonnets* (Cambridge, MA: Harvard University Press, 1997).

Vickers, Brian, *Appropriating Shakespeare: Contemporary Critical Quarrels* (New Haven: Yale University Press, 1993).

_____, *The Artistry of Shakespeare's Prose*, two editions (London: Methuen 1968 and 1979).

_____, *Classical Rhetoric in English Poetry*, two editions (London: Macmillan, 1970 and Carbondale: Southern Illinois University Press, 1989).

_____, *Coriolanus* (London: Edward Arnold, 1976).

_____, *'Counterfeiting' Shakespeare: Evidence, Authorship, and John Ford's 'Funerall Elegye'* (Cambridge: Cambridge University Press, 2002).

_____, *English Renaissance Literary Criticism* (Oxford: Oxford University Press, 1999).

_____, *Essential Articles for the Study of Francis Bacon* (Hamden, CT: Archon Books, 1968).

_____, *Francis Bacon and Renaissance Prose* (Cambridge: Cambridge University Press, 1968).

_____, *In Defense of Rhetoric*, three editions (Oxford: Oxford University Press, 1988–1997).

_____, "Incomplete Shakespeare: Or, Denying Coauthorship in *1 Henry VI*," *Shakespeare Quarterly*, 58:3, Fall 2007, pp. 311–52.

_____, *Occult and Scientific Mentalities in the Renaissance* (Cambridge: Cambridge University Press, 1984).

_____, *One King Lear* (Cambridge, MA: Harvard University Press, 2016).

_____, "Recreating a Tradition: Some Reminiscences on Editing *Shakespeare: The Critical Heritage*," *Shakespeare Newsletter*, 44:2, Summer 1994, pp. 23–4, 32, and 34.

_____, *Returning to Shakespeare* (London: Routledge, 1989).

_____, "A Rum 'do': The Likely Authorship of 'A Lover's Complaint,'" *Times Literary Supplement*, 5 December 2003, pp. 13–5.

_____, *Shakespeare, "A Lover's Complaint," and John Davies of Hereford* (Cambridge: Cambridge University Press, 2007).

_____, *Shakespeare Co-Author: A Historical Study of Five Collaborative Plays* (Oxford: Oxford University Press, 2002).

_____, *Shakespeare: The Critical Heritage*, six volumes (London: Routledge and Kegan Paul, 1974–1981).

_____, "The Shakespeare Reflex," *The Times Literary Supplement*, 24 April 2015, p. 11.

_____, "Shakespearian Consolations," *Proceedings of the British Academy 82* (Oxford: Oxford University Press), pp. 219–84.

_____, *Towards Greek Tragedy: Drama, Myth and Society* (Harlow, UK: Longman, 1973).

Vickers, Brian, ed., *Rhetoric Revealed: Papers from the International Society for the History of Rhetoric* (Binghamton, NY: Medieval and Renaissance Texts and Studies, 1982).

Vickers, Brian, review, "Stanley Wells and Gary Taylor (eds.), William Shakespeare, *The Complete Works* (Oxford, 1986), and id., William Shakespeare, *The Textual Companion* (Oxford, 1987)," *Review of English Studies*, 40:159, August 1989, pp. 402–11.

Virgil, *The Thirteene Bookes of Aeneidos*, Thomas Phaer and Thomas Twyne, translators (London: 1596).

_____, *Eclogues. Georgics. Aeneid: Books 1–6*, H. Rushton Fairclough, translator and G. P. Goold, reviser (Cambridge, MA: Loeb, 1999).

Voltaire, Lettre à l'Académie française, 1776.

Waldron, Francis Godolphin, *The Virgin Queen, a Drama in Five Acts Attempted as a Sequel to Shakespeare's Tempest* (London: 1797).

Walker, Alice, *Textual Problems of the First Folio: Richard III, King Lear, Troilus & Cressida, 2 Henry IV, Hamlet, Othello* (Cambridge: Cambridge University Press, 1953).

Wallace, Malcolm, *The Life of Sir Philip Sidney* (Cambridge: Cambridge University Press, 1915).

Walsham, Alexandra, *Church Papists: Catholicism, Conformity and Confessional Polemic in Early Modern England* (Martlesham, UK: Boydell Press, 1993).

Walton, J. K., *The Copy for the Folio Text of* Richard III: *with a Note on the Copy for the Folio Text of* King Lear (Auckland: Auckland University Press, 1955).

_____, *Quarto Copy for the First Folio of Shakespeare* (Dublin: Dublin University Press, 1971).

Warren, Roger, *Staging Shakespeare's Late Plays* (Oxford: Oxford University Press, 1990).

Webster, John, *The Works of John Webster, Volume One: The White Devil, The Duchess of Malfi*, David Gunby, David Carnegie, and Antony Hammond, eds. (Cambridge: Cambridge University Press, 1995).

_____, *The Works of John Webster, Volume Two: The Devil's Law-Case, A Cure for a Cuckold, Appius and Virginia*, David Gunby, David Carnegie, and MacDonald P. Jackson, eds. (Cambridge: Cambridge University Press, 2003).

_____, *The Works of John Webster, Volume Three: Anything for a Quiet Life, Monu-*

ments of Honour, Induction and Additions to the Malcontent, A Monumental Column, Shorter Poems, New Characters, David Gunby, David Carnegie, and MacDonald P. Jackson, eds. (Cambridge: Cambridge University Press, 2007).

Weimann, Robert, *Author's Pen and Actor's Voice: Playing and Writing in Shakespeare's Theatre* (Cambridge: Cambridge University Press, 2000).

Wells, Stanley, *Coffee with Shakespeare* (London: Duncan Baird, 2008, reprinted under the title *Shakespeare ... Off the Record* by London: Watkins Publishing, 2011).

_____, *For All Time: Shakespeare and his Legacy* (London: Macmillan, 2002).

_____, *Great Shakespeare Actors: Burbage to Branagh* (Oxford: Oxford University Press, 2015).

_____, *Is It True What They Say About Shakespeare?* (Ebrington, UK: Long Barn Books, 2007).

_____, *Looking for Sex in Shakespeare* (Cambridge: Cambridge University Press, 2004).

_____, *Re-Editing Shakespeare for the Modern Reader* (Oxford: Oxford University Press, 1984).

_____, *Shakespeare: A Dramatic Life* (London: Sinclair-Stevenson Ltd, 1994, published in the U.S. as *Shakespeare: A Life in Drama*, New York: W. W. Norton & Company, 1994).

_____, *Shakespeare and Co.: Christopher Marlowe, Thomas Dekker, Ben Jonson, Thomas Middleton, John Fletcher and the Other Players in His Story* (London: Allen Lane, 2006).

_____, *Shakespeare on Page and Stage: Selected Essays*, Paul Edmondson, ed. (Oxford: Oxford University Press, 2016).

_____, *Shakespeare, Sex and Love* (Oxford: Oxford University Press, 2010).

_____, *Shakespeare's Tragedies: A Very Short Introduction* (Oxford: Oxford University Press, 2017).

_____, *William Shakespeare: A Very Short Introduction* (Oxford: Oxford University Press, 2015).

Wells, Stanley, ed., *Shakespeare in the Theatre: An Anthology of Criticism* (Oxford: Oxford University Press, 1997).

Wells, Stanley, and Gary Taylor, eds., *William Shakespeare: A Textual Companion* (Oxford: Oxford University Press, 1987).

Wells, Stanley, and Lena Cowen Orlin, *Shakespeare: An Oxford Guide* (Oxford: Oxford University Press, 2003).

Werstine, Paul, "A Century of 'Bad' Shakespeare Quartos," *Shakespeare Quarterly*, 50:3, Autumn 1999, pp. 310–333.

_____, *Early Modern Playhouse Manuscripts and the Editing of Shakespeare* (Cambridge: Cambridge University Press, 2012).

_____, "Narratives about Printed Shakespeare Texts: 'Foul Papers' and 'Bad' Quartos," *Shakespeare Quarterly*, 41:1, Spring 1990, pp. 65–86.

_____, "Plays in Manuscript." *A New History of Early English Drama*, John D. Cox and David Scott Kastan, eds. (New York: Columbia University Press, 1997), pp. 481–97.

_____, "Shakespeare," *Scholarly Editing: A Guide to Research*, David Greetham, ed. (New York: Modern Language Association, 1996), pp. 253–82.

_____, "The Textual Mystery of *Hamlet*," *Shakespeare Quarterly*, 39:1, Spring 1988, pp. 1–26.

West, E. J., ed., *Shaw on Theatre* (New York: Hill and Wang, 1958).

Whelan, Peter, *The School of Night* (London: Josef Weinberger, 1992).

Whitaker, Virgil K., *Shakespeare's Use of Learning: An Inquiry into the Growth of his Mind and Art* (San Marino, CA: The Huntington Library, 1953).

White, Hayden, *Tropics of Discourse: Essays in Cultural Criticism* (Baltimore: Johns Hopkins University Press, 1979).

Wickham, Glynne, Herbert Berry, and William Ingram, eds., *English Professional Theatre, 1530–1660* (Cambridge: Cambridge University Press, 2000).

Wilders, John, review, *Shakespeare and the Traditions of Comedy* by Leo Salinger, *Review of English Studies*, 27:106, May 1976, pp. 207–9.

Wilkins, George, *The Painfull Aduentures of Pericles Prince of Tyre* (London: 1608).

Williams, George Walton, "The Year's Contribution to Shakespearian Study: Textual Studies" *Shakespeare Survey 36*

(Cambridge: Cambridge University Press, 1983), p. 182.

Williams, Gordon, *A Dictionary of Sexual Language and Imagery in Shakespearean and Stuart Literature,* three volumes (London: Athlone Press, 1994).

Williams, Phillip, Jr., "The 'Second Issue' of Shakespeare's *Troilus and Cressida,* 1609," *Studies in Bibliography 2,* 1949, pp. 25–34.

_____, "Shakespeare's *Troilus and Cressida:* The Relationship of Quarto and Folio," *Studies in Bibliography* 3, 1950, pp. 131–44.

Williams, Raymond, *Modern Tragedy*, two editions (London: Chatto and Windus, 1966, Brooklyn, NY: Verso Editions, 1979).

Wilson, John Dover, *What Happens in Hamlet* (Cambridge: Cambridge University Press, 1935).

Wood, Nigel, *Theory in Practice: The Tempest* (Maidenhead, UK: Open University Press, 1995).

Woodbridge, Linda, *Women in the English Renaissance: Literature and the Nature of Womankind, 1540 to 1620* (Champaign, IL: University of Illinois Press, 1984).

Woodring, Carl, and James Shapiro, eds., *The Columbia Anthology of British Poetry* (New York: Columbia University Press, 1993).

World Shakespeare Bibliography, https://www.worldshakesbib.org

Worthen, W. B., *Shakespeare and the Authority of Performance* (Cambridge: Cambridge University Press, 1997).

_____, *Shakespeare and the Force of Modern Performance* (Cambridge: Cambridge University Press, 2003).

Wray, Ramona, "Nostalgia for Navarre: The Melancholic Metacinema of Kenneth Branagh," *Literature/Film Quarterly* 30:3, 2002, pp. 171–8.

Wright, George T., *Aimless Life: Poems 1961–1995* (Minneapolis, MN: North Stone Editions, 1999).

_____, *Hearing the Measures: Shakespearean and Other Inflections* (Madison: University of Wisconsin Press, 2001).

_____, *The Poet in the Poem: The Personae of Eliot, Yeats, and Pound* (Berkeley: University of California Press, 1960).

_____, *Shakespeare's Metrical Art* (Berkeley: University of California Press, 1988).

_____, *W. H. Auden*, two editions (New York: Twayne, 1969 and 1981).

Wycherley, William, *The Plays of William Wycherley*, Peter Holland, ed. (Cambridge: Cambridge University Press, 1981).

Yachnin, Paul, *Stage-wrights: Shakespeare, Jonson, Middleton and the Making of Theatrical Value* (Philadelphia: University of Pennsylvania Press, 1997).

Young, Edward, *The Revenge: A Tragedy* (London: 1721).

Zabus, Chantal, *Tempests After Shakespeare* (London: Palgrave, 2002).

Zagorin, Perez, *Francis Bacon* (Princeton: Princeton University Press, 1998).

Personnel Index

Title Index